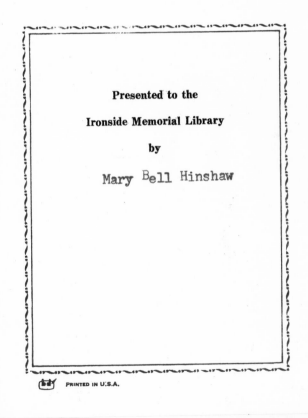

ALEXANDRE DUMAS'

Adventures
in Czarist Russia

Czarist Russia

Translated and Edited by

Alma Elizabeth Murch

Those raised on *The Three Musketeers*
and *The Count of Monte Cristo* will welcome this first translation of Dumas' *Adventures in Czarist Russia,* which follows his
three other travel books.

Alive is the only word for Dumas *Père!*
Gourmet, sophisticate, art lover—whatever
his role, he hurls himself into it with fantastic zest.

In 1858 Dumas was invited to attend the
wedding, in St. Petersburg, of the famous
American spiritualist Home to a god-
daughter of Czar Nicholas II. After two
months of indefatigable sightseeing in and
around the capital, he visited Finland before
going on to Moscow, en route to Nijni-
Novgorod, Astrakhan, and the Caucasus.

ALSO BY ALEXANDRE DUMAS

Adventures in Switzerland

Adventures in Spain

Adventures in Algeria

One minute sneering at Russian cooking, *Pets*
the next praising Russian architecture, he
storms along from Finland to the steppes of
Asia. French to the core, he blasts any personal discomfort with rage or daggers it
with invective. Sensitive artist and kindly
bourgeois, Dumas is revolted by the cruelty
and subservience which hung over 19th-
century Russia like a cloud.

But Dumas can never abandon life for
long, even in Holy Russia. He rushes about
in strange vehicles, seizes the chance to talk
to (or at least about) every pretty woman
he sees, and behaves as if he owns everything
he inspects. Bits of legend, myth and history,
much of it grim and bloody, are interwoven
with the personal narrative, but the pace
never flags. The reader is carried along as if
by a hurricane swept by the torrential writing of that Genie of the Globe-Trotters, the
Towering Tourist—Alexandre Dumas.

A country is known by its past, and Russia's past was never more clearly sketched
than by Dumas, whose novelist's skill is en-
hanced by extraordinary perception and a
camera eye.

Those who have already adventured with
Dumas will want to add this to their shelves.
Those who are discovering his perfection as
a traveling companion for the first time will
want to experience the pleasures of Dumas'
*Adventures in Spain, Adventures in Algeria,
Adventures in Switzerland,* and, at home and
abroad, his *Adventures with My Pets.*

The Haymarket, St. Petersburg.

The Nevskoi Prospect, St. Petersburg.

ALEXANDRE DUMAS'

Adventures
in Czarist Russia

Translated and Edited by

ALMA ELIZABETH MURCH

CHILTON COMPANY — BOOK DIVISION
Publishers
Philadelphia   *New York*

CONTENTS

27946

ILLUSTRATIONS

★

★

INTRODUCTION

In the spring of 1858, when Alexandre Dumas was 55 and one of the best-known literary figures in Paris, he was frequently entertained by a Russian nobleman and his family who were making a prolonged stay in the French capital. On the eve of their return to St. Petersburg they warmly invited Dumas to go with them and spend several months exploring their country.

Dumas was, as always, deeply immersed in literary work that could hardly be left, but, on the other hand, he had a passion for visiting distant countries, getting to know men of different races in their own homes, and such an offer as this was unlikely to come his way again. Russia had already made a deep impression on his mind. As a boy of twelve he had watched a Cossack regiment galloping down the highroad near his home in Villers-Cotterets, and even in late manhood he retained a vivid memory of "those long-bearded horsemen with pointed caps and wide red trousers who were the terror of our childhood as they swept through the plains and towns of France."

The average Frenchman of the mid-nineteenth century knew very little about Russia, except for a smattering of her history, gleaned from Voltaire's short treatise on Peter the Great, published a hundred years earlier, and impressions of the land and its peoples, from the reminiscences of those veterans who returned from Napoleon's march to Moscow. But by 1858 all nations of Western Europe, particularly France, with her zeal for *"Liberté, Egalité, Fraternité,"* felt a mounting curiosity about conditions inside Russia, where a vast social experiment, the emancipation of the serfs (ten and a half million men and their families), was due to be completed in 1861.

Dumas had already published accounts of his tours in Switzerland, Italy, Spain and North Africa,[1] and was planning a voyage round the coast of the Eastern Mediterranean, but he instantly

[1] *Adventures in Switzerland* (Chilton, 1960); *Adventures in Spain* (Chilton, 1959); *Adventures in Algeria* (Chilton, 1959).

7

shelved that project and set out for St. Petersburg, devoting the next nine months to travelling up to Finland, across to Moscow, down the Volga to the Caspian Sea, and on through Astrakhan to the Caucasus, journeys that he described in two separate works, *En Russie* and *Le Caucase*.

The first of these, published in 1860, consists of four volumes, each containing some 300 pages of close print. Dumas was determined to give his compatriots the clearest possible picture, not only of the places he visited and the people he met, but also of Russia's history and development from the Middle Ages onward. He included the life stories of her Czars, their conquests abroad, their rule or mis-rule of the empire; the successive revolutions whereby tyrant replaced tyrant; her outstanding generals and their campaigns; the careers of her famous statesmen; her social problems, with particular reference to the question of emancipation. He introduced his readers to Russia's journalists, novelists and poets, giving biographical details and an assessment of their work, even going to the length of translating many Russian poems into French verse, choosing those he considered most typical of their authors or most expressive of the Russian character. He discussed methods of local government, the various religious groups, problems of education, the neglect of agriculture, labour difficulties and many other aspects of life in Russia.

Apart from a few stories of dramatic historical events,[1] this is the first translation in English of *En Russie*, and to bring it within the compass of a single volume it has been necessary to concentrate almost wholly upon Dumas's travels inside Russia, his account of the places he saw, the exciting events he witnessed, the social and economic conditions that roused his interest, the men and women of every walk of life who entertained him in their palaces, homesteads, inns or tents. In brief, to give a colourful panorama of that vast empire of a century ago, which has now become the U.S.S.R.

A.E.M.

---

[1] Translated by Mikael Gortshakov. *Celebrated Crimes of the Russian Court* (London, Hurst and Blackett, 1906).

8

I

THE KOUCHELEFS AND THEIR CIRCLE

Before we start, I must tell you something of our travelling companions. If, towards the end of last winter, you happened to pass through the *Place du Palais Royal* between midnight and four in the morning on almost any day, you must have noticed the whole first floor of the hotel *Les Trois Empereurs* blazing with light, resounding with music and gaiety till the very cab-drivers and road sweepers, the only human creatures frequenting the streets at such an hour, stood dumb with amazement. On the balcony, decked waist-high with flowering shrubs, four great windows stood wide open to the cool freshness of the night air, except when Sivori was playing his entrancing violin solos, or Ascher his wonderful melodies on the piano.

From the roadway, the passer-by could look through the open windows, between the blossoms, into the salon where a dozen men were talking, pacing up and down, gesticulating, discussing art, literature, politics—everything except the bourse and the stock-exchange—in a word, enjoying conversation, an art that is rarer than you may suppose, one that has never existed outside France. Even there, I greatly fear, we are beginning to lose it, thanks to the growing popularity of cigar-smoking and late suppers.

Now and again a young girl of 23 or 24, slender as an English-woman, graceful as a Parisienne and languid as an oriental, would rise from her reclining chair, take the arm of the nearest guest and stroll idly to the balcony to take a deep breath or two and gaze for a moment at the sky before returning to her seat, her pose half Asiatic, half European. True, if the music changed to a polka or a waltz, this listless child of the far North would dance with all the verve and lightness of a daughter of Seville or Cadiz until the last notes had died away. In these moments of exhilaration, obviously far from being a habit with her, her velvet eyes, usually so still, would flash like black diamonds; her cheeks, pale as camellia petals grew bright as a rose; her finely chiselled nostrils would dilate and her lips part to reveal her tiny white teeth. At such times she seemed a lady to be feared, rather than a woman to be loved.

When she moved about the room she would often contrive to pass close to a young man aged about 25, of average height, very slender and pale, whose eyes shone with a strange light. When motionless, they possessed the hypnotic force of a Manfred or a Lord Ruthven. His delicate, transparent hands were loaded with rings; his feet small and narrow, betokening his aristocratic breeding. As she passed she would offer him her brow or her hand, and he, with a smile that brought a second's warmth to his pallor, would lightly touch that brow or that hand with his lips, as delicately as if it were a flower.   She is the Countess, he the Count Kouchelef-Bezborodko. Both are Russian aristocrats of ancient lineage.

The first man to bear the name Bezborodko was one of those Cossack chiefs who fought the Turks in the 16th century. In one fierce battle his chin was slashed away, hence his name, which means "the chinless one." Here, you see, is nobility in the grand manner. What a man sows on the field of battle, he has the right to reap in history. His descendant, André Bezborodko, was the last Supreme Judge of those same Cossack tribes and father of the Alexander Bezborodko who served as personal secretary to the Czarina Catherine II. On her death he transferred his allegiance to her son, Paul I, whose succession he secured by trickery, whereupon he was rewarded by the title of Prince, the position of High Chancellor of the Russian Empire and a gift of vast estates with 20,000 serfs.

The Kouchelef family has an equally distinguished ancestry; dating from the time of Ivan the Terrible.   When Catherine II exiled Paul to Catchina a group of young nobles accompanied him, among them the grandfather of the present count, and once Paul was on the throne he heaped wealth and honour on these old friends. A marriage was arranged between Count Kouchelef and the niece of the childless Prince Bezborodko, and so, in due course, the vast fortunes of both families were inherited by the present Count Gregory Kouchelef, whose windows, last winter, blazed till dawn in his hotel in Paris. A year ago he decided to tour Europe from Poland through Austria and Italy to France, and set out with his family and retainers, twelve persons in all.

Next in blood to the count and countess are a girl of eighteen and a little boy of six. The young lady, pleasant rather than pretty, with a perfect figure, charming smile and delightful personality, is the countess' sister, and it is to her wedding that I am invited. It behoves me, therefore, to speak of her as delicately and discreetly as I would of the crown of orange blossom she will wear as she walks to the altar. Her name is Alexandrina.[1]

The little boy is a miracle of good breeding and careful training, never in your way or under your feet. He never climbs on your knee, pulls your hair or throws a toy at your head; never pokes a stick in your eye, deafens you with his drum or bothers you with questions. He may be in the salon with you, but where? Playing quietly behind an armchair or under the piano. He may share your table at lunch, but you never hear him. As soon as his hunger is satisfied he slips from his chair and disappears. I wish all the parents whose homes I visit had children like him, even more for my sake than theirs. He is called Alexander, Sacha for short.

After these close relatives come the family retainers, with Dandré at their head, of French ancestry as his name suggests, but with some Russian blood in his veins. He is the count's chamberlain, who takes charge of money matters, checks expenditure and pays the bills. Never by any chance does he carry less than a hundred 1,000 franc notes in his wallet, ready for any little emergency that might arise. In addition he is responsible for reserving compartments in trains, choosing suitable cabins in ships, sending a courier ahead to arrange relays of horses when the count travels by coach. Dandré has a free hand and smooths out every difficulty. If there are bandits on the road, as happens sometimes, he comes

---

[1] She was the youngest daughter of the Count de Kroll, a general in the Russian army, and a god-daughter of Czar Alexander I, given the name of Alexandrina at his request. The Czar made the same stipulation when he agreed to stand as god-father to the baby daughter of the Duke and Duchess of Kent, at her christening in London in 1819. The child was named Alexandrina Victoria, but the first of these was dropped before she ascended the throne as Queen Victoria.—Ed.

to terms with them in advance. Is the only inn a poor one? He improves it beyond recognition. No inn at all? He creates one, and the party arrives to find a perfect dinner just ready to be served, wines and all! For the rest, he is a young man of twenty-five or six who combines shrewdness with imperturbable good humour, a born *raconteur* who knows Russia, Turkey and Persia like the back of his hand and never tires of travelling.

Next in status to Dandré is Doctor Koudriavtzef, a Russian of 28 or 30 who cannot speak a single word of French, an amiable man with a heart of gold. He has no qualifications other than a natural aptitude for tending the sick, and a certain amount of experience. He treats little Sacha's bumps and bruises, the countess's headaches, any cuts or scratches sustained by members of the household. Just at the moment he has no other patient but myself, and is looking after a carbuncle the size of a pigeon's egg that, oddly enough, has swollen up on my right cheekbone. The good doctor gives me every hope that, thanks to his skilled attention, I may escape with nothing worse than a scar like the one that disfigured the Duc de Guise. God grant he is right! For a moment I was afraid he meant to amputate my head to save the rest of my body.

Next comes Professor Reltchensky, formerly the count's tutor, who found the household so much to his liking that he simply stayed on. Now his only occupation is collecting—every discarded or broken *objet d'art* he can lay hands on. He has a vast accumulation of inlaid strong boxes with broken locks, beautifully carved tables with a leg missing, pottery from Faenza carefully mended (as I hope to be) without a scar, all acquired by the worthy professor at no cost, simply by using patience, soap and good strong glue. The day he offers his collection in a Paris saleroom he will net a fortune.

The remaining ladies of the party are Mlle Hélène, a friend of the countess's mother, now companion-housekeeper to the daughter, relieving her of such tasks as dispensing tea to the constant stream of visitors; and Mlle Annette, a typical young Russian girl, calm, plump, passive and devoted to the countess whose ward she has been for the past twelve years. The other members of the suite brought by the count from St. Petersburg are two valets, Simon and Missam; two personal maids for the countess, Annouchka and Louise; and two secretaries whom I never saw and whose names I forgot to ask. Finally, the countess's little pet spaniel, *Doucha,* of the aristocratic King Charles breed. As the result of a clandestine *affaire* she was in whelp before leaving St. Petersburg, to a greyhound, said some, a poodle, said others, but when she produced her litter in Vienna their paternity was no longer in doubt. It was the poodle after all, and the pups were hideous. Still, the most presentable of them was adopted by Louise, the second chambermaid, who gave him the name of *Charick*—"little ball."

In the course of their travels through Europe, this group was increased by three human beings—Polovski, the Russian poet; Millelotti, an Italian musician; and the spiritualist, Daniel Dunglas Home. The others you will not know, but you must have heard of Home, who can conjure up the spirits of the dead. I will try to describe him for you, his physical appearance, that is. Only God, who creates exceptional beings and knows why He did so, can assess their moral worth.

Home is a young man of twenty-three or four, guileless as a child, of average height, slenderly built, frail and highly strung. His skin is pale, faintly tinged with pink and freckled here and there. His hair has a lovely warm colour between gold and auburn; his eyes a clear blue, his brows lightly marked, his nose small and *retroussé*. His moustache, of the same colour as his hair, hides the sensitive curve of his mouth, and behind his rather pale, thin lips he has good teeth. His hands, white and ladylike, are beautifully kept and covered with rings. Though he has adopted a Parisian elegance in his dress, he usually wears a Scottish bonnet with a silver crest representing an arm brandishing a sword, surrounded by the motto: *Vincere aut mori.*

How did Home join the count's *entourage*? I will tell you. After his astonishing career as a medium in America he came to France in April, 1855, a very sick man hoping to recover his health. In September he went to Florence, where his psychic power returned in full force. He performed marvels—I profoundly regret

13

that I did not witness them myself—at the home of Mme Orsini, daughter of Gregory Orloff, when the spirits not only lifted tables from the floor, played the piano and created a steeplechase of sofas and armchairs, but prevailed on the spirit of Orloff to write a short message to his daughter in handwriting that his friends recognised as characteristically his. But in Florence it is dangerous to work miracles—Savonarola was burned alive for indulging in this exercise —and Home was informed that the Holy Inquisition was growing concerned about his activities, so he left for Naples with Count Alexandre Branicki, who is not afraid of spirits, nor, I fancy, of anything in the world.

Home's health had greatly improved during his stay in Italy, and his powers as a medium brought him the interest of the French court. He was the man of the hour, the latest fashionable celebrity, fêted everywhere. An elderly Englishwoman bequeathed to him an income of £6,000 a year for life! The favours he received from so many kings and queens caused a great deal of jealousy, spiteful rumours about him began to spread, and Home judged it prudent to retire while he could do so with dignity. While in Rome, Count Kouchelef heard of him, met him, liked him, entertained him, and a month later a marriage was arranged between Home and the sister of the countess, to take place later in the year at St. Petersburg. Home, as a prospective brother-in-law and so a member of the family, travelled with the count to Paris, where I came across him in the salon of *Les Trois Empereurs,* playing like an ordinary mortal with Sacha and three of the countess's pets that I have not yet mentioned: Signorina, her lovely white cat; Muichka, a tiny coal-black terrier bitch; and Tchérépacha the tortoise, a rather sulky creature with no social graces, apt to retire into corners to nibble a lettuce leaf or a slice of carrot.

How did I make the acquaintance of all these unusual people? I will tell you as briefly as I can. Daniel Home, when at the height of his powers, had often invited me to his séances and expressed a desire to meet me, but I had never managed to go, not from any lack of desire but simply because of my endless work. One day, two very good friends of mine, Delaage and the Count of Sancillon, said to me in the course of conversation: "By the way, we will bring Home to call on you tomorrow."

"Good," said I. "Bring him to dinner." That is my favourite way of meeting people. Like all men whose work is intensive and demanding, I detest any intrusion while I am busy, though I usually have to endure, with whatever grace I can muster, the irritation of being interrupted fifty or sixty times every day. Since one always has to dine—well or otherwise, hastily or in leisurely fashion—I have made it a habit to meet old and new friends around my table, unless they prefer some more formal occasion. (My own reputation as a cook exerts a certain attraction!) So the next evening Sancillon, Delaage and Home arrived at six-thirty and I made the acquaintance of the magician as we enjoyed our *consommé*. (One of these days I will give you the recipe.)

It would have been tactless—and might have disturbed his digestion—to talk to Home of his former triumphs at court and in society, since his powers were temporarily in eclipse, so I led the conversation to his travels in Italy. He told me how he had met the Count and Countess Kouchelef in Rome, went on to speak of his fiancée, and added that they all wished to meet me.

"Bring them to dinner tomorrow," said I, faithful to my principles.

"Would it not be better to give them the invitation yourself?"

"Certainly. I will do myself the honour to call on them at *Les Trois Empereurs* in the morning."

"Why not tonight?"

"Because you will all be with me, I hope, till almost midnight."

"But that is quite early in the evening for the Kouchelefs. They never go to bed till six. Let us all go there together." I turned to Delaage, an old friend of the count, who assured me with a gesture that the suggestion would be entirely acceptable.

"Besides," Home continued, "we have already arranged to present M. de Sancillon to the count tonight, so we can kill two birds with one stone." Without even asking whether I should be the first or second bird, I accepted.

That same evening I was introduced to the count and countess, and it was five in the morning when I left *Les Trois Empereurs,* promising myself never again to visit a house where they kept such hours. I went again next day and stayed till six. The day after, it was seven before I left, but on that occasion Sivori was playing his violin and Ascher the piano, and Méry spoke. Still, all that would not get my novels written and I stayed away for three days. On the third day, Home and Sancillon arrived in a cab to fetch me. I protested, but the flesh is weak, and with a sigh for my neglected work I followed my two custodians and was soon back at *Les Trois Empereurs* where the scene was more festive than ever.

As I entered, the count and countess rose and came to greet me, then placed me on a chair between them, while the count remarked: "M. Dumas, we noticed that you seemed tired when you stayed with us till six or seven in the morning."

"I must confess," I replied, "that it does disturb my normal routine."

"Then," said the countess, "we must let you go at midnight."

"That, countess, is very easy to say! Still, I will try."

"But on one condition," the count went on.

"Namely," the countess broke in, "that you come to St. Petersburg with us! I thought that would make you jump!"

"That's simply impossible," I stammered.

"Why isn't it possible?" the count persisted.

"But you are leaving next Tuesday! How could I prepare for such a journey in five days? Besides," I went on, half to myself, "if I were to go to Russia I should want to see more than St. Petersburg."

"You're quite right," he said. "St. Petersburg is not Russia."

"No, I continued, "I should want to visit Moscow, Nijny-Novgorod, Kasan, Astrakhan, Sebastopol, and return via the Danube."

"That fits in extraordinarily well," replied the countess. "I have an estate at Koralovo, near Moscow; the count has land near Nijny, steppes at Kasan, fishing grounds at the Caspian Sea and a country house at Isatcha. That will give you thousands of square miles to explore!"

It was enough to turn the head of a traveller like me, tied to Paris by nothing stronger than a single hair, and a woman's hair at that, the most fragile of all bonds. "Countess," I exclaimed, "give me two days to decide."

"I give you two minutes," she teased me. "Either we shall refuse to give our sister to M. Home, or you will be best man at the wedding!"

I rose, went out on the balcony, and pondered. There was my proposed visit to the Eastern Mediterranean, but it would be a year or eighteen months before that would be possible. I reflected that nothing could be more interesting than to explore Russia under such conditions as the count proposed. Finally it struck me that the whole idea was crazy, and I rather fear it was this last thought that decided me.

"Well?" asked the countess, as I returned two minutes later.

"Well," I returned, "I will come with you." The count shook me by the hand, Home threw his arms round my neck, the next few days passed like a dream, and we were off!

❊ ❊ ❊ ❊

2

FROM PARIS TO BERLIN

On June 20th we set out from Paris by the overnight express for Cologne, in which Dandré had reserved three entire coaches for our party. The count and countess travelled in the middle one with Dandré and myself. Dandré had taken tickets for the two dogs, Douchka and Muichka, and the railway official in charge of such matters made no difficulty about letting them travel in our compartment as the count suggested, instead of in the guard's van. Moynet, whom I brought with me,—you remember Moynet, the artist whose charming décors you have so often admired at the *Opéra Comique* —was in the coach in front, with the doctor, the tutor, the maestro and the magician. Mademoiselle Hélène and the other ladies, with the maids and little Sacha, travelled in the rear coach. Among them they had managed to smuggle in the three remaining pets unobserved; the puppy, Charick, wrapped in a rug till he could settle down on Louise's lap; Signorina, in her basket; and Tchérépacha in a box that had once held pots of jam. Missam, the valet, had been sent on ahead to make sure a good meal would be waiting for us at Cologne. Where Simon and the two secretaries were, I have no idea.

The heat was stifling, but Dandré—a resourceful man—had provided three baskets of refreshments for us; one with champagne and ice-water; one full of roast chickens, hard-boiled eggs, sausages and a few bottles of Bordeaux; and the third with grapes, peaches, apricots and almonds. At Pontoise we had supper; at Creil we drank a little soda-water, and by the time we reached Compiègne we were all asleep.

I was wakened at the Belgian frontier by a shout—in the sort of French you know only too well—ordering all passengers to alight for their luggage to be searched. Out in the customs shed the sight of my name on my trunk and travelling bag had its usual effect, and, accepting without question my assurance that I had nothing to declare, the official scrawled on them the hieroglyphic that showed I was free to continue my journey. An hour later, once more settled in our seats, we were rolling on towards Aix-la-Chapelle.

At Verviers, on the Prussian frontier, a porter appeared at our carriage door to check our tickets. Dandré produced them, for four passengers and two dogs. The porter glanced round the compartment, but no dogs were to be seen, so he assumed they were duly in the van and passed on. At Aix-la-Chapelle our troubles began. While another porter was punching our tickets, Douchka poked her little nose out between the lace shawls that had covered her and yawned under the Prussian's very nose. "A dog!" he exclaimed, and his voice grew ominous. "You have dogs in here with you!"

"As you know," replied Dandré. "You have just seen their tickets."

"But dogs are not allowed to travel with the passengers."
"Why not?"

He had no time to explain, for a whistle blew and the train began to move. As long as he could he hung on the step, repeating fervently: "Dogs are not allowed to travel with the passengers," until he was forced to drop off, unless he wanted to cling on till we reached Cologne.

All through the next stage of our journey we discussed this enigma. Since dogs could travel with passengers in France and Belgium, why not in Prussia, too? But there was no one among us who could think of a reasonable explanation.

At the next station an official rushed to our carriage door and jumped on the step before the train had even stopped, furiously shouting at us: "Dogs! You have some dogs in there with you!"

"Yes. Here are their tickets, and ours." But no-one was bothering about us any more. "Dogs are not allowed to travel with the passengers," he cried, in the very words and intonation of his predecessor.

"Why not?" asked Dandré. "Give me one good reason."

"Because they might annoy other travellers."

"But that is not so in this case," said the count, speaking for the first time and in excellent German. "There are no passengers here but ourselves. We have reserved three coaches for our exclusive use, and we wish our dogs to remain with us."

"The rule expressly forbids it."

"To push a rule to such lengths is absurd," returned the count. "Fetch the station-master."

The station-master came to our window. He wore fearsome moustaches, three medals and an iron cross. "You have two dogs," he stated curtly. "They must be handed over and shut up in the guard's van."

"But we sent for you because we wish to keep them here with us."

"Quite impossible!"

"Why?"

"Dogs are not allowed to travel with the passengers!" He sang the same tune as the lesser employés we had already listened to, and was equally impervious to reason. We were on the point of letting him take our pets when the whistle blew. "All right, all right," the station-master snapped in exasperation. "Wait till the next station!" and as the train drew out his voice followed us, *diminuendo.*

We waited for the next station in a state of some anxiety. The train had barely slowed to a halt when two officials rushed to our compartment flung open the door and shouted for the dogs. There was nothing we could do. One of the Prussians snatched up Douchka, but Muichka seemed to have vanished. "The other dog!" shouted the second Prussian, his tone as threatening as though he meant to search us to the skin. "Where is the other one?"

Dandré had a bright idea. "In the next coach," he replied, and led the official to where Louise sat with Charick on her lap. With a sigh of relief the Prussian seized the puppy despite the protests of Louise, shut him up in the guard's van with Douchka, and then, his good humour restored, the worthy fellow came back to close our door behind Dandré and wish us a pleasant journey, satisfied that the rule was now being obeyed.

Now we could hope for a little peace. We nibbled some fruit, drank a glass of cool wine, and were comfortably dozing when, at the next station, a cry startled us into wakefulness. A fresh porter had come to keep an eye on us. "Why!" he exclaimed in shocked surprise, pointing an indignant finger at Muichka, who had rashly emerged from her hiding place, "there's another! You must have three dogs!" There was nothing for it but to own up, accept the Prussian's stern reprimand with humility and an apology, buy a ticket for a third dog and allow Muichka to be carried off to join Douchka and Charick in the van. Then, as the train moved off, we settled ourselves once more.

Towards noon we were nearing Cologne, a place I first visited with poor Gérard de Nerval[1]—it must be eighteen years ago, now. Two personal memories link me with this town of the three kings, one from my childhood, the other from the days when I was a lusty young man. In 1814, at the time of the German invasion, my mother was afraid to stay at Villers-Cotterets, thinking—why, I do not know—that we should be safer at Crépy-en-Valois, a little town

[1] Gérard de Nerval, the French poet and mystic, was a close friend of Dumas. They travelled extensively in Germany together in 1838. In 1841 his mind became unhinged and he committed suicide by hanging in 1855, some years before Dumas wrote this book.—Ed.

well away from the main routes through France. We hid our linen and silver in a cellar with one or two pieces of furniture more valuable than the rest, then my mother set out on a donkey, with me riding pillion behind her.

Three and a half hours later we reached the end of our journey. We stayed first with the mother of some of my school friends who had offered us hospitality, Madame de Longpré, the widow of a former *valet-de-chambre* of Louis XV. Perhaps she had once been pretty enough to win a glance of approval from His Majesty. Be that as it may, among the presents he gave her was a splendid dinner service of old Chinese porcelain. I can still see those huge soup plates, immense dishes and gigantic salad bowls with their fantastic flowers painted by some unknown Diaz, and dragons devised by a nameless Ariosto. It would have made a modern collector of bric-a-brac swoon with delight. But there was no market for bric-a-brac in 1814. The poor woman, and she really was poor, (unfortunately she had a weakness for the bottle), had many times tried to sell this royal dinner service complete, with no success, and when we knew her she had been reduced to selling it piecemeal. Whenever she managed to get 40 sous for a piece worth 200 francs, she would rush off in great delight to the nearest wine shop where she would drink two, four, or even six glasses of brandy one after the other, never coming home till she was dead drunk.

We remained only a day or two with her. My mother, who never drank anything stronger than water and has bequeathed to me a preference for the same beverage, could not tolerate, and, above all, could not permit me to witness, the hideous spectacle of drunkenness. She moved to the house of a doctor's widow, a Madame Millet, who let us have a little room on the first floor where there were two beds. It overlooked the courtyard, but also had a little window giving on to the main road from Crépy to Villers-Cotterets. We were to take our meals with the family, paying our share of the cost. Madame Millet's two sons had both followed their father's profession, the elder as a civilian doctor, living with his mother and two sisters, Amélie and Adèle, the younger as an army surgeon, now on active service. The whole family were keenly anxious, for they had had no news of him since the eve of the battle of Brienne, two months ago, and feared he might be killed or wounded, or taken prisoner.

On our first night, towards one o'clock in the morning, there came a heavy knocking at the street door. In great alarm everyone was instantly afoot, expecting the enemy to burst in at any moment. The knocking persisted, and at last Doctor Millet, as the only man in the house—I was eleven at the time—ventured to go down and open the door while the rest of us waited in terror. Then came a cry of joy, M. Millet called his mother and sisters, and a handsome young man of twenty-five or so rushed into the salon, threw off his cloak and stood revealed in his major's uniform—Madame Millet's younger son. As they all threw their arms around one another with happy tears and a babble of excited laughter, my mother silently drew me away, for any stranger is an intruder at such a moment. No one noticed us or saw us go. They had forgotten us completely.

In the morning they described to us what had happened, as though we had not been present. The young officer belonged to an army corps commanded by Marshal Mortier, that had suffered a surprise attack the night before at Villers-Cotterets. After fierce fighting, the corps had been utterly routed, the scattered survivors escaping as best they could in the darkness. Frederic Millet had naturally made for his own home, only a few miles away. Now, at the dawn of a new day, he was anxious to rejoin his regiment. But where would he find it? If he ventured out to look for it, he would almost certainly run into a party of Prussians and lose his liberty, if not his life. Would it not be better to wait for news, or, failing that, the roar of cannon? That sound he would certainly recognise, and then he would rally to the guns, as they say in the army.

While waiting, expecting the enemy to appear from one moment to the next, Frederic shaved off his moustache and changed into civilian clothes to avoid being recognised as belonging to the French army. His uniform, carefully folded, was hidden away with his sword in the bottom of a cupboard. Scarcely were these precautions completed when word reached us that a small detachment of French infantry and cavalry had just entered Crépy. Frederic ran out to question them. They were part of a force commanded by the Duke of Raguse, but had been cut off from their comrades. They had just posted sentinels round the town and were hoping for a short spell of rest.

But the enemy were close on their heels. Frederic had barely got back when we heard a shot and saw the sentinel, who had been stationed at the far end of our street, rushing back towards the town shouting *"Aux armes!"* From our upper window we caught sight of a corps of Prussian cavalry coming at full gallop. I can still see those soldiers in their blue coats, white collars and grey trousers, thundering towards us over the metalled high-road, while every house-holder in their path hastily fastened doors and windows. The sentinel would surely be overtaken and run down before he could warn his comrades camping in the town centre. The elder M. Millet dashed to our street door, flung it open and signalled to the man, who darted through into the garden, while behind him, swiftly as a trap on the stage, the door slammed shut.

Only just in time. The horsemen wheeled round the corner into our street and roared past the house like a whirlwind. Millet opened a back door, pointed out a byroad leading to the town centre, and the soldier, pausing only to drink a glass of wine and reload his gun, slipped through to rejoin his comrades. Once more the door was shut and bolted. You can imagine the tense interest we all took in this drama. We were all eyes and ears. Soon we heard the same thunder of hoofs again. It was the Prussians, riding back even faster than they came, with our French huzzars at their heels.

In spite of all my mother could do to hold me back, I ran to the window and saw that sublime, terrible sight, a melée, hand to hand fighting with swords and pistols. The Prussians tried desperately to form their ranks again and beat off the attack, but were forced to give ground. They fled, closely pursued by our cavalry, and the confused mass of men vanished round a twist in the road, noise, smoke and all, leaving nothing behind them but a few bodies lying on the cobbles outside the house. Three of those lay motionless in pools of blood. A fourth began to drag himself towards our door, doubtless hoping to rest his head on the stone step as on a pillow, and die peacefully dreaming of his native land. He was a young man in a blue coat—a Prussian, then—bleeding profusely from a wound in the forehead.

Dr. Millet and his brother rushed to open the door and drag the wounded man inside. From that moment, all our attention was given to tending him; the women made bandages, the two surgeons devoted their skill to dressing the gash that had split his skull and trying to restore him to consciousness, all of us oblivious of the battle once more raging in the street outside. Though no-one gave it a thought at the time, the situation was to our advantage. If the French won, we had nothing to fear; if the Prussians, our charity towards their comrade would safeguard us.

The patient opened his eyes and tried to speak. His French was very poor, but the elder Millet spoke German fairly well, so that doctor and patient could understand each other.

We had heard French bugles sounding the charge, and two or three detachments of our Light Cavalry galloping past our door, then a great burst of firing. Shortly after, there came a pounding on our door. When M. Millet answered it, we found that this time the Prussians were masters of the town, and demanding food and shelter for their men. He led the newcomers to the salon, where the patient, who proved to be an officer, ordered one of them to remain outside the house to prevent any intrusion. (When the time came for this sentry to be relieved, I need hardly add, he found a good meal waiting for him in the kitchen.)

For a month, the young Prussian was nursed like a son and a brother. Then, his wound quite healed, he left us, telling us his name and address. He was Antoine-Marie Farina, of Cologne, nephew of the celebrated Jean-Marie Farina, the finest distiller of perfume in the world.

In 1838, when I was visiting the banks of the Rhine, I went to Cologne and called on Antoine-Marie Farina, who had become a distiller of eau-de-cologne, like his uncle. The boy in the shop told me the *patron* was at dinner, but nevertheless, on hearing that I wished to see him, he came with a gracious smile to learn the reason for my call. My eyes sought his forehead. There was the scar. It was the right man. I asked him about his wound, and he told me where he received it. "Do you remember the Millet family?"

Indeed he did, with the utmost gratitude. "Do you recall a boy of ten or eleven, who held the basin when they dressed your wound? I hardly suppose you would recognise him now?" I added, laughing.

"Was that you?" he exclaimed, seizing both my hands in his. He threw his arms round my neck, called his wife and two charming daughters, explained the position to them in two words—those comprehensive German words, of course—and instantly I was the centre of a general embrace. They dragged me into their dining room, plied me with spiced bread, veal served with fruit jelly, hare stuffed with plums, washed down with the finest bottle of Johannesburg their cellar could produce. We talked all day round the table and spent the evening drinking tea and nibbling sweets until one o'clock in the morning. Never in living memory had anyone stayed up so late in Cologne!

My second memory is more recent. In 1840, while I was living in Florence, I was told that a German priest had called to see me. "What can a German priest want with me?" I wondered. "Never mind. Show him in." I expected to see a venerable old man with a long white beard, and was getting ready to ask his blessing when in came a fair-haired, pink cheeked fellow of thirty or so, striding across the room with a smile and an outstretched hand. I shook it cordially and asked what I could do for him.

"You can make it possible for me to see Rome. From a child, that has been my dearest wish, but I shall never be able to make it come true unless you are the sort of man I take you for."

"Sit down, then, and tell me all about it."

"My name is S -. - -," he told me, "I am the son of the famous German tragedienne S - - -, and a brother of that popular comedian D - - -."

"Why, then," I exclaimed, "I know your whole family."

"That is what encouraged me to come to you," he went on. "I am the *curé* of a poor parish in Cologne and my income is very small, but by living with the utmost frugality I managed to save a thousand francs for a visit to Italy. I have got to Florence, but all the money I have left is my fare home. Yet my whole heart is set on seeing Rome, so I have come to ask if you will lend me five hundred francs to take me there, though I must warn you I do not know how I shall ever pay you back, unless I live on bread and water for the next five years—not an inviting prospect."

I laughed. "You felt sure I should not be so hard as to insist on that! You shall indeed see Rome, without having to deny yourself a glass of Rhine wine now and then, or a little beef to follow your soup. Come with me." I took him to Messrs. Plowden and French, who held my letters of credit, had them count out six hundred francs into the good pastor's hand, and pointed out to him the road to Rome. He embraced me with tears of joy. "Off you go," I said. *Bon voyage,* and remember me in your prayers."

"Do such kind hearts need to be prayed for?" he replied. "I shall think of you and love you. You need not ask for more."

Two years later I was passing through Cologne with my son, and went to call on the curé. As he had told me, his home was poor, but easy to find. I walked straight in, and he rose to welcome me with a cry of delight. Then he faltered: "You haven't come to ask me for your six hundred francs, I hope?"

"No. Only to ask if you got to Rome, and whether it pleased you?"

"What a city!" he cried, raising his eyes to heaven. "And, but for you, I should have died without ever seeing it! Come, let me show you something."

He took me to his bedroom and showed me my portrait, hanging between pictures of Hugo and Lamartine. "But," I remarked, "these gentlemen have proper frames. Why have I only passe-partout?"

"You," he answered, "have my heart for your frame."

Finding myself once more in Cologne with an hour to spare, my first thought was to visit these two old friends again. Alas! Antoine-Marie Farina, that handsome young man I had tended in 1814, died a year ago at the age of 70; the pastor, S - - -, had been given a better living in a village outside the town. May the first rest in peace, and the second dwell happily in his new presbytery, with a couple of hundred extra francs a year!

On my return to the station where the train for Berlin was due to leave at four in the afternoon, I found Dandré deep in a serious discussion with the railway authorities. To avoid any repetition of our earlier embarrassments he had resolved to take tickets for all the pets, but when he mentioned Signorina the booking clerk gave a cry of shocked surprise. "But," he protested, "cats are not allowed to travel by train! Impossible! They are not on the tariff!" No argument could move him! Dogs, yes! Cats, no! At last Dandré sent for the station master. Once that functionary had recovered from his stupefaction at the question he was not unhelpful, and promised to refer the matter to the administrative council. Meanwhile, to avoid the risk of any political repercussions, he would, as a special concession, allow the cat to continue her journey, provided Dandré bought a dog's ticket for her.

The next problem was Tchérépacha. On its bed of salad the tortoise lay motionless. The officials turned it this way up, then that, but it gave no sign of life and at last they decided to classify it as a shell, a 'curiosity', an item of personal luggage. It struck me as odd that, in the country of those celebrated naturalists, Humboldt and Zimmerman, a cat was classed as a dog, and a tortoise as a shell. I must remember to tell my biologist friend, Saint-Hilaire, about it when I get back to Paris.

As soon as this scientific discussion was settled to the satisfaction of the authorities, we took our seats and the train began to move. Of the journey to Berlin I can tell you nothing of interest, for the heat was so fierce, the dust so choking, that we were obliged to draw the curtains and amuse ourselves as best we could until ten o'clock, when we wished one another goodnight and tried to sleep. I have a vague impression that during the night Dandré brought me a strawberry sherbet—delicious, but fleeting—and once, when I drew aside the curtain for a moment, I saw a family of hares performing a fantastic dance by moonlight in a field beside the track.

It was eleven in the morning when we arrived in Berlin, to find carriages waiting for us at the station and a good meal being prepared at the Rome Hotel, thanks to Missam. Our first cry was for baths, and there were some actually in the hotel, in a deliciously cool basement. I was on the point of getting into my bath when there came a knock on the door, and a manservant brought in a visiting card. My presence in Berlin was already known! On the card I read: Alexandre Dunker, Bookseller. My intention was to see absolutely no-one in Berlin, not from any lack of respect for the town, but because the carbuncle on my cheek was now so enormous that I dreaded facing the public eye in such a state. But a bookseller wouldn't worry me! Practically a member of the family! So I called him in.

Having heard of my arrival in Berlin—I have no idea who told him—he had come to offer to show me the town. I showed him my carbuncle. Gravely he inspected it and expressed the opinion that it had passed the stage of being merely a personal disfigurement, and become a natural curiosity. Far be it from me to deprive Berliners of a sight of any phenomenon of nature, so I promised the good bookseller that I would come to his shop at two o'clock, with Moynet, and we would all explore the town together.

The first place I wanted to visit was the New Museum, where Kaulbach[1] was busy painting his sixth fresco. If Théophile Gautier had been in my place, with his admirable talent for appreciation of sculptured forms, he would have told you everything about these frescos from Alpha to Omega; but all I did was to walk in front of them in shoes that were pinching me, and all I remember is that I thought them very beautiful. The German School of painting, especially in Berlin, excels in murals, and M. Kaulbach's figures symbolising Architecture, Poetry, Painting and Music are magnificent. If I might be allowed to offer a hint of constructive criticism, it is that in the fresco of Architecture there are two almost identical winged figures, one presenting the Parthenon, the other, Strasbourg Cathedral. That seems wrong to me from several points of view, artistic, archeological and religious. Each figure should have been given some affinity with the masterpiece it displayed; one should have been a genie; the other, an angel.

We mounted the staircase to the Greek Room, for this museum possesses not only modern frescoes of great value, but also antique statues of great beauty. Alas! Here, as everywhere else, to bring Greek sculpture near modern works is to emphasise how inferior contemporary sculptors are by comparison. Nowadays, a sculptor studies anatomy in lecture rooms for years; he must know as much

---

(1) Wilhelm von Kaulbach (1805-1874).—Ed.

as any doctor about bone structure and movements, the play of muscles under the skin. Yet not one of them since Michael Angelo has managed to avoid making mistakes in depicting muscular action.

The Greeks, on the contrary, had no scientific knowledge of anatomy. Worshippers of beauty, they would have thought it a sacrilege to dissect a corpse. Hippocrates himself has told us that to learn anything about the internal structure of human beings he had to follow the army and examine the wrecks of bodies on the battlefield. Whence, then, came that physical perfection we see in the works of Praxiteles, Phidias, and a score of other sculptors who left behind them whole groves of marble masterpieces? From a never-ending study of the nude, an instinctive love of beauty, and a memory for shapes, three things it is impossible to find in modern art. But there! We have steam-power, electricity, railways, balloons, daily papers,—things the ancients never knew. One cannot have everything.

Of Berlin itself I cannot tell you more than you will find in any guide-book, but would you believe that in such a large city I could not find a room and a bed? Yet that is the truth! Moynet and I searched for hours! By eight o'clock tonight we were on the point of asking the King of Prussia for hospitality—with a palace 460 feet long and 100 feet high, how could he have refused?—when I suddenly thought of the cool bathroom and large baths where we enjoyed such a refreshing hour this morning. Were the bathrooms empty? They were. Could the manager send down two mattresses and four sheets to make beds for us in two of the baths? With pleasure. So now, unperturbed by belated Berliners peering in amazement through the ventilator, I am writing to you from my bath, and looking forward to a luxurious night's rest. Tomorrow evening we shall leave for Stettin, where we shall board a ship at one o'clock the next afternoon. If the Baltic is friendly, I shall be able to continue writing as we sail on to St. Petersburg.

*   *   *   *

3

BETWEEN STETTIN AND ST. PETERSBURG

Begun aboard the *Vladimir,* June 25th.
Between Denmark and Courland.

The Baltic, though grey and sombre as befits a northern sea, is as smooth as a mirror, so that, as I hoped, I can continue writing on board. We are on the better of the two steamers that make regular crossings between Stettin and St. Petersburg, the *Vladimir.* (The other is the *Eagle.*) Ours is named after Vladimir the Great, St. Vladimir, who, if I remember rightly, was the eldest of the three sons of Sviatoslav, Prince of Russia, from whom he inherited Novgorod. The history books will give you details of how Vladimir won his title of "the Great"; I will confine myself to telling you how he became a saint.

First he killed his brother and usurped his lands. Then he married six wives, and, like Solomon, had eight hundred concubines. One of his wives was a princess of Polotsk, whose family he massacred, and whom he raped to force her consent to the ceremony. He had twelve sons. (In all probability he forgot to count his daughters.) Clearly, such a man was an ecletic in matters of culture, and the time came when he felt an urge to embrace a religion. He was offered a choice of four. Would he follow the teachings of Mahomet? Vladimir shook his head: "I have no liking for a faith that forbids the use of wine. Strong drink is indispensable to Russians. It is their only joy."

The Roman Catholic Church? Again he rejected the suggestion. This time the difficulty was the existence of the Pope. "I am quite willing," said Vladimir, "to acknowledge a God in heaven, but one here on earth? No!"

Judaism, then? "There seems to me no sense in taking sides with those fugitives from the wrath of heaven. Why should I share their punishment for a crime I did not commit?"

Finally someone proposed the Greek Church, and though I have no idea what reasons swayed Vladimir this time, I know he accepted it. He was not the sort of man to do things by halves, so he had every false god in his kingdom cast into the Dnieper. Then the new convert, in his zeal to ensure that the grace that had so miraculously touched his own heart should be extended to his subjects, had them all herded up in droves on the banks of the nearest river. There they were baptised in thousands, one crowd crawling out of the water as the next was forced in, every man emerging with the same christian name—that of some saint or other. All these good deeds received due recognition, Sviatoslav's son was canonised, and the name of Saint Vladimir was added to the calendar.

So much for our ship's patron saint. Now for some of our fellow passengers. First I should mention Princess Dolgorouky and her three daughters, the eldest just sixteen. The princess claims to be fifty—a subterfuge to safeguard her while travelling, I presume, for she cannot be more than thirty-five or forty. She is very well-educated, and can be gracious when she relaxes her customary severity. The Dolgorouky family is one of the oldest in Russia. One of their ancestors, Prince Grégory, defended the Convent of Saint Sergius from 1608 to 1610 against 30,000 Poles and Cossacks commanded by the four greatest leaders of the time: Sapieha, Lissovsky, Tyszkievicz and Constantin Visnioviecki. In 1624, a princess of the House of Dolgorouky was married to the Czar Michael Romanoff, founder of the dynasty that still rules Russia today. Prince Jacques Dolgorouky was a friend and counsellor of the Czar Peter I, and that ruler's grandson, Peter II, made Prince Jean Dolgorouky his closest companion. When Empress Anne came to the throne and handed her power over to that infamous Biren, who caused the death of eleven thousand Russians, Prince Jean and his family were exiled to Siberia. Nine years later he was brought back to die by torture. His wife, Princess Nathalie, who had shared his exile, returned to Kiev and became a nun. The day before she took her final vows she climbed a steep cliff overhanging the Dnieper, slipped her wedding ring from her finger and cast it into the water. Then she entered a convent where, for thirty years, she lived praying for the man she loved.

Today, there are three members of the Dolgorouky family holding important government posts: Prince Nicolas, formerly Governor-General of Lithuania and now Governor-General of Little Russia; Prince Elia, Commander-in-Chief of the Imperial Artillery; and Prince Basil, who has accomplished several diplomatic and military missions with distinction.

On board with us, too, is Prince Pierre Troubetskoi, returning from Paris with despatches. He is still a young man—33 or 34, I should say—as distinguished in appearance as in his qualities of mind. Few men have his detailed grasp of the problems involved in emancipation, the question everyone is discussing at the moment, and though he stands to lose an income of a million a year, no one views the project more broad-mindedly than he does.

The Troubetskoi family belong to the ancient aristocracy of Russia, and are descended from Olgerd, Grand-Duke of Lithuania, father of the famous Jagellon. Another ancestor, Prince Dimitri, was one of the most brilliant leaders in the War of Independence at the beginning of the 17th century, and one of the three candidates for the throne in 1613, when Michael Romanoff was chosen to be the Czar.

After these two important personages, the next most remarkable passenger on board is an English globe-trotter, who was recently hunting crocodiles, elephants and hippopotami on the banks of the Blue Nile. He wants to see the sun shining at midnight, as one can in the extreme north of Europe on the night of the summer solstice. Then he is off to Borneo. Oddly enough, this is the second time our Englishman has come north for this purpose. The first time, he reached Mt. Ava-Saxa—the best spot for observing this astronomic phenomenon—at ten o'clock at night, in a state of such complete exhaustion that he fell asleep, telling his servant to wake him just before midnight. The conscientious fellow stood by, watch in hand, and at five minutes to twelve tried to rouse his master. In vain! The Englishman might have been dead for all the notice he took, except for his snores. His servant shook him and at last evoked the murmur: "Stop it, John! Let me sleep!"

"But, my lord, you told me to wake you! This is the day! Tomorrow will be too late."

"Never mind! I'll come back next year!" The following year he was busy in some other part of the globe, but now, three years later, he has come to keep his promise, still followed by his faithful John.

Reverting to Stettin, where this stage of our journey started, I strongly advise you not to stay in that town. God! What beds! A badly stuffed sofa, draped in a sheet and covered with a quilted counterpane! The sheet may be washed from time to time, the counterpane never. Luckily we spent only one night there, but it seemed very long!

At eleven precisely our boat began to glide down the Oder, whose emerald-green banks were dotted with groups of red-roofed houses, surprisingly like Normandy, and five or six hours later we were out in the Baltic. Another hour or two and we could see the shores of Pomerania sloping gently down to sea level, merging with the waves as night began to fall. This passage from Stettin to St. Petersburg cost 232 francs per person, including meals. Indeed, for 400 francs one can go from Paris to St. Petersburg, inclusive of hotels and food—about four *sous* a mile, which is not absolutely ruinous.

At nine o'clock we drank a cup of tea, and stayed chatting on deck till midnight, enjoying the first fresh air we had breathed since leaving Paris. At two in the morning it began to rain and a gale sprang up. It seemed to me a good time to follow the example of the Englishman and refuse to re-open my eyes, which I did to such good purpose that it was seven in the morning when I woke. I dressed and went on deck, where the first thing I saw was Home, pale as death, having spent the whole night in direct communication with the Baltic.

Fortunately, the fine weather had returned. The sun, rather pale, I thought, was climbing above the horizon. The sea was blue, vast and empty. A tall, handsome, fair-haired young fellow of 26 or so came to make my acquaintance. He was Prince Galitzine, and we soon found a mutual interest. He was a great hunter before the Lord, and while we were talking of hunting he pointed out to me a stretch of land appearing on our port side. It was the island of Gotland.

Soon we could make out the outline of its craggy coast, and I was trying to see all I could of the place through a telescope, for it was fifteen or twenty miles away, when a Swede, a corn-merchant from Visby, the capital of Gotland, came up and offered to tell me anything I might want to know about the island. My friends know how patiently I listen, even to people who bore me. When I am interested, as I was then, I am insatiable. My questions came thick and fast, and I soon gathered a good many entertaining details about this Swedish territory. Visby is one of the oldest towns in the North, but now shorn of its ancient prestige and full of ruins. Its cathedral, my informant told me, is purest Gothic, begun at the end of the 14th century and completed early in the 15th. (How many Paris corn-chandlers could tell you the date and architectural style of our own great churches?) Agriculture is the main industry, My friend made his money out of wheat, or, rather, rye, which in Gotland grows almost white. A peculiarity of the soil there is its large proportion of lime. The earth retains the sun's heat and would dry up completely if the fields were not protected by a covering of leafy branches. I should add that Gotland has no lakes or rivers, only little brooks that run dry in summer. Besides its commerce in grain, the island breeds silkworms and cattle. Personally, I dislike mutton, but my Swedish friend assured me I should enjoy the meat of the woolly sheep I was watching through my glass as he spoke. It seems they have a special flavour, something between hare and venison, due to the salt pastures where they graze.

In Visby, and everywhere in Gotland, there is a great festival on the night of June 23rd. Each patch of high ground has its bonfire or firework display, in memory, some say, of the funeral pyre of Balder, son of Frigga, goddess of Norse mythology. Others claim it is a ritual to welcome summer. Tradition says that on this night a young Swedish girl may obtain a prophetic glimpse of the man she will marry. To conjure up this vision she must gather, in utter silence, a magic bouquet of nine different flowers plucked from nine different fields and sleep with it under her pillow. In her dreams her future husband will appear, take out the bouquet, lift it to his lips, and then gently replace it. Or she may choose a different method and spend that night sleeping on her balcony, wrapped only in a sheet, having placed beside her a bowl of water and a white towel. If she dreams that a young man draws near and asks permission to wash his face and hands in the basin, he is the one she is destined to wed.

While I was hearing about these customs, both, I believe, of pagan origin, Gotland was vanishing into the distance. The gong sounded for dinner, we went down, and when we came back on deck there was no land in sight, though Sweden lay to our left and the coast of Courland to our right. By and by we managed to make out what seemed at first a patch of fog rather than solid ground— the Island of Oesel, our first glimpse of Russia! Long ago, Oesel, like Courland, was conquered by the Teutonic Knights, who yielded it to Poland in 1561. Later it passed to the Danes, then to Sweden, and in 1721, under Peter the Great, it became Russian, as it has remained ever since.

As tea was served I glanced at my watch and decided I must have forgotten to wind it. Nine o'clock? Ridiculous! It was still broad daylight! I asked a man who stood near me. His watch told an even more extraordinary tale—eleven! But he had set it to St. Petersburg time, which is two hours ahead of French time. The further we went, the more we should see of those luminous nights I had heard so much about, which, for a whole month, give Northern Russia twenty-four hours daylight every day. I glanced towards the west, where the sun was setting. In three hours, they told me, it would rise again. I had no desire to sleep, so I had my tea brought up on deck, picked up a book and settled down, reading and dreaming, to wait for the sunrise. At midnight by my watch the horizon grew red as the sun's rim rose, not due east, as we see it in Paris, but several points further north. The transparency of the night robbed the dawn of the majesty it has in other latitudes, and the sun seemed hardly more brilliant than the full moon does, with us, in July or August. I waited till it was well above the horizon, then I went to bed.

Three hours later I was up again. So, indeed, were all the other passengers. It looked like being a beautiful day. Once again we were out of sight of land, but towards ten o'clock we saw a lighthouse on our right—the Kokchar, built on sea-girt rocks—and on our left a brown strip of land—Estonia, reunited to Russia by Peter the Great after the Peace of Nystadt, in 1721. It was here that Alexander I made his first experiment in emancipation, giving the Estonians their freedom in 1816.

As we drew nearer we began to make out a shore covered with trees that seemed to spring from the sea itself. The waters of the Baltic have no harmful effect on vegetation, I was told. True, the influence of the Neva affects the whole Gulf of Finland, and all the way from St. Petersburg to Kronstadt the water is fresh enough to drink. The sea proper begins below Reval, and at St. Petersburg only freshwater fish are offered for sale.

Towards noon we could see houses here and there against the dark green of the forest, and soon the outline of a town with three steeples towering above the tangle of roof-tops—Reval. It was Waldemar I of Denmark who, in 1200, seized the Castle of Lindanisse, the key to Estonia, and built round it a town to be the capital of his new kingdom, calling it *Rehfall*—"The Hind's Leap"—after an incident he saw while hunting there. The people of Reval, unconquered, made peace on honourable terms, retaining their rights and liberties which they guarded jealously, as the following legend testifies.

One of their rights was the freedom to maintain justice without respect of persons. It happened in 1525 that a certain Baron Uxhul of Riesenberg flouted their laws by strangling a peasant within the boundaries of the town. The tribunal of Revalian justice considered the matter and pronounced Baron Uxhul a blood-guilty outlaw. The baron contemptuously ignored the ban and boldly walked into the town, but before he had gone a hundred yards he was arrested. Brought to trial, baron though he was, he was convicted of murder and sentenced to death. His family, beginning to realise the matter was serious, bestirred themselves, appealed to the authorities, begged for clemency, offered money to wipe out the stain of blood and to ransom Uxhul, but all in vain. The baron was duly hanged, and buried beside the Blacksmith's Gate, under a stone recording the details.

A hundred years or so later the nobles held sway for a time and had the Gate walled up to conceal Uxhul's memorial, but in 1794 the burghers won back their power and ordered the Blacksmith's Gate to be re-opened so that all men might see this monument to public justice.

A further instance showing the free exercise of the rights of the common people existed till last year in Reval, actually in the Church of St. Nicholas, which can easily be seen from the steamer. It was the mummified body of Charles-Eugène, Duke of Croy, Prince of the Holy Roman Empire, Marquis of Monte-Corneto and Renti. This corpse was the property of a worthy sexton who used to display it to visitors for whatever honorarium they cared to give.

The Duke of Croy, a son of that ancient and illustrious Belgian family whose ancestors were allied to the King of Hungary, was born in the middle of the 17th century. He served Christian V, King of Denmark, who made him a Lieutenant-General, and Leopold I, for whom he waged a victorious campaign against the Turks. From Austria he went to Saxony, then to Russia, where he was wounded at Narva, taken prisoner by Charles XII and interned at Reval, where he died on January 20th, 1702.

During his brief sojourn at Reval the duke contracted debts that he could not pay, and died insolvent. The Town Council, by virtue of the existing laws, decreed that his body must remain unburied until those debts were paid. Accordingly he was placed in a corner of St. Nicholas's Church, still dressed in the clothes he had worn when alive: a black velvet cloak over the military uniform given him by Peter the Great, a long curled wig on his head, silk stockings on his legs and a fine linen cravat round his neck.

When the Marquis Paulucci came to Reval in 1819 as Governor of the Baltic Provinces, he pleaded for greater charity towards this poor corpse, so pitilessly exposed for more than a hundred years to the curiosity of generation after generation, but the city fathers would brook no interference with the exercise of their civic rights. The utmost concession they would grant was to allow Paulucci to have the body decently laid in a wooden niche, and there it still was, three years ago, when Prince Troubetskoi, who told me this story, actually saw it.

What particularly impressed the prince was the sexton's devoted care for the corpse that had become his livelihood. By this time, the church was almost as far gone in decay as the Duke of Croy, and the roof leaked badly. Mindful, no doubt, of the gravedigger's comment in *Hamlet*—"your water is a sore decayer of your dead body"—the sexton constantly moved it away from the damp. And that was not all. Like a nurse tending an invalid, in fine weather he would take it outside for an airing, and on summer days would stand it in the sunshine. Unfortunately for the poor sexton, the young emperor Nicholas decided this exposure, and, indeed exploitation, of a corpse was sacrilege. He over-ruled the local authorities and commanded that the Duke of Croy, in debt or not, must be given Christian burial. Nowadays, there is nothing more remarkable in the Church of St. Nicholas than a painting of *The Flight into Egypt,* in which the artist, instead of following tradition and showing the Virgin seated on a donkey with the infant Jesus in her arms, followed by St. Joseph leaning on his staff, chose to portray the Holy Family riding in a magnificent carriage drawn by four horses. St. Joseph in a powdered wig, is holding the long reins, while angels circling round the carriage are fanning Mother and Child with their wings and sheltering them from the sun.

When I went up on deck at 5 a.m. the first thing I saw was the Russian Fleet on manoeuvres in the Baltic. The Flagship was commanded by the Grand-Duke Constantin, who enjoys being at sea. He seemed in no hurry to return to port, for he was idling along under top-sails only, and though the *Vladimir* was not a fast ship we soon outstripped the fleet. Towards seven we began to make out the fortifications of Kronstadt, that impregnable Russian naval base, rising up from the rough and dark-brown sea. That was as far as our steamer could take us, for only vessels of shallow draught can navigate the Neva.

Count Kouchelef, who has such facilities at his command, had written from Paris ordering that a boat should be waiting for his party at Kronstadt, so, leaving all our effects to follow later, we were able to continue our journey without delay. As it happened, our departure for St. Petersburg did not lack ceremonial honours. The Grand-Duke Constantin, coming into port behind us, saluted Kronstadt with a salvo of twenty-one guns; Kronstadt replied with an equal burst of artillery, making forty-two explosions in all. Only a very exacting man would ask for more.

The sight of Kronstadt reminded me of the *affaire* between M. de Villebois and Empress Catherine the First. M. de Villebois was one of those hardy adventurers who went to Russia in the eighteenth century to make their fortunes. He was the son of a Breton nobleman, and as a lad joined a band of smugglers. After a skirmish in which three coastguards were shot, he fled to England, volunteered for the navy and rose to the rank of a non-commissioned officer. On one of its voyages his ship put in at Texel, and Peter the Czar, who, at the time, was working at Saardam in the guise of a dock-yard labourer to obtain practical knowledge of ship-building, came to look at the English man-o'-war. Finding that she was on the point of sailing, he contrived to go aboard her *incognito*, presumably to gain an an insight into the science of navigation.

Providence gave him more than he bargained for. Such a fearful tempest blew up that after battling against it for three days the captain, officers and crew found themselves at the end of their resources, physical as well as scientific. At a moment of peril it was Villebois who seized the helm and executed a manoeuvre that saved the ship.

The Czar had already noticed the quarter-master as a man of spirit and hardihood, swift to think and act, as empire builders or reformers need to be. Once the emergency had passed he went up to Villebois and greeted him warmly. The haughty Breton was disposed to repulse this advance from a humble Dutch seaman, and the Czar revealed his identity. It says a great deal for Villebois' perspicacity that he recognised royalty through such a disguise, and when Peter returned to Russia Villebois went with him as his aide-de-camp and chief adviser in naval matters.

Our gentleman from Lower Brittany had all the good and

bad qualities of his compatriots. He was a good officer, audacious to the point of recklessness, headstrong, fond of drinking to excess. If, by some mischance, he failed to reach that stage of intoxication when he rolled peacefully under the table, he was capable of any outburst of passion, as Peter himself was—one reason why the two men were such boon companions in war or at table. At such times Villebois was beside himself, hardly aware of what he did, and on three occasions he killed three men, but the Czar took a lenient view of crimes like that and readily forgave him.

Unfortunately for Villebois, drink did always move him to homicide. One day, when the Czar was at his castle of Strelna, in the bay of St. Petersburg, he entrusted Villebois with a mission to the Empress Catherine, who was at Kronstadt. It was in the depth of winter, the temperature was ten or twelve degrees below zero, and the gulf was frozen, so Villebois set out in a sleigh, taking a bottle of brandy with him to keep out the cold. When he reached Kronstadt the bottle was empty, but for Villebois that was sobriety, and he seemed perfectly composed to all the officers of the guard when he presented himself and asked to be taken to the Czarina.

The Empress was asleep, and while her maids of honour prepared to wake her, Villebois sat waiting in a room as over-heated as rooms always are in St. Petersburg in winter, and the change of temperature had a profound effect on him. When Catherine's maids conducted him to her bed-chamber and left him alone in her presence, he forgot he was looking at an Empress, saw her only as a very lovely woman, and immediately felt a strong urge to express his admiration for her beauty. Villebois was a man of rapid execution, and though the Czarina called her women, he had already given proof of that admiration by the time they arrived.

Instantly he was arrested and a swift courier despatched to tell the Czar as tactfully as possible what had occurred. The Czar listened to the whole story with no sign of anger, and then asked: "What have you done with him?"

"Sire," replied the messenger, "he was bound hand and foot and thrown into prison."

"What did he do then?"

"The moment the cell door closed behind him he fell fast asleep."

"That's my Villebois!" cried the Czar. "I'll wager that when he wakes in the morning he will have forgotten why he is there." To the courtier's amazement, Peter gave no sign of anger, but stalked up and down the room in perplexity. Then he went on: "I suppose I must make an example of him, though the great dolt is innocent enough and had no idea what he was doing. But the Czarina would be furious if he were not punished. Let me see. Suppose I send him to the galleys for a couple of years and then forget all about it." But before Villebois had been away six months, the Czar found he could not do without him and recalled him to court, begging the Czarina to pardon him as a favour to her husband. Thereafter, Villebois was as much in the Czar's confidence as he had been before being sent on the mission that ended in such a singular fashion.

As yet we have not set foot in Russia, and already we are talking of Peter the Great, that giant whose personality still broods over the mouth of the Neva. "St. Petersburg," said Pushkin, "is a window opening upon Europe." When, in 1469, Ivan III married Princess Sophia, heiress of a realm that stretched from Greece to Constantinople, he took as his emblem the imperial double-headed eagle, one head looking towards Asia, the other towards Europe. The symbolism is clear, but in those days Pushkin's "window" did not exist. The place where it now stands was nothing but a marsh commanded by a Swedish fortress called Nienschantz. Peter captured the fort and at once began to lay the foundations of a second capital for Russia, destined to become more important than her first. On 27th May, 1703, the Day of Pentecost, it was named St. Petersburg in honour of the Czar's patron saint. Pushkin, whose lyrics in praise of Peter the Great I have translated into French verse,[1] was a fine romantic poet comparable to Byron or Goethe. Unfortunately, he died after a duel fought when he was only 38 and his powers were at their zenith. Russia is unlucky. All her great poets, painters and musicians die young, by violence or from natural causes, as though the branches of her

(1) The original text contains Dumas's translations of Pushkin's work.—Ed.

culture are not yet strong enough to bear such fruits.

All that most Frenchmen of today know about this northern empire is gleaned from Voltaire's *History of Russia,* which gave details of Peter the Great's public life, and to that extent was of value, but said almost nothing about his personal affairs, even when these had a bearing on matters of state. Could you tell the history of Troy, and suppress all mention of Helen's elopement with Priam's son on the grounds that it concerned merely the private life of Menelaus? The savage murder of the Czarevitch Alexius by his father's orders so appalled Voltaire that he wrote to Count Schouvalef: "Until I can edit the details of this terrible affair I have put aside my *Histoire* and started work on another book." What it was he did not say, but even if it had been the *Dictionnaire philosophique* he could have spared enough time to relate the facts. In my view, to edit history is to falsify it. Write the whole truth as far as you know it, or do not write at all.

The facts were simple, and easy to understand, once you accept the truth that this Russian colossus was utterly ruthless. Alexius, the only surviving son of Peter I and his wife, Eudoxia, became the figure-head in a revolt that threatened to assassinate the Czar and split Russia by civil war. At last he was made prisoner, and on July 6th, 1718, was brought before a tribunal that condemned him to death. By the next day, the whole population was up in arms, clamouring that Alexius must be set free, and a deputation humbly petitioned Peter to pardon his son. "So be it," replied the Czar at last. "I will sign a warrant for his release. Let this good news be conveyed to the prisoner."

As the deputation turned to leave him, Peter the Great summoned the court physician. "Doctor," he said, "you know the czarevitch is highly strung. This unexpected pardon may prove too much of a shock to him. Quick! Go to the prison. Bleed him well, as a precaution." Then, as the doctor reached the door, the Czar added in a voice throbbing with hatred for the hapless prince: "Bleed him thoroughly—in all four limbs." Two hours later, the czarevitch was dead.

Peter's choice was clear. If his son lived, Russia would die—the Russia he had hewn out of chaos and welded into a nation. With

Alexius dead, his work survived. The Russian Empire, first formed by the hand of Peter the Great, now covers a third of the globe and glorifies its founder in 30 different languages while Alexius sleeps, forgotten, in six feet of quiet earth in a corner of the Church of Saints Peter and Paul.

*   *   *   *

The boat sent from St. Petersburg to pick us up at Kronstadt was *The Cockerel,* and Count Kouchelef invited Prince Troubetskoi and Princess Dolgorouky to travel in her, an offer they both accepted. Dandré, our charming, efficient major-domo, was left behind to do battle with the customs officials over our 57 pieces of luggage. Compared with the *Vladimir,* the *Cockerel* was a mere nutshell, and the gangway placed from deck to deck sloped as steeply as a Paris roof. The only way to negotiate it was to slide down on one's posterior, a mode of locomotion that the ladies refused to adopt. After some discussion, one end of the gangplank was raised from the *Cockerel's* deck to her bridge, whence we could descend via the captain's ladder. Even that proved difficult, for a high wind swept down on us from Finland, whipping up great waves that threw the boats now against each other, now apart. Still, with two stout sailors clutching each end of our improvised bridge, we managed to cross without mishap.

Lunch for twenty persons was ready in the mess, but it was decided—most imprudently—to delay our meal until we were on the move. Curiosity kept everyone on deck while the *Cockerel* gave a cough, belched out a little smoke, churned the water with her paddle wheels and began to pull away from her huge neighbour. Dandré, surrounded by luggage, gazed sadly down at us as we passed. We gave him one last wave of encouragement, then we were under way, en route for St. Petersburg. (What has become of him? God knows! That was three days ago, and our only collars, cravats and shirts are those we were wearing.) Here is a copy of a letter I have just written to a charming compatriot I will tell you of later, who invited me to her birthday party:

"To the fairest of angels from the filthiest of mortals:

We are expecting our trunks at any moment. If they arrive, it will give me great pleasure to accept your invitation. But if they do not, how can we presume to sully the festivities? Wire me the name of the patron saint of the Customs Office, and I will light in his or her honour a candle as thick as my body and as tall as an obelisque. Do not expect us, but lay our places at table just the same.

I kiss your hands. Moynet kisses your feet, aspiring to reach my level one day.

Alexandre Dumas."

Soon the wind reached gale force and the *Cockerel* pitched and rolled in the heavy seas. The ladies pleaded indisposition and retired below. Poor Home turned from pink to yellow, then to pale green, and clung with both arms to the *maestro* Millelotti. The other men clutched the rigging, while I started off in the direction of lunch, for a high sea always gives me a good appetite. Unfortunately, at the very moment when, after miracles of balancing, I set foot in the dining room (probably my left foot!) everything on the table, food, plates, bottles, glasses, slid to the deck with a mighty crash. Not a single piece of glass or china remained unbroken. From the debris I picked up a slice or two of bread and ham and ate them as I went back up on deck. There I found Home—his occupation the exact opposite of my own—and a group of passengers with good sea-legs standing in the bows. I strolled forward to join them. Through the haze Moynet had caught sight of a gilded dome and was pointing it out to the rest of us. I boldly expressed the opinion that it must be the cupola of Saint Isaac, built by our countryman, Montferrand. Prince Troubetskoi, coming up just them, confirmed that I was right, led me aside and invited me to join him on a wolf-hunt in the woods of Gatchina, where, I am told, wolves are as plentiful as the hares in our forest of Saint-Germain.

Hunting wolves in a favourite sport of the Russians and, loving danger for its own sake, they have invented a method that doubles the danger. The hunter may be devoured by wolves or battered to death in his carriage. This is how their ingenious invention operates—always in the winter time, of course, when wolves are ferocious from lack of food. Three or four hunters, each with a double-barrelled gun, crowd into a troika—that is a carriage of any sort, *drojky*, *kibitk*, *calèche* or *tarantass*, drawn by three horses, for the name depends on the team, not on the shape of the vehicle. The horse in the middle must always trot; the ones on the left and right must always gallop. The middle one trots with his head down, and is called "the snow eater"; his companions, harnessed to the shafts by their girths and each driven with a single rein, gallop along tossing their heads and are called "the furies." A dependable driver—always supposing that such a man exists—takes the reins, and a young pig is tied on behind with a rope twelve yards long, or a chain for greater security. The pig travels comfortably inside the carriage as far as the place where the hunt is to begin, then he is put out. The horses start off again and the pig, unaccustomed to such a pace, protests loudly. His squeals swell to a lamentation; the first wolf pokes his nose out and chases the pig, then a second, a third, a dozen, fifty, all striving to get close enough to nip him with their smoking jaws. The poor creature's cries become shrieks of hopeless terror, shrill enough to pierce the deepest recesses of the forest and rouse every wolf within a radius of seven or eight miles. Soon the troika has a great pack in pursuit, and that is when the driver's skill is of vital importance, for horses have an instinctive dread of wolves and will bolt if they can. All this time, the hunters are firing at random, for there is no need to take aim. The snow whirls up around them in a dense white cloud, while the pig screams, the horses neigh, the wolves howl, the guns flash and roar—a devil's concert to rouse the envy of Mephistopheles himself. As long as the driver remains master of his frenzied horses, all may be well; but if, for a single instant, he loses control and the carriage overturns, that is the end. To-morrow, the next day, or a week later, a search party will find the debris of the troika, the rifle barrels, the skeletons of the horses, the arm and leg bones of the men.

Last winter, Prince Repnine very nearly met his death on a hunt like this, out on the steppes that form part of his own domain. Their vehicle was a sledge large enough to hold three hunters, and the prince sat facing the rear while his two friends faced to the left and right respectively, each man armed with a pair of double-barrelled guns and a hundred and fifty rounds of ammunition. Their young, powerful horses were in the charge of a coachman born in the neighbourhood, a shrewd man with vast experience. It was night when they reached the snow-covered desert, but the full moon shone brilliantly. The pig was turned out, the sledge moved on, squeals arose and one or two wolves appeared, timidly at first and at a distance, but soon there were twenty closing in and the first shot rang out. There is a proverb that says "wolf does not eat wolf," but the starving pack surged round to devour the body, and the smell of blood brought more wolves from their holes. They seemed to spring out of the very earth till there were two or three thousand howling beasts with flashing eyes and pointed noses pursuing the sledge. As they came within range, the hunters kept up a running fire, but though every shot told, the pack grew larger and larger. The pig was dragged into the sledge, for his cries seemed to redouble the ferocity of the wolves. They were running in the shape of a great crescent, and in spite of the speed of the horses the two points of the crescent out-distanced them, threatening to close in and form a circle round the hunting party, whose ammunition began to run short. Had one of the horses stumbled, all would have been over.

"What do you think of it, Ivan?" the prince asked his coachman.

"It's not good. Those devils have tasted blood, and the more you fire, the fiercer they will be. With your permission, *mon prince,* I'll give the horses their heads. I can depend on them."

"And on us?" asked the prince, but the coachman did not reply. The noble creatures seemed to redouble their speed as he urged them on with a shrill whistle and changed course to cut athwart one tip of the crescent. The wolves, puzzled by this manoeuvre, fell back as the sledge plunged through their ranks. The hunters raised their guns. "For your very life, sirs, hold your fire" cried the driver, and was obeyed. It was a moment or two before the wolves could form their ranks again, and in that time the horses covered almost a mile. Try as they might, the pursuers could not lessen the gap, and a quarter of an hour later the castle was in sight. Next morning, the prince rode out to the scene of the hunt and found the skeletons of more than two hundred wolves.

So you see, hunting wolves can be an exciting business. However, in case any of my readers are kind enough to be anxious for my safety, I will add that it is a *battue,* not a wolf-hunt in a *troika,* that we are looking forward to in the woods of Prince Troubetskoi.

❀　　❀　　❀　　❀

4

FIRST IMPRESSIONS OF ST. PETERSBURG

While Prince Troubetskoi was telling me of this wolf-hunt, I watched St. Petersburg slowly rising above the water line at the far end of the gulf. Soon I began to notice other domes, lower than the first one, shining here and there, some of them gilded like the cupola of St. Isaac, others covered with bright stars. St. Petersburg has a multitude of religious buildings—two cathedrals, forty-six parish churches, a hundred other places of public worship and forty-five private chapels, with six hundred and twenty-six bells between them!—but the general effect is by no means picturesque, for the place is flat and low-lying.

As we drew nearer, the most striking landmarks that caught our eyes were two frightful yellow buildings like barracks, and two green domes crowning the chapels of a cemetery. The Russians are particularly fond of green paint for their churches and the roofs of their houses—not a happy choice, for the domes clash with the blue sky and the roofs swear at the green of the trees. True, the sky is seldom blue and the trees are not green for long.

We entered the mouth of the Neva—six times as wide as the Seine, and a moment later ran alongside the English Embankment and tied up just below the Nicholas Bridge, built eight years ago.

In Peter the Great's lifetime there was no bridge over the Neva. That obstinate old sailor expected everyone who lived in his town to be as much at home in a boat as he was, dangerous though the crossing might be. Twenty-five or thirty people were waiting on the quay to greet us, and suddenly Home, now fully recovered from his generosity towards the fish in the Gulf of Finland, clapped his hands, jumped with joy and threw his arms around my neck. In the group he had caught sight of his fiancée, who had left Paris before we did. No-one had come to meet me, nor had I expected anyone would.

This time it was a simple matter for us to cross the gangway, since we had no luggage to hamper us. On the quay we said good-bye to Princess Dolgorouky and Prince Troubetskoi (who reminded me of his invitation to shoot wolves with him at Gatchina), then we climbed into three or four of the count's carriages that stood waiting to take us to his country house, Bezborodko, which lies on the right bank of the Neva outside St. Petersburg, not much more than half a mile from the Arsenal and almost opposite the Convent of Smolnoi.

Any foreigner landing at St. Petersburg must at once notice the one-horse carriages, called *drojkys,* their drivers wearing long robes tied at the waist with a sash edged with gold braid—unless the gold had worn off. Their hats are like pots of *pâté de fois gras,* and hanging down their back is a lozenge-shaped copper badge with their number on it. Should any passenger wish to make a complaint against his *cocher,* all he has to do is to take the badge hanging so conveniently to hand and send it to the police. It goes without saying that the police in Russia, as in France, are unlikely to side with a driver of public transport. These drivers, like every-one else in St. Petersburg, are very seldom natives of the town. Usually they are peasants from Finland, Estonia, Livonia or distant parts of Russia, serfs whose masters have allowed them to under-take this work. For this semi-liberty, each *isvotschick* must pay his overlord an annual duty, called an *obrok,* of anything between twenty-five and sixty roubles.

There are two different kinds of *drojky.* One is a sort of low-slung gig, no higher than the go-carts children have in France—

and barely wide enough for two. The other looks like a riding saddle extended at the back to take two or three pillion passengers. You bestride this saddle as though you were mounting a horse, but your feet rest on wooden bars instead of stirrups. The driver, perched in front, looks like the eldest of Aymon's four sons taking his brothers to a grand tournament at the court of their uncle, the Emperor Charlemagne. This type of vehicle is obviously native to the country and of Tartar origin; the other has been imported from abroad and modified to suit the taste of Russian travellers or the hazards of Russian roads.

Driving along the quay, we were soon in Admiralty Square. I had never been in St. Petersburg before, but I had studied every description of the town that I could find, and at once recognised the Imperial Winter Palace on my left, the Senate on my right, the Cathedral of St. Isaac in the background and the two monuments standing before me—a column in memory of Alexander I and the magnificent statue of Peter the Great by our French sculptor, Falconet. A moment later we were crossing the Field of Mars, dominated by the barracks of the Paulovski—the famous regiment created by the Mad Czar, Paul I, tyrant and military fanatic. To this day, no man can join the Paulovski unless he has a snub nose like that of their imperial founder.

I saw the Red Palace (painted yellow now), which Paul built to honour his mistress, Anna Lapuknin, who loved wearing red gloves; and St. Michael's Palace, where Paul was murdered in his bedroom on March 11th, 1801, by a band of army officers. I could see the corner window of that very room, still closed and with the blinds drawn as they have been for the last fifty-seven years. At one time, passers-by were strictly forbidden even to pause and look up at this window. A young man from Livonia who rashly did so was seized and dragged inside the palace—now the College of Engineers—and stripped to the skin. His head was shaved and he was forced to serve in the army for twenty years. That was during the reign of Nicholas. Now Alexander II is on the throne, and Moynet will be able to sit in a corner of the Summer Garden and make a sketch of that window openly, in broad daylight, without being conscripted or even sent to Siberia.

On we went, crossing the Neva by a wooden bridge, glancing at the old fortress and the steeple of the Church of Saints Peter and Paul, at present embellished by an elaborate wooden scaffolding that seems to me as fine a work of art as the steeple itself will be when it is finished. From this bridge, the Neva is a splendid sight as it rolls majestically on towards the sea. Thanks to this magnificent river, St. Petersburg has an air of grandeur that few other capitals can equal. Note that I said "an air of grandeur." Later I must touch on the difference between appearance and reality.

There is one thing in which appearance is borne out by reality—the way the roads of St. Petersburg are paved. Imagine oval cobblestones, some as large as the skull of a Patagonian giant, others as small as the head of a tiny child, all laid side by side and left loose, so that carriages—and the passengers inside them—bounce up and down like dried peas. And that's not all. Along the middle of the road are deep ruts, with heaps of pebbles standing by, like army reserves, waiting to be drafted to active service. Some stretches are covered with long loose planks that seesaw as wheels run over them. Beyond, you will find a couple of hundred yards of macadam that has disintegrated into grit; then more cobbles, more ruts and heaps of stones, more planks, and finally another furlong or so of dust. There you have a typical thoroughfare of St. Petersburg in 1858, capable of shattering the sturdiest English or French coach to bits in less than three years.

Painfully acquiring personal experience of this *pavé*, we passed in front of the Arsenal—the architect of this huge building had the good sense to leave its bricks in their natural colour—and soon found ourselves once more following the bank of the Neva, with the lovely Convent of Smolnoi facing us on the opposite shore. A little more than half a mile further on we came to a great villa with two semi-circular wings curving out from the main structure and flower gardens all around it. Our carriages followed one another in a procession up the long drive between great clumps of lilac in full bloom, for the spring that said goodbye to us in Paris two months ago is here in St. Petersburg to greet us again.

On the wide stone steps leading up to the main entrance all

the count's household servants were assembled in full livery, while at the foot of the steps twenty-five or thirty *mougiks* stood waiting to welcome their master. The count and countess alighted from their carriage and the ceremony of hand-kissing began. When it was over we all mounted a staircase to the first floor and entered a great salon where an altar had been erected. In front of it stood a Russian priest, and as the count and countess crossed the threshold he began to celebrate mass, while the whole company gathered before the altar and listened devoutly. It was a special mass to give thanks for the safe return of the count and his family, and after the short service their friends crowded round to add their felicitations and exchange greetings. Then the count ordered servants to conduct us to the rooms already prepared for us.

My apartment is on the ground floor and opens on to a garden full of spring flowers. It comprises a huge salon large enough for a theatre, a small drawing room and antechamber, a billiards room complete with billiards table, a bedroom for Moynet and another for me. Doubtless I may have to make do with a bivouac on the steppes later on, but at the moment I am in the lap of luxury, as you see.

After a short interval, lunch was announced. You may recall the sad fate of the meal sent to Kronstadt for us earlier in the day, but the count's major-domo was not a man to stint supplies and he had prudently prepared another *déjeuner* in case we might fancy some refreshment on arrival. I must confess I went to table with certain misgivings, having heard very poor reports of Russian cooking. A great deal could be said on this subject, not only from a gastronomic point of view, but even more in respect of hygiene. We shall return to it later, and meanwhile I will abstain from comment.

When the meal was finished, my first spontaneous action since I arrived in Russia was to run to the balcony of the *salon*, overlooking the Neva. The view was breathtaking. Below me lay an anchorage with two flights of granite steps leading down to the water's edge. Above them towered a fifty-foot mast flying a flag with the count's coat of arms. It was at this private landing stage that Catherine the Great stepped ashore when she graced with her presence a fête that Prince Bezborodko gave here in her honour. The Neva, eight or ten times as wide as the Seine at the *Pont des Arts,* rolled placidly by, crowded with boats whose long red pennants floated in the breeze. Among them were barges loaded with pinewood for building or for fuel, coming from central Russia through the system of canals constructed by Peter the Great. These craft never return whence they came, but are sold with the wood they carry, to be dismantled and used or burned like the rest. The bargemen must go back home on foot. These barges hugged the bank, usually the left one, leaving the main stream to the count-less sailing boats tacking up and down. In and out between them darted a swarm of skiffs, swift as tiny fish, their sails striped with green, yellow and red like the *caiques* of Constantinople.

On the further shore stands the most beautiful religious build-ing in St. Petersburg, the Convent of Smolnoi, the work of the Italian architect, Rastrelli, in the reign of Catherine II. It was originally a cloistered retreat for the widows of Russian aristocrats, and is now a boarding school for the daughters of noble families, a great, square, eastern-looking edifice crowned by a central dome covered with stars. Four smaller domes, one at each point of the compass and five hundred yards apart, mark the corners of the high walls enclosing the grounds.

To the left of the convent, as I stood facing it, lay the Tauridus Palace with its squat rotunda and its vast, well-wooded park, beyond which, as from a dark green carpet, rose the golden cupola of Saint Vladimir. Seen at close hand, this granite improvisation of Count Potemkin looks somewhat crude, but at a distance the details are softened, and the sheer mass of it claims a certain majectic place in the landscape. As everyone knows, this palace, with its magnificent furniture and marble statues, its ponds full of goldfish, an owl of solid gold that could twist its head and roll its eyes, a golden peacock that spread its jewelled tail, a gold cock that crowed—all this was a gift from Potemkin to the Empress Catherine to celebrate the conquest of the Crimea. (Those three triumphs of the goldsmith's art, with the golden tree that sheltered them, were later moved to the Hermitage where we can see them still.) The most astonishing thing about the whole affair was not the prodigality of the giver, for Potemkin had accustomed Catherine to receiving lavish presents from him—every year, in mid-January, he used to send her a basket of cherries costing ten thousand roubles!—but the way the project was kept secret. That great palace, covering six acres, was built in the middle of her capital without Catherine knowing anything at all about it! One evening the minister invited the empress to a fête in her honour at a place she knew only as a marshy field. She arrived to find a fairy palace dazzling with light, throbbing with music, resplendent with banks of flowers.

While in Russia, I had the good fortune to meet Potemkin's niece, Countess Braninka, now an old lady of 86, who described his death to me. Commanded by Catherine to negotiate for peace in the Crimea, (though his whole heart was set on continuing the war), Potemkin, a sick man of 54, set out in October 1791 for Jassy, accompanied by his niece, a girl of 19, who had been nursing him. Out on the windswept steppes, 40 miles from Jassy, Potemkin felt too ill to continue his journey and stopped the carriage, spread his fine blue cloak on the frozen ground beside a ditch, lay down and died there in his niece's arms. (I did not ask her whether there was any truth in the rumour that his death was hastened by his having eaten a whole goose while in a state of high fever.) However, let me return to my enjoyment of the view from the count's balcony. Two or three miles away to my left, the Neva curved out of sight in the direction of its source in Lake Ladoga, more than 112 miles from where I stood. There were few buildings on this right bank of the river, and, except for two steeples, they were all low and unpretentious (remember, the count's villa was outside the town), but magnificent masses of verdure gave great charm to this flat stretch of country. On my extreme right, as far as eye could see, lay St. Petersburg, an immense jumble of houses divided by the river and surmounted by the weathervane on the Admiralty building, the golden dome of Isaac and the star-spangled cupolas of the cathedral of Ismaelovski, all standing out clearly against a pearly-grey, faintly blue sky that lent a luminous quality to everything except the pale green roofs.

It is not simply out of pride at having invented a 53rd shade of green—nature, I believe, has 52—that the people of St. Petersburg are so devoted to this colour. Their roofs, being of sheet-metal, had to be painted, and in a colour that would withstand as long as possible the effects of snow, rain and frost. Black was cheap and long-lasting, therefore, at one time, half the roofs in north-western Russia looked as if they were in mourning. But the Emperor Nicholas found the effect depressing, and forbade the use of black paint except on castles belonging to the crown. Red was an alternative choice, with the advantage of looking well against the trees and the sky, but red is inclined to fade, and those who used it had to re-paint their roofs after three years. Green, which contains arsenic, lasts for seven—as long as the average pope.

I should have remained on the balcony longer, but a servant brought a message inviting me to join the others in a walk around the park, which so far I had not seen, except for a limited view from my bedroom window. Arriving on the terrace at the head of the flight of steps leading to the main entrance, I admired an avenue of lime-trees more than half a mile long and twenty feet wide. To right and left of it, above a thicket of shrubs surrounded by flowerbeds, rose, each on a marble pedestal, two bronze busts four times life size, one of Prince Bezborodko and the other of Count Kouchelef, the two founders of the present count's family.

The park wall is seven or eight miles long, and encloses a river, a corinthian temple enshrining a colossal bronze statue of Catherine the Great as Ceres, (Prince Bezborodko was not miserly in his use of metal), two villages and a hundred and fifty or two hundred scattered houses, each in its own garden. Eighty servants, from the major domo down to the kitchen maid who does the washing up, are attached to the chateau itself. Two thousand others live their whole working life inside the park, and the whole community adores the count and countess. Every face I saw was beaming with smiles, positively radiant.

Forty or fifty acres of the park are reserved for the private use of the count and his family, but on Sundays these gardens, like the rest of the park, are thrown open to the public. Military bands from the garrison in St. Petersburg play in front of the château at the end of the avenue. At the moment, as in May-time in France, the lime trees are in flower and alive with the hum of bees. When the band plays on Sundays, three thousand people circle round the house, enjoying the music and the flowers. The children are almost all dressed in the traditional Russian costume —a little hat with a peacock's feather, a short smock of red or yellow silk, wide striped trousers tucked into high boots with turn-over tops of red. The children are all charming—not one of them ever tramples on a flower-bed—and the women—I wish I could say they were charming, too—never pick a single bloom. Among the gaily dressed crowd stroll family nurses wearing the old national garb: a bonnet of gold cloth and a gown patterned with huge flowers. All families of any status, even shopkeepers (those who are well-to-do), take a special pride in having their nurses richly dressed, and some of these costumes are worth a thousand, fifteen hundred, even two thousand francs.

The strangest thing, especially to us—for we Frenchmen are born chatterers—is the utter silence of the crowd. I almost said they are like ghosts, but ghosts, as you know, are often quite noisy, dragging chains, groaning, upsetting the furniture, even making long speeches as Hamlet's father did. The Russians are not ghosts, but spectres, walking solemnly beside or behind one another, neither sad nor glad, never letting a word escape their lips, never lifting their hands to make a single gesture. Even the children do not laugh. True, they do not cry, either.

In St. Petersburg is one short arcade that runs from the Prospekt —one of the three main arteries of the town—to the Rue Italienne. At the Prospekt end is a café where French people meet for a drink or a chat, and there the arcade is gay with life and movement, but only a step or two further in the walls close soundlessly around you, and the end of the passage is as cold and silent as a tomb. The very drivers in the streets do not shout as our French *cochers* do, to scatter pedestrians or make other traffic give way. Now and again they may plaintively murmur *"bereghissa"*—"mind your-self"—but that is all.

You poor Russian people! Is it because you have so long been slaves, that you have this habit of silence? Then talk, sing, be happy, for today you are free! Yes, I quite understand that you still have to get used to being free. If I say to a *mougik*: "Well, so you're a free man now," he replies: "So they tell me, Your Excellency." But he doesn't believe it. To believe in a thing, one must know what it is, and the Russian serf has no conception of liberty or democracy. During the revolt of 1825, the only way Mouravief, Pestel and Ryléyef could get the peasants to shout *"Vive la Constitution!"* was by making them believe *"la Constitution"* was the name of Constantin's wife! Still, this ignorance will not prevent Alexander II's decree of emancipation from coming into effect, though it may bring about unforeseen consequences.

I forgot to mention that the count's park contains a theatre, too, where there is to be a performance of *Invitation to the Waltz* and a Russian play written by the count, as soon as my friend the Viscount of Sancillon arrives from Paris.

When dinner was served we could hardly credit the time was six o'clock, and even at midnight it still seemed afternoon. Nothing can give you any idea of a June night in St. Petersburg. The pen of a writer, the brush of an artist, cannot hope to depict its magic. Imagine that the sky and the air around you are pearly-grey, shot with opal, quite unlike dawn or dusk; a light that is pale, yet not wan, encircles every object but casts no shadow. There is a transparency revealing the whole landscape for miles around, almost like an eclipse of the sun, but without the disquiet that an eclipse always causes in the world of nature; there is a calm that refreshes your very soul, a peace to fill your heart, a silence so profound that one instinctively listens for the song of angels or the voice of God. To make love on such a night would be a two-fold joy.

I have known many wonderful nights, gliding before the faintest breath of wind over the Bay of Naples, off Palermo and in the Straits of Messina; or lying flat on the deck of my craft, rich in my youthful dreams (for I was young in those days), trying vainly to count the myriads of stars shining down on Sicily, Calabria or Greece. From off the coast of Africa I have watched Algiers with her white houses and her gardens of banana trees and sycamores, and Tunis sleeping fitfully where Carthage sleeps for ever; I have gazed on the Roman arches of Djemdjem's amphitheatre starkly etched against the desert sand under a brilliant August moon. But never have I seen anything to equal the nights of St. Petersburg.

The first of these nights—that of my arrival—I spent entirely upon my balcony in the Villa Bezborodko, never for one moment thinking of sleep, in spite of the fatigues of the preceding nights. Moynet was beside me, as entranced as I was by a spectacle so new to us. We were both lost in an admiration so profound that neither of us spoke a single word. The vast expanse of the Neva—a river of silver—rolled at our feet; great boats, like swallows, swept noiselessly up and down with billowing sails, leaving a faint ripple in their wake. Not a single light gleamed from either bank, not one star kept watch in the sky. Suddenly a sphere of gold appeared far to our left, rising above a dark green wood, cleaving a mother-of-pearl sky while the waves of foliage were still strongly outlined against it. Slowly this great shining breastplate climbed the sky, but added nothing to the transparency of the night. Only, a long line of molten gold lay trembling on the water, giving a touch of flame to the boats that crossed it, for the brief moment of their passing. At last, majestically, proudly, serene as a goddess, the moon glided slowly down behind the domes of Smolnoi, which remained sharply outlined against her brilliance for the whole time it took her to sink from the cross crowning the pinnacle and submerge herself in the depths of the sea on the horizon.

Pushkin, that great Russian poet I have mentioned before and shall speak of again, tried to depict such a night in noble verses. But, fine as they are, they are only the poetry of Man; the nights of St. Petersburg are the poetry of God Himself.

✿　　✿　　✿　　✿

5

IN ST. PETERSBURG

So far we have no idea what has become of Dandré and our fifty-seven pieces of luggage. Consequently I am reduced to exploring St. Petersburg wearing a hard felt hat, white corduroy jacket, grey trousers and my celebrated carbuncle. If only I had the count's panama! With a 500 franc panama I should at once be taken for a nobleman by every one in St. Petersburg! Still, such as I am, I bestride a *drojky* and start out. From studying maps of the town I know St. Petersburg like my own pocket; I can say *na prava* (to the right), *na leva* (to the left), *pachol* (go on), *stoi* (stop) and *damoi* (drive back to the house). With this repertoire and the much-vaunted intelligence of *mougiks* I count on managing my excursion very creditably.

At the very moment my *drojky* begins to move, I notice a charming little steam-boat of about ten horse-power leaving the count's landing stage and skimming over the Neva like a swallow towards the Summer Garden, which gives me an idea for my next outing. Not being in a boat at the moment, I can pause on the wooden bridge spanning the river and admire once again the finest view in all St. Petersburg. As before, my eyes are drawn to the scaffolding around the steeple of the Church of Saints Peter and Paul, now being restored. It has been there for a year already, and will probably remain for two or even three years more. It has become what the Russians call a "current expense."

The Russians have no equivalent for our phrase: "cutting down expenses." With them, expenses either go on as they are, or increase. In Tzarsko-Celo there is a Chinese-style bridge, decorated with half-a-dozen life-size wooden figures, each on its own pedestal. One day, Catherine remarked as she was crossing the bridge: "Those grotesques need re-painting. Their colour is flaking off." The very next day a painter set to work on the figures, and throughout the life-time of that Czarina the paint was renewed on the same date every year. She has been dead for sixty-three years, yet on the due date the work is still carried out. The poor carvings, now buried under eighty coats of paint, have completely lost not only their features but any semblance to human shape. You would have to cut away two inches of cobalt or vermilion to get down to the original wood! (One day I will go to Tzarsko-Celo just to see them!) That is was the Russians consider a "current expense"!

To give you another instance, Catherine II detested candles and forbade their use in the palace. Two years later, she chanced to notice in the household accounts the item: "Candles, 1,500 roubles." Determined to discover who had had the audacity to ignore her orders, she made enquiries and found that, one day, the Grand Duke Paul, on his return from a hard day's hunting, found the seat of his leather breeches peeling from their contact with the saddle, and called for a candle to wax over the damage. His candle cost only two sous, but thereafter a new one was provided every day. "A current expense."

A similar thing happened to the Czar Nicholas. Checking over the palace account books with Prince Wolkonsky, he came across a note of 4,500 roubles spent on lipstick during the year, which struck him as excessive. The Czarina assured him she never used cosmetics, nor did she permit her ladies in waiting to do so. At last an explanation came to light. The Grand-Duke Alexander, now the reigning Czar, recalled a certain occasion when he came home to the Winter Palace with his lips badly chapped from the cold, and asked for something to soften and soothe them. Henceforward, lipsticks were a "current expense." As far as the scaffolding on the steeple is concerned, the surprising thing will be not whether it stays in place, two, three, or even ten years, but if it is ever taken down!

Leaving the wooden bridge and proceeding along the quay from east to west towards the green expanse of the Summer Garden, one crosses a very hump-backed bridge over the Fontanka, constructed by Peter the Great. Formerly, a wooden bridge crossed this river, and one day, when Peter, driving his own *drojky,* was taking the Chief of Police to dine with him at his "Little House" (not to be confused with his "original house," now preserved under glass near the fortress), the bridge collapsed and threw both of them into the water. Peter got out first and helped the Chief of Police to do the same, but once the official stood safe and sound on the bank, the Czar belaboured him with the cane he always carried to inflict correction. It was the responsibility of the police department to maintain the bridge in good condition! Having thrashed him soundly, the Czar went on: "Now let us go on to dinner. I was punishing the Chief of Police, not my guest." The legend does not mention whether the guest still had an appetite for the meal.

The Summer Garden is the Luxembourg of St. Petersburg, square in shape, bordered on one side by the River Fontanka and on another by a deep ditch. The interior, too, is laid out on lines as straight as a bowstring, and visitors would find the walks very dull if it had not occurred to Catherine to place, here and there, some of the busts and statues seized by Russia after the partition of Poland. This whole collection of marble gods, goddesses and nymphs seemed to me quite grotesque in their present setting, with their pompadour atmosphere, their stiff hair and heart-shaped mouths, though some of them are well worth seeing, for example, a statue of Lechery with leering eyes, a gently smiling Dawn and a Saturn devouring its young. Among these Polish marbles interned in a Russian pleasure garden is a bust of John III, Sobieski, the saviour of Vienna.[1]   One day (it was in 1855), the Emperor Nicholas was strolling through the Summer Garden with his *aide-de-camp*, Count Rzevouski—a Pole, as his name indicates—and paused a moment to look at this bust. Then, turning to his *aide,* he remarked: "Do you know who, after Sobieski, is the world's greatest dolt?" The count, faced with an *embarras de choix,* hardly knew how to reply. "Well," continued the Czar, "'Tis I, for I saved Austria a second time!"

If, on entering the Summer Garden, you turn left, you will find the Little Palace of Peter I—the same monarch who thrashed his Chief of Police in such fatherly fashion after their mishap on the

---

(1) John III (1624-1696), eldest son of James Sobieski, became King of Poland in 1676.

Fontanka bridge. For twenty kopeks, a disabled war veteran will show you a clock carved by Peter the Great himself, the cupboards and tables he used, even the oven where Catherine, who did not forget she was once a pastry cook, used to bake her little pies.[1]

One thing you must get used to, when you set foot in Russia, is their *"Na tchay,"* the equivalent of *"baksheesh"* among eastern peoples, *"trinkgeldt"* in Germany, and our French *"pourboire."* Literally, it means "for the tea," tea being the national beverage of Russia, where no home is so poor that it has no *samovar*. You have no conception of what tea means to a *mougik*, or how many half-pints of boiling water he can absorb with the help of a couple of lumps of sugar. He never puts these bean-sized morsels in his glass (in Russia, men drink tea from glasses, women from cups. Why this distinction, I have no idea), but holds them in his mouth to be dissolved as he drinks. So the Russian begs "for tea" at every opportunity, without having done anything to deserve reward, without rhyme or reason, save the hope that perhaps he may be given it. There is a Russian legend that when God created the first Slav, the man at once turned to his Maker with outstretched hand, whining: "Please, Your Excellency, *na tchay.*"

Twenty paces from Peter I's house is a monument to the poet Krylof, its pedestal decorated with four bas-reliefs depicting the creatures brought to life in his fables—monkeys, chickens, tortoises, lizards, hares, dogs, foxes—while the poet himself is seated on a sort of rock surrounded by this troupe of birds, beasts and reptiles. The statue, not a good one, has a further disadvantage in its site. Placed as it is, in front of what I imagine are the only water-closets in all St. Petersburg, it seems to stand as a trademark for that useful establishment.

Let us leave the Summer Garden and walk down the quay again

---

(1) Catherine I, Empress of Russia, was of humble birth, daughter of a peasant farmer who died of plague when she was a baby. The child grew up in the home of a certain Pastor Gluck, where she became a kitchen maid. After her marriage to a Swedish dragoon she was captured with other prisoners of war, and sold to Prince Menschikov, at whose home in Moscow she was seen by Peter the Great, who made her his mistress. In 1711, Peter divorced his wife, Eudoxia, and married Catherine.

as far as the famous statue of Suvarov. I do not know who the sculptor was, and do not care to enquire, so I will just say a word or two about the man the statue represents, for Suvarov is almost as popular in France as in Russia. The well-known song in memory of M. de Marlborough also immortalises the Russian Field-Marshal's victories over Macdonald and Joubert; and "Suvarov boots" were fashionable wear for nearly a year. His grandfather was Jean Suvarov, a priest in the Kremlin and one of the conspirators who supported Princess Sophia in her bid for power. This priest had a son who enlisted in the army, became an officer and consequently a gentleman, and rose to the rank of general. His son, born in 1729, was the man commemorated by this bronze Achilles, a military genius who gained every honour a man can win in Russia, short of becoming Emperor.

As I stood musing on Suvarov's forty years of victorious campaigns, his iron discipline, his total disregard for human lives, the eventual defeat and humiliation that killed him at the age of seventy, I suddenly felt a touch on my shoulder, turned, and uttered a cry of joy. It was Blanchard! [1] You must know the name, or at least the work, of that fearless artist-explorer who has crammed his portfolios with drawings in the four corners of the world. Our last meeting was in Madrid in 1846, since when he has been to North America, Mexico and parts of South America. Now he was on his way home from the very places I was going to visit —the Caspian Sea, Tiflis and the Caucasus. He told me that our old friend, the Duke of Ossuna, [1] was also in St. Petersburg, and hearing of my arrival had sent Blanchard to find me and bring me to see him. I protested that I was hardly suitably dressed for such a visit, but my objections were brushed aside, and I finally agreed on condition that we first called at Blanchard's *atelier* in Little Morskoi Street. There, he showed me a hundred or more sketches, and told me of the Russian Album he had just completed for the Empress herself. What a pity it was that Moynet was not with us! The delay at the Customs Office had inconvenienced him even more than myself.

---

(1) Cf. *From Paris to Cadiz,* Chs. 4 & 6.—Ed.

At length we set off again in our *drojky* for the Maison Larsky on the English Embankment, where the Duke was staying, and ten minutes later the Swiss Guard ushered us into an anteroom where a magnificent bear stood like a footman to do the honours. An inscription informed us that this gigantic beast, some seven feet tall, had had the favour of being killed by the imperial hand of His Majesty Alexander II, who is famous as a very brave, very skilful hunter of this species of big game. D'Ossuna, having waited for me until two o'clock, had just gone out, so I left my card in the bear's paw and went away.

Bear-hunting is a veritable passion with the Russians, and those who take to this sport can never give it up. It is the first proposition they make to any foreign hunter who arrives in Russia, to try out their man, as the army phrase goes, and usually the foreigner, if he is a Frenchman, accepts. The Count of Vogué did so, a couple of years ago, and not only upheld our country's honour, but won a reputation for courage that generations of Russian hunters will talk of with awe.

That hunt took place on the estate of Count Alexis Tolstoi, in the government of Novgorod, and the actors in the drama were Count Melchoir de Vogué, the Count de Bylandt, *chargé d'affaires* from the Dutch Embassy, and Count Seuchtelen, of the Imperial Russian Court. Word had reached them of a she-bear of enormous size, doubly ferocious since her cubs were still at heel. Driven out by the beaters, this huge creature passed in front of the Count de Brylandt, whose first shot wounded it slightly, so that it left a trail of blood on the snow as it went on to cross the line of fire of Count de Vogué, who from a range of scarcely forty or fifty yards scored hits with both barrels.

Hearing the three shots, and thinking his friends might be in some difficulty, Count Seuchtelen, stationed a hundred yards away with two loaded guns, sent his servant with one of them in the direction of the firing. As the man came up, Count de Vogué threw aside his empty weapon, snatched the fresh one, and set off in pursuit of the bear, following its bloody tracks easily enough. The bear plunged into the forest, and weakened by its three wounds, paused to take breath. Count de Vogué, with the *mougik* close behind him, ventured within forty yards of his quarry, took careful aim and fired.

The bear gave a terrible roar and, instead of trying to escape, turned to charge the hunter, whose second shot had no effect except to increase the animal's speed and fury. Vogué now had no weapon he could use, other than a yataghan that the Count of Bylandt had lent him, so he took to his heels, still followed by the *mougik,* but the bear was far swifter than either. The Frenchman, young and nimble, had outdistanced the peasant when he thought he heard a cry behind him and turned his head. All he could see was the bear. The serf, on the point of being overtaken, had plunged deep into a snowdrift and crouched down with his arms covering his head as the bear rushed on him with open jaws. The man was silent now. All hope had left him. What chance was there that a nobleman, a Frenchman with nothing to lose by the death of a Russian slave, would risk his life to save a poor *mougik*?

But the Count de Vogué was not the man to let a human being, serf or not, be killed before his very eyes without trying to rescue him. "No!" he shouted, as if to fortify himself against a twinge of hesitation, "that will not do at all!" Drawing his yataghan he threw himself at the bear and plunged the sword up to the hilt between its shoulders. The beast turned on him and felled him with one blow of its heavy paw, but the count kept hold of his yataghan and rained furious blows on the bear's head. Fortunately, instead of seizing him in a crushing grip, the animal seemed intent on biting him. The count said later that he had no idea how long the struggle lasted. He lost all count of time and was aware of nothing but the creature's bloodshot eyes, its bleeding muzzle and dripping jaws, while he struck blow after blow, mechanically, ruthlessly, desperately.

Suddenly he heard de Bylandt's voice and yelled to him for help. The Dutchman, waist deep in snow, managed to get within ten yards, then de Vogué heard a shot and instantly felt as if a mountain had rolled down on him. A moment later, his friends dragged him out from beneath the crushing weight of the dead

Tower of Ivan Velekoi, Moscow

The Kremlin, Moscow.

bear. All this time, the *mougik* had given no sign of life, but when he in his turn was pulled out of the snow and saw de Vogué standing safe and unharmed, he fell on his knees before him and kissed his feet.

When the hunters reached home that night, Count de Vogué wished to return the yataghan to its owner, but de Bylandt refused to take it. There is a Russian superstition that forbids one friend to give another any sharp or pointed blade, so, to ward off ill-luck, de Vogué "bought" the weapon with a twenty-*kopek* piece, and de Bylandt at once had the coin mounted in the butt of his gun as a souvenir.

I could tell you a dozen tales of the courage and endurance of Russian bear-hunters if only I had room, of Hamilton, for instance, who scorned fire-arms and used to set out on snow-shoes armed only with a lance, the man who presented to the Natural History Museum in London a great black bear, eight feet tall, that he killed almost single handed. He was an officer in the Imperial Guard, son of a Russian admiral, and he slew more than a hundred and fifty bears before he tired of this sport, married a charming girl, a Miss Anderson, and settled down on an estate in a quiet corner of Ireland, where he could hunt nothing more exciting than foxes, hares and snipe.

The bear a Russian hunter fears the most, no matter how brave or cunning he may be, is his fortieth. A man may kill thirty-nine without even a scratch, but the fortieth is Nemesis and will avenge all the others, or so tradition says. This belief is so strong, so widespread throughout Russia that the most intrepid hunter, who has tackled thirty-nine without turning a hair, faces his fortieth in such fear and trembling that he may very well miss his aim. The bear, undisturbed by any such qualms, has the advantage and will not miss the man. There must, indeed, be some truth in it, for my Russian friends could tell me of thirty, fifty, a hundred hunters killed by their fortieth bear. If, however, a hunter succeeds in killing that particular adversary his confidence is fully restored. He even grows *blasé*, and instead of a carbine he will try using

C

a pocket pistol, or if his former weapon was a hunting knife, he takes to a penknife.

The Cossacks of Siberia actually do hunt bears with knives. When a Cossack has found a bear's den, he covers himself with a long leather hood to protect him from the beast's claws, takes his *ragatina* (a kind of short-handled pitchfork) in his left hand, and gets his wife or mistress to lash his hunting knife securely to his right forearm. Then he marches off to attack the bear at close quarters, fending off its head with the *ragatina* while, with his right hand, he slits up the animals belly from navel to breastbone with one swift, straight cut, so as to kill the bear without spoiling its skin. Krylof wrote a charming little tale on the subject, but unfortunately I cannot put my hand on it just now. Instead, I will tell you another, and a true, story of a Siberian hunter.

This Cossack, a man of fifty, went out to hunt his fortieth bear. Such an occasion called for special precautions, so he chose a gun as his weapon and took with him his twenty-year-old son, armed with a *ragatina* and a hunting knife. Suddenly, instead of the bear they expected, a huge leopard sprang towards them. (In all probability it had strayed from its native India across the steppes, as such creatures sometimes do.) The lad, who had never before set eyes on such a terrifying wild beast, fled in panic. The Cossack, with the iron nerve of an old hunter, waited until the leopard was only twenty yards away, then fired. It gave one tremendous leap, fell limply back and lay still. The father looked round, expecting his son to rejoin him on hearing the sound of the shot, but the young man did not even turn his head or pause in his headlong flight.

Carefully the Cossack reloaded his gun, gripped the knife between his teeth and crept towards the great cat, on his guard against any cunning move, but it was quite dead, an immense creature very finely marked, its fur worth at least 75 roubles. The hunter skinned it, slung the pelt across his shoulders and strode away homewards, deep in thought. What punishment should be meted out to a coward who abandoned a friend in peril? Worse still, a son who deserted his father? By the time he reached home his mind was made up.

His son had shut himself in his room, but opened the door at his father's command and fell at his feet. "Take this pickaxe and come with me," said the Cossack, shouldering a similar tool himself and leading the way to a clearing a few hundred yards from the house. There in the frozen ground he marked out a rectangle six feet by three, and both men set to work to hollow out the earth.

"That will do," said the old man at last. "Now, make your peace with God." The trembling lad began to understand, yet such was his father's stern resolution that he offered no resistance, but fell on his knees to pray. After giving him ample time to complete his devotions, the hunter paced out the same distance there had been between him and the leopard, took careful aim, and shot his son through the head at the exact spot where his earlier bullet had pierced the animal. He laid him in the grave, covered him with earth, returned home, put on his Sunday clothes and went to tell the local magistrate what had happened.

The official was appalled at the old man's tale. "Miserable wretch!" he exclaimed. "What have you done!"

"I have performed an act of justice, as God would have me do."

"You must go to prison and await the decision of the governor-general." The Cossack, still perfectly serene, obeyed without a word, while the magistrate instantly sent an account of the matter to the governor-general of Siberia, who has power to decide the life or death of any prisoner. In due course he gave his verdict, but because the circumstances were so unusual he sent to the Czar Alexander a copy of the magistrate's report and of the sentence he had passed. It was as follows: "For three days and nights the father shall sit holding on his knees the head of his son, severed from the trunk. If the ordeal kills him or drives him mad, that will be the judgment of God. But if he remains unmoved, it can only be because he acted not in anger, but as a conscientious father performing a duty, in which case he is not guilty of murder."

So for three long days and nights the old Cossack held the head of his dead son upon his knees without batting an eyelid or showing the slightest sign of emotion, whereupon he was immediately set free. Three months later, the magistrate received word direct from the Emperor, confirming the decision of the governor-general. The old man lived to be 80, perfectly serene, perfectly happy; killed his fortieth bear and many others; and died as recently as 1851, his deathbed quite untroubled by remorse, a true Russian patriarch.

We owe this story to General Samanky Bykovetz, an officer in the mines of Siberia, who was an eye-witness of the hunter's behaviour during his ordeal. Not a diverting tale, but you must remember that Russia, in spite of her veneer of civilisation, is not like any other country in the world.

✻   ✻   ✻   ✻

6

ASPECTS OF LIFE IN RUSSIA

After leaving my card with the bear in the Duke of Ossuna's anteroom, I went to visit my compatriot, Dufour, one of the two principal booksellers in St. Petersburg, the other being the Russian, Issakov. I was hoping Dufour could supply me with certain books I needed. (I had been careful not to bring too many with me, because Russian customs officers have a reputation for seizing books brought in by travellers, under a ban imposed by the Emperor Nicholas. My precaution, I learned, was quite unnecessary, for the present Czar, Alexander, has considerably relaxed these and other restrictions.)

Dufour was at home, and already aware of my arrival. A charming young Frenchwoman—a friend of mine for 25 years, though she is only 33 now—had called on him to enquire whether he had seen me or knew where I was staying in St. Petersburg. She was Jenny Falcon, sister of Cornelia Falcon, who starred for ten years at l'Opéra in Paris. I have known Cornelia ever since her début in

1832, when her mother was still one of the loveliest women in France, and Jenny was the prettiest, most roguish seven-year-old in the world. At 16, Jenny appeared in one of Scribe's plays with great success, and St. Petersburg, always on the look-out for young talent, prevailed on her to go to Russia. She retired from the stage when she was 26, and her *salon* is one of the most elegant in this northern capital, her parties are the gayest, her horses and sleighs are the finest that ever skimmed across the bridges of the Neva. Every distinguished Frenchman visiting St. Petersburg in the last ten years has been welcomed by Jenny Falcon at her home in the Place Michel.

Sharing the honours of the *salon* with her is another old friend of mine (I have known him for 20 years), Dmitri Paulovitch Narychkine, whose family, if not one of the oldest, is one of the most illustrious in all Russia. The Narychkines have never wished to become counts or princes, preferring to be simply 'the Narychkines,' but they have the Russian eagle as their coat of arms. That fearless queen, Nathalia Kyrile, who saved her little son from the massacre of the strelitz, was a Narychkine. She was the second wife of the Czar Alexis Michaelovitch, and her son became Peter the Great.

There is a rather charming tradition, possibly untrue—I cannot answer for history, let alone tradition—that tells how Nathalia came to the Russian court. The *boyard* Matheof chanced to be driving one day through Kirkino, a little village in the province of Riazan, a place almost entirely inhabited by noble families fallen on evil days. (Such people are called *odnovortzi*, which means: "nobles who possess only one house.") While waiting for fresh horses, he noticed a lovely little girl of 12 or so, sitting on a doorstep sobbing bitterly, and asked a bystander the reason for her grief. He learned that the child was the sole survivor of an aristocratic family from the Crimea, and that morning her last remaining slave, her nurse-companion, had hanged herself. Matheof dried the girl's tears, took her away with him, brought her up as his daughter and presented her at court. Alexis Michaelovitch, by that time a widower, saw her, fell in love and married her. Is the story true? All I can vouch for is that in the village where the Czarina Nathalia Kyrile was born there is still a popular proverb which says: "If a serving maid had not hanged herself in Kirkino, there would never have been a Peter the Great."

Reverting to my call on M. Dufour, Jenny had left word with him, begging me not to lose an instant in coming to see her, adding that my friend Narychkine would be there too, both of them longing to embrace me. At once I hurried to the Place Michel, where four arms were outstretched to welcome me, not to mention a third pair belonging to *Maman* Falcon, who, on hearing my voice, rushed from the dining room and gave me a hug. They had been expecting me for days. (How they knew I was on my way to Russia I simply do not know.) Jenny and Narychkine were on the point of leaving for Moscow, but had postponed their departure in the hope of seeing me first. If I could be ready to leave St. Petersburg in a fortnight's time, they would wait and take me with them, warmly inviting me to stay at their villa in Petrovsky-Park, for as long as I remained in Moscow. That's Russian hospitality for you! The old Russian aristocrats are the most courteous people I know. I begged my friends not to put themselves to any inconvenience for my sake and gladly accepted their invitation, though I could not yet be sure when I should be ready to leave St. Petersburg. The next day was Jenny's birthday, and it was agreed that if the Customs officials released my clothes in time I would come and share in the festivities.

On leaving the Place Michel I asked my *mougik* to take me to a money-changer. I had with me a considerable sum in French gold that I needed to change into Russian paper. (In Russia, that land of gold and silver mines, there is practically no metal coinage, only paper money—a bewildering variety of notes ranging in value from one to a hundred roubles.) I knew that my gold pieces were each worth 5 roubles, and you can imagine my astonishment when, in addition to the 750 roubles I expected, I was handed a profit of 25 or 30 francs. The value of gold had risen.

I looked at the honest money-changer with increased attention. He could speak a few words of French, and as he tried to explain the details of the transaction I noticed his sparse beard and his high, clear musical voice such as one sometimes hears in the Sistine Chapel. At once I realised I was dealing with a member of the sect known as the *scopsi*. You are unlikely to find the word in your Russian Dictionary, even in the singular, *scopetz*, so I will try to explain what these people are, though the subject is somewhat delicate.

Do you happen to have as a family pet a fine, long-haired Persian tom-cat that never wants to chase over roof-tops in pursuit of lovesick tabbies, and does nothing but eat, sleep and grow fat? He could belong to the *scopsi*. At table, do you sometimes enjoy one of those plump capons from Maine that Béranger praised so much, tender, succulent and roasted to a turn? A fine-looking bird, even when alive, but bereft of a cock's virility. The *scopsi* would regard him as a brother. When King Louis-Philippe was a little boy, he once asked his governess, Mme. de Genlis: "What is a bull?"

"He is the father of a calf."

"And a cow?"

"She is the calf's mother."

"What is a bullock?"

The lady hesitated a moment. A precise definition would be embarrassing. At last she thought of a tactful periphrase, and replied: "A bullock is the calf's uncle." Well, the *scopsi* are the bullocks of the human race. Do you catch my meaning?

Why do men chose of their own accord to join such a sect? I will tell you all I know. The *scopsi* are one of the many groups of "heretics" who refused to accept a modernised version of the Holy Scriptures prepared by the patriarch Nikon during the reign of Alexis Michaelovitch, and rigidly adhered to the old texts in spite of persecution. Travellers who have written about Russia have said little or nothing of these "heretics"—*raskolniks*—but I expect I shall tell you several things that have not been mentioned before. Officially, Russia has five million *raskolniks*. In fact there are eleven million, and their numbers are increasing every day. Such a multitude can hardly be ignored, particularly since, in my opinion, they are destined to play an important part in the social development of Russia.

These *raskolniks* are subdivided into many different sects, all violently opposed to one another, all with their own peculiar creeds, some merely odd, some terrible. The *scopsi* are the strangest and most terrible of all. They believe that until the time of Paul I, Christ, the Virgin Mary and John the Baptist were still living on earth in the persons of three illiterate Russian peasants. Opposite the Church of Znamenia, near the Prospekt Nevskiy, was a great wooden house with its shutters always closed, where the *scopsi* met to enact their mysteries on feast days. On entering, they prostrated themselves before the throne where their "Christ" was seated with his "mother" close at hand; they listened to an impassioned discourse exhorting them to be true to their faith; then came their feast, followed by their secret rites.

Theirs is a baptism of blood and consists of emasculation. As soon as a married couple has produced a son to carry on the family name, their religion demands that the man must be rendered impotent and the woman sterile. The priest, an ignorant barbarian, performs the operation in barbarous fashion with a length of red-hot brass wire, and one initiate in every three dies under his hands.

At their festivals they still partake of a "feast" consisting solely of fruit, vegetables and food made from milk. Meat and fish, indeed anything that has lived, is forbidden to them. The only exception is that, very rarely and only for medical reasons, they may take a little fish—raw, so as not to overheat the blood.

After this feast comes the *strady,* the "dance of martyrdom." At first the worshippers encircle the throne in a slow and stately march, but soon they are whirling like dancing dervishes, delirious with mingled extasy and anquish, till one by one they fall utterly exhausted. It is during the *strady* that new members undergo mutilation.

It was generally believed throughout Russia that Peter III was impotent, and that the son of his wife, Catherine, was adulterous and a usurper, though he ascended the throne as Paul I. The *scopsi* refused to acknowledge him as their rightful czar, and Paul commanded that the *mougik* whom they regarded as their "Christ" should be brought before him. Finding that this fanatic fully believed in his own divinity, and his right, not only to a heavenly crown, but to that of all the Russias as well, the Czar banished him and his "mother" to Siberia, whence few exiles ever return. (The *scopsi* believed they had ascended into heaven and are still awaiting their "second coming.") As for their "John the Baptist," he was sent to Olonetz—a province adjoining St. Petersburg—where he died. His tomb has now become a place of pilgrimage for the devout.

This sect, though banned by law, still flourishes and is extremely rich. (The law, in Russia, is like Atalanta, and will always stop to pick up a golden apple.) Almost all money-changers are *scopsi*, and they hold most of the gold and silver in the kingdom—hence the scarcity of these metals. Since their religion forbids the pleasures of the table, and their condition denies them the pleasures of love, they spend practically nothing and amass colossal fortunes which they hoard in readiness for the "second coming." Meanwhile, they hate their rival sects and their orthodox compatriots even more than they hate foreigners, which is really saying something!

To return to our missing luggage, it had not been confiscated after all, nor had Dandré been banished to Siberia. When we had waited impatiently for three whole days he duly reappeared with everything safe. I leapt on my package of books. Most of them were banned in Russia and I feared the customs might have laid hands on them, but not a single one had been opened! Evidently the order had been given that my trunks were not to be inspected, though how the authorities knew I was coming I never discovered.

What had delayed Dandré was the countess's wardrobe of 80 gowns and 36 hats, but nothing had been damaged—except the count's panama. Like all panama hats, his was double, and the customs officers, suspecting that the space between the layers might contain contraband—a few yards of lace, perhaps—had cut half a dozen holes right through it! The count has taken his loss philosophically and has ordered another panama, this time of Russian manufacture. Very naturally he prefers straw to felt in this weather —86 in the shade!

I took possession of my three items of luggage and had them taken to my room. Now that I have clean shirts and fresh clothes I shall be able to go to Jenny's birthday party.

In Russia, nothing is done as it is elsewhere. This morning, towards seven, I heard the sound of marching feet in the corridor, like a patrol. They halted at Moynet's door—his room is nearer the corridor than mine—and voices were raised in a mixture of French and Russian. Apparently Moynet, believing I was still asleep, was forbidding them to enter my room, but he was obviously over-ruled, for, a moment later, my door opened and a troop of 12 men came marching in wearing red or pink smocks and carrying equipment for cleaning the parquet. They were the count's polishers, and, taking possession of my room, all twelve of them started rubbing the floor, some upright, some on all fours, while I took refuge on a chair like a man clinging to a rock in a stormy sea, and sprang from one spot to another as the work proceeded. In five minutes they had finished and the floor shone like a mirror. (In France I should have been disturbed for at least an hour.) Then they did Moynet's room with equal rapidity. This multiplicity of polishers has its advantages, but also its drawbacks, for *mougiks* have that characteristic smell known in France as "Russian leather." (Whether this distinctive odour comes from the *mougik* or the leather is a deep mystery not yet solved.) At all events, my freshly polished room smelt so strongly of *mougik*—or of Russian leather —that I had to fling open the windows and burn some aromatic vinegar. In two or three hours, the whole ground floor of Bezborodko—some three acres at least—was freshly polished, a gigantic task that would have kept one man busy for a whole week.

You have no conception of the army of servants of every kind always at work in a Russian house such as Bezborodko. Even their master does not know how many. I said earlier that there were 80, but that only referred to the day staff. The night staff is in addition to this. In towns, these are called *dvorniky*—porters—and in the country, *karaoulny,* or watchmen. Porters can sleep at home every other night, for each has an understanding with his neighbour and they take it in turn to guard both houses. Whatever the weather, in driving rain or 30 degrees of frost, the porter must spend the night out of doors, sheltering as best he can. He carries a flat piece of wood in one hand and a drumstick in the other, and at intervals raps out a little tune, always the same one, to prove he is awake and on duty. Sometimes he plays his rhythmic signal against the wooden pillars standing in front of the houses, which makes just as much noise. He wakes you up every hour, but at least you can sleep peacefully in between, confident that the porter is on guard. The *dvornik*, then, is a kind of policeman employed and maintained by a private householder, not by the government.

One advantage of this system is that if you are looking for a particular house at night, one *dvornik* will pass you on to the next until you reach the place you want. Better still, if you have a specific purpose in mind the *dvornik*, who holds the keys of both the houses he is guarding, will let you in (providing, of course, he likes the look of you) and if you are not quite sure of the way he will conduct you personally to the apartment you require. For a rouble, or even less, he will forget he ever saw you, and since these porters are all men—not women, as they so often are in France—one's amorous secrets are not bandied about the streets.

The country watchman, or *karaoulnoi*, is usually an old soldier. In Russia, the majority of the rank and file come from the serfs, of whom eight out of every 1,000 are commandeered for the army. Veterans who survive their 18, 20 or 25 years of service are sent back as free men to the places they left as slaves. In France, we, in our sentimental way, speak of an old soldier returning to his hearth and home, but alas, up to the present at all events, there is no home in Russia for a poor veteran. He has no right to a place of his own, no right to plough his six *arpents* like other men, no rights at all. Having served his country he becomes a pariah, cast off by government and landowner alike.

There is, indeed, on the Tsarsko-Celo road, a hostel for disabled soldiers, built like those we have in France and large enough to take 3,000, but in it there are, to date, 150 staff and 18 patients. It happens in other countries, but to a greater extent in Russia than elsewhere, that the primary function of philanthropic institutions is to provide a living for a certain number of employees. The people for whom such places are nominally intended are considered later, if at all. But what of that? The institution exists, that is all that matters.

Russia is a vast facade, and no one bothers about what goes on behind the scenes. Anyone who tries to find out learns no more than a kitten that catches sight of itself in a mirror and then looks behind it to see where the other cat has gone. Curiously enough, in Russia, the home of abuses and injustice, everyone from the emperor down to the humblest *dvornik* is forever urging that corrupt practices must cease, but they go just the same. The people, with some justification, had great hopes that when Alexander II came to the throne he would abolish these evils, and he tried hard to do so, but it was more easily said than done. Carrying out reforms is like eating an artichoke bristling with sharp points. The hardest, thorniest leaves must be tackled first, and you can seldom get to the heart of it without pricking your own fingers.

To return to our poor veteran, if he has any family and they take pity on him, he joins them. If he still has all his limbs he shares their labour, hoping to be tolerated for the sake of the work he does. But if he has no family, he has nothing. He cannot even hire himself out as a *rabotnick*—a day labourer. A veteran with no medal to his credit has no option: he becomes a thief. If he has two or three medals he may take to begging, kneeling on the highways or in church porches, kissing the ground as you pass and trying to exist on the four or five *kopeks* a day that charitable men may throw him if he is lucky. But if he can show six or eight medals he has a chance of finding employment as a *karaoulnoi*.

Here, at the count's home, all the *karaoulny* are eight-medal men. Day and night—in relays, I imagine—they are constantly on guard, on the landing stage, beside all the main doors, in the hall, at every corner of the garden, and the moment we appear, whatever the time may be, the poor devils jump smartly to attention with their right hands at their peaked caps in a stiff military salute. If Moynet and I, on an evening stroll through the moonlit grounds, feel the need to relieve ourselves, before we have finished there will be a *karaoulnoi,* or even two, standing watching us, blank-faced, a couple of feet away. It is embarrassing at first, like watching funerals go past your window, but you get used to it in time.

Incidentally, in the streets of St. Petersburg there are none of those convenient concave columns that ornament the boulevards of Paris. Nor is smoking allowed. On one occasion the Czar Nicholas, driving alone in a *drojky* as was his custom, noticed a French tourist luxuriously puffing a choice Havana. Nicholas picked him up, drove him to the Winter Palace, took him to the smoking room used by the young Grand-Dukes and said: "Finish your cigar here, monsieur. This is the only place in St. Petersburg where smoking is allowed." Not until the Frenchman was leaving the palace did he discover that he had been taken there by the emperor himself.

This ban on smoking is readily understandable in a land where buildings are generally of wood, and a cigar stub, carelessly thrown down, could burn a whole village. Fires are frequent and terrible in Russia. The famous fire of Moscow defied the efforts of an army of 120,000 desperate men fighting it for their very lives. Here and there in all Russian cities you can see towers surmounted by pulleys and ropes to haul up the spherical signals that serve as fire alarms. When these are hoisted, the nearest fire-engines rush in at once, followed by others from outlying districts that stand by to give help if the fire seems likely to get out of hand. Our friends assure us we are certain to see at least one magnificent fire before we leave Russia, and they add that five or six forest fires are raging at this moment in the country around St. Petersburg.

As soon as I had changed my clothes I hired a *drojky* and, with a friend to act as interpreter, set off to visit the oldest church in St. Petersburg, the "Little House" of Peter the Great, and the fortress, all of them in old St. Petersburg, near the right bank of the Neva and quite close to one another. The church has some historic interest but no artistic value, and while Moynet made a sketch of it I strolled on towards the "Little House," Peter's first shelter on the shore of the Neva, built with his own hands. As one might expect from this imperial carpenter, fresh from his sojourn in Saardam, it is a typical Dutch house, made of wood painted red to look like bricks. To protect this tiny dwelling from the ravages of the weather, a sheath of wood and glass has been erected over and around it, and there it stands, very clean and well-cared for, bright and freshly painted. There is something profoundly moving about the way Russians preserve relics of Peter the Great, as though to give posterity every possible proof that the founder of their empire was a genius. A great future may stem from this veneration for the past.

The house has four rooms: a tiny hall, a living-room, dining-room and bedroom. In the living-room you can see his wooden armchair, his work-bench and the sail of his boat. The dining-room, now a sort of chapel, contains the image that Peter I carried everywhere with him, convinced that it had miraculous powers. There is always a procession of common people, sailors for the most part, filing into this room to pray there. Displayed on one of the inside walls of the house is the little skiff the czar used to sail across the Neva, now affectionately known as "the grandmother of the Russian fleet."

Around the house is an open space bounded by a hedge and shaded by magnificent lime-trees, now in full flower. Among their branches, myriads of bees are working with a busy hum, well aware that their time is short, for the blossom comes late and winter early. In the shade, deep in the untroubled sleep of men who own nothing in the world but their faith in God, lie two or three *moujiks,* while I sit on a little seat, savouring the thoughts that come thick and fast in this garden, probably planted by Peter the Great in the intervals of building St. Petersburg on the opposite bank of the river. It is terrifying to reflect what Russia could have become, if Peter's successors had shared his genius or carried out his progressive, far-sighted schemes.

It was an hour or more before I turned away from this cradle of modern Russia and wandered on towards the Fortress of St. Peter and St. Paul. Like all prisons, it stands as a visible testimony of enmity between the people and their rulers. Built on a little island in the fast-flowing river, it once served to defend the town against the Swedes, but now its function is to threaten and those it imprisons are Russians. It is the Bastille of St. Petersburg, and, like our own Bastille in the faubourg Saint-Antoine, it symbolises tyranny, above all, the suppression of men's right to think. If ever its secret records are revealed; if the time comes when its dark, foul, icy dungeons are flung open to the light of day like those of our Château d'If, then Russia will begin to learn her true history. All she has now is legend.

The tales one hears of cruelties practised in this fortress would be too terrible to believe—if we were not in Russia, where power and ruthless inhumanity have in past centuries gone hand in hand. To look no further back than a hundred years or so ago, the notorious Ernst Biren, Duke of Courland, during his ten years of power as the Queen's favourite, had more than 25,000 people murdered or banished to Siberia. He even invented a new form of torture—a feat rarely achieved since the days of Nero—made possible by the biting cold of the Neva, where in the depth of winter the temperature may be 25 or 30 degrees below zero. He ordered that water should be poured upon his victim's head till the living body slowly froze into a statue of solid ice. In 1764, the lovely Princess Helena Tarakanoff, then a girl of 20 whose strain of royal blood was considered a danger to the reigning monarch, was snatched from her Italian home by Gregory Orlov, brought back to Russia and thrown into this very fortress, where her cell was below water level, her bed a few wisps of straw on the muddy floor. There she endured twelve long years of agony, her only companions the slimy reptiles that crawled over her at night, until at last, while the Neva was in flood, she slowly drowned in the water seeping through her dungeon wall. Her grave is a simple mound just outside the fortress, where today the guards sit chatting or playing cards.

A former officer of the Paulovski, Dimitri Alexandrovitch, told a fearful story, fifty years after the event, of an execution carried out by the orders of the Czar Paul I in 1798. A certain aged political prisoner—the gaolers who had guarded him for years knew him only as "number eleven"—was taken from the fortress and driven, gaunt and almost naked, to the middle of the frozen Neva. There, with pickaxes and levers, a hole was cut through the ice and the proud, silent old man thrown into the water below. Not until the ice had reformed as thickly as before could the officer withdraw his men and return to the Red Palace to report to the waiting Czar that his orders had been obeyed.

People still talk of prisoners confined in egg-shaped cells where a man can neither sit nor stand, but must support himself on one twisted foot till his weight dislocates his joints; of naked captives chained by the waist astride a beam within ten feet of the rushing waters of the Neva. Nothing of all this is still true, heaven be thanked, but I hear that Alexander II complains bitterly of such rumours, which, in his reign, are entirely false. But if I had the honour to be in his presence and heard him make this protest, I would say to him: "Sire, there is a very simple way of silencing these sinister reports. A monarch such as yourself, who began his reign by freeing all who had been imprisoned by his predecessors, and in his three years as Czar has sentenced no-one, has nothing to fear from his people or from history. Throw open every cell in the fortress for all men to see; call in workmen to fill up the underground dungeons, masons to brick up the prison doors. Proclaim to your people: "My children, czars of the past maintained such places because, in their day, nobles and serfs alike were slaves, but now you are all free men and your ruler has no further use for this prison-fortress." Then, sire, such a cry of joy—more, of admiration—would rise from the shores of the Neva that its echoes would resound throughout the four corners of the world."

✽   ✽   ✽   ✽

7

THE ROGUERY OF OFFICIALS.
A VISIT TO A PRISON

Leaving the fortress on Petersburg Island, I made my way across the Isaac Bridge, along the Prospekt Nevskiy, and so to the Place Michel to spend the evening at Jenny's birthday party. The dinner was as delightful as any you could find in Paris, made memorable by the addition of two delicacies very highly prized in Russia—a sterlet brought alive all the way from the Volga at fantastic expense and a dish of superb strawberries that cost even more! But you would hardly be interested in hearing details of this private gathering of old friends and compatriots, so, instead, I will talk about a more intriguing subject—robbery!

I am not thinking of pickpockets who snatch your watch or your purse—Russian thieves of that sort are no cleverer than ours in France; nor of Stock Exchange gamblers, bulls and bears making fortunes by fleecing the general public, promoters of bogus companies to ruin small investors, for nothing of that sort exists in Russia as yet, and in any case, no country in the world, except possibly America, is worse than France in this respect. What I mean is licensed robbery, carried on openly and respectably under a government commission or royal warrant.

Alexander I, speaking of his subjects, used to say: "Those rascals would even steal my ships, if they could think where to put them!" Something of the sort did actually happen to the Emperor Nicholas! In April, 1826, some six months after he came to the throne, he was holding a review at Tsarsko-Celo, when he noticed four bearded men in long smocks making fruitless but persistent efforts to come near him, while all the officials made common cause to push them back. Curious to know what they wanted, he sent an aide-de-camp to bring them to his presence and questioned them privately.

"Sire," replied the *mougik* acting as their spokesman, "We have come to tell you of the incredible amount of stealing going on at Kronstadt under the very eyes of the Director of Naval Construction and his brother, the Commissioner of Supplies."

"Take care," warned Nicholas. "That is a serious accusation."

"We know the risk we run, Sire, but as your faithful subjects we saw our duty plainly. If the accusation is false, we shall be punished."

"I am listening," said the Czar.

"Well, the *gastinoi-dvor,* the town market, is crammed with crown property stolen from your shipwrights, naval stores, even from the arsenals. There is everything there: ropes, sails, gear and tackle, brass fittings, iron-work, anchors, even cannon."

The emperor began to laugh, recalling what his brother

Alexander had said, and the *mougik* went on: "If you doubt it, father (*batiouch*), I could buy it back for you up to any value you care to name. The thieves hide supplies in double bulk-heads, and . . ."

"I do not doubt you," replied the Czar, "but why did you not lay the information before the officers of justice?"

"Because the rogues are rich enough to buy justice. You would never have heard the facts, and one fine day we should have been sent to Siberia on some trumped up charge and never heard of again."

The Czar sent a trusted envoy, M. Michael Lazaref, to Kronstadt with a force of 300 men to carry out a full investigation. Lazaref found the *mougik's* story perfectly true, so he sealed every booth in the market, set a guard on each, and reported back to the emperor, who had the offenders punished with the utmost rigour of the law. He may well have regretted this impulse later, for on the night of the following June 21st fires broke out at Kronstadt and utterly destroyed all the government stores of rope, timber, hemp and tar—a "legitimate reprisal,' apparently, for Nicholas took no further action, and the official *St. Petersburg Gazette* did not even mention the blaze, though it was clearly visible from every corner of the Gulf.

When I mentioned to a Russian friend of mine that I should like details about any corrupt practices in local government, he at once offered to put me in touch with magistrates and administrators who could tell me of their own methods.

"What?" I exclaimed in surprise. "Will these twisters tell me how they work?"

"Why not?" he laughed. "Provided, of course, you can gain their confidence and promise not to reveal their names. The day after tomorrow I am expecting a visit from the magistrate of a large village belonging to the crown and adjacent to my own estates. We'll give him a drink or two to loosen his tongue, I'll go off to my club on some pretext and leave you together, then you may get him to talk."

A couple of days later my friend invited me to dinner. His *bailli* had arrived. After a glass or two of Kummel and champagne our man was just in the right mood to talk freely, and my friend slipped away while I engaged the official in conversation. He gave two or three heavy sighs, then observed, sadly: "Times have changed, brother, and things are not as simple nowadays as they used to be. The serfs are growing artful . . ."

"Tell me about it," said I. "You will find me most sympathetic."

"Well, honoured sir, I used to be in charge of a district head-quarters and my salary was 350 roubles a year. I had a family of five to feed, and we all lived as well as anybody in the world. In those days, everyone understood that an honest man in a government post was entitled to eat and drink, but it's not the same now. You have to tighten your belt. 'Reform,' they call it, but to my mind its the abomination of desolation."

"What can you expect?" I remarked. "These devils of philosophers preach liberal ideas; liberalism begets republicans; and republicans are forever urging economies, reforms, the suppression of abuses, all sorts of frightful words that I hate as much as you do." We solemnly shook hands like men who find they share the same views, and he opened his heart to me. "My district was a long way from the capital—from Moscow, I mean, for St. Petersburg will never seem the capital to me. No one bothered to poke their noses into local affairs. All I had to do was to go to the government offices once a year with a few gifts for my superiors, then I was left in peace till the next year came round. No interference at all. The people are better off now, so the 'progressives' say. (That's another new word they've invented, that never existed in our good old Russian language.) Pah! 'They are more conscientious.' More crafty, that's all. Working-class they are and always will be. True, we used to touch their pockets a little, but no one can claim to be perfect. I ask you, is it better not to steal, and just sit doing nothing? No! The chance to make a little money gives you a good heart for work.

In the old days, we officials were like brothers, whether our grade was high or low, and that gave us strength. If we happened to lose two or three thousand roubles at cards . . . a thing that can happen to anyone, don't you agree?"

"Yes, indeed, except to those who don't gamble."

"But what else is there to do in these outposts? A man must amuse himself somehow! Supposing, then, you have a loss like that. No hope of paying such a sum out of your salary of 350 roubles a year! Well, we used to go to our *bailli* and tell him. (I hadn't been promoted, then, and was just a simple *stavanoi*.) He was angry, or pretended to be, so we would add: 'You understand, sir, that we do not expect your help for nothing. There would be 500 in it for you'."

" 'You dogs,' he would say, 'always losing your money on drink or at cards. Idle good-for-nothings!' "

"Not idle, sir," we would reply, "and to prove it, just give us an order to raise a levy immediately and we'll manage to make your share 1,000."

"And you actually imagine that for a paltry 1,000 roubles I would authorise you to harass those penniless serfs . . .?"

" 'All right! 1,500! That's our final word'." Now and then a *bailli* might be hard and stand out for 2,000, but sooner or later he would pass an order for the immediate payment of taxes. (That word 'immediate' alone was worth 4,000!) Back we would go to our villages and announce that the emperor needed money urgently. In his kindness to his subjects, his little pigeons, he had allowed arrears to remain unpaid, but now we were ordered to collect them at once, together with the current dues. The groans and lamentations were enough to break a heart of stone, but fortunately we were used to them. The serfs would bow, withdraw, confer among themselves for an hour or two, but if they seemed unduly reluctant we would enter each hut, or *isba*, make an inventory of their few miserable possessions as though to force a sale, and in the evening their *maire* would arrive with 10, 20, or 25 kopeks from every serf. From ten villages we would get a total of three or four thousand roubles, pay the *bailli*, settle our debts, and send the balance to the emperor, who, but for our efforts, would have had to wait a year or perhaps two. Everyone benefited, the state and ourselves, and what difference could a few kopeks more or less make to a wretched serf?"

"But," I asked, "what if the peasants really could not pay?"

"Then their master would, if he were kindhearted."

"And if not?"

"Then, since my area was Sarato, I used to sell the peasant into slavery as a *bourlak,* to haul boats up the Volga."

"But," I persisted, "surely this extortion—I beg your pardon, this devotion to duty—was rather risky?"

"What risk was there, honourable sir?"

"Couldn't the peasants complain?"

"Certainly they could, and sometimes did, but any complaints had to pass through our hands, and we saw that they went no further."

"I see. Indeed I do. And you tell me that sort of thing is not so easy, nowadays?"

"It certainly isn't. The serf, fool though he may be, is beginning to learn. One wretch told me only yesterday that the birds in the fields no longer fear the scarecrows, now they have the sense to fly in flocks. The serfs have banded together. Half a village, sometimes a whole village, will appeal to their overlord, who may be a man of some importance at court. He goes over the head of the *bailli,* straight to the Finance Minister, who may not cancel the demand, but will at least give them time to pay. So, as I was saying, now we have to use our wits to make ends meet."

"You look to me, comrade, like a fellow with plenty of imagination! Tell me some of the bright schemes you've thought of."

"Well, I can't complain, though I've had a bit of luck to help things along. One day, for instance, I came across the body of a new-born child on the bank of a river. Accident? or infanticide? Someone not so sharp as I am would probably have hunted out the guilty party and demanded money, threatening to hand her over to justice if she did not pay. But a mother who throws her child into the water must be too poor to feed it. Even if she had any money, it would not be much."

"What did you do?"

"It was very simple. I carried the body upstream to the next village, where I had the right to search every house if I thought fit. I announced that, to identify the criminal, I proposed visiting every *isba* and examining the breasts of every woman of child-bearing age. If I found any woman whose breasts were flowing with milk, she must show me her living child, bring witnesses to prove it had recently died from natural causes, or be charged with the murder. You may not know what a strong repugnance our women have to uncovering any part of their bodies. Each of them paid well to be excused the examination, and I made 1,000 silver roubles out of that little affair. Then I had the child buried and that was the end of the matter. Wasn't that better than handing over some poor woman to die under the knout or in the mines? Punishing the mother would not have restored life to the baby."

"With an imagination like yours, you must have thought of several ideas."

"Yes, indeed. Last winter, for example, when we had 32 degrees of frost, I called the serfs of my village together and said to them: 'Little brothers, our emperor, as you know, drinks nothing but champagne that has to be brought from France, and this wine must be iced to bring out its flavour. Therefore, he commands his subjects to bring him ice from every province in the empire. We must divide the work fairly. Some of you must hew ice from the Volga, and those who own horses and sledges must take it to St. Petersburg. Only, my little pigeons, they will have to be quick or the ice will melt.' You can imagine how they argued! No one wanted to hew ice, still less to take it to St. Petersburg, but I urged, insisted, threatened till they felt they had no choice. Then I called them together and said: 'My friends, I have had an idea that will please you.' They listened with breathless attention. 'Our emperor,' I went on, 'has called for ice, but ice is not like wine, good in one province and poor in another. Ice is just ice, whether from the Volga or anywhere else. So I can arrange to have it taken from Lake Ladoga, which is much nearer to St. Petersburg and the transport will be cheaper.' 'Hurrah!' they cried. 'Long live our *stavanoi*!'

"But," I went on, 'I must employ labourers to get the ice, hire horses and sledges to take it to St. Petersburg, and that will cost at least 2,000 roubles.' They broke into horrified protests. 'One thousand five-hundred at the very least. I give you three days to decide. Think of the thaw!' Three days later, the *maire* brought me the 1,500 roubles."

"Most ingenious," I murmured.

"But sometimes I helped them," he went on. "One day, a peasant at Savkina set fire to his house and burned down the whole village. Why did he do it? Well, you know, sometimes a serf imagines he has cause for complaint against his overlord, who, perhaps, has coveted his sister, scourged his wife, or had his son drafted to the army. Then, in revenge, he may burn his home and turn vagabond as this fellow did. On behalf of the serfs who remained, the *maire* wrote to the *pomeschik*, the local landowner, asking permission to fell enough trees to rebuild the village. The *pomeschik* agreed, but stipulated that the trees must be cut from a forest five or six miles away instead of from the one close at hand. What did my bright lads do? Cut down the nearest trees, of course! One fine day, when they had just finished building their new homes—some 200 of them—word came that the *pomeschik* had heard a rumour of what had happened and was sending his supervisor to investigate. As you can imagine, it makes a hole in a forest when you fell enough trees to build 200 houses at 60 or 70 trees per house, and the rascals were desperate. It meant the knout for each of them, and for some at least, Siberia. Who could they turn to? Only to me, knowing me a man of infinite resource.

"How much time have you, my pigeons?" I asked.

"Just a month."

"Then you are saved," I replied, and they jumped for joy.

"Yes," I went on, "but you know our Russian proverb that good counsel is worth whatever it costs?" They listened, but stopped jumping. "It will cost you 10 silver roubles each." They groaned aloud. "Take it or leave it," I went on, "but remember the supervisor will be here in a month, and unless you get busy in the next three days my plan will be useless." Next day they offered me five roubles, and eight the day after, but I was adamant and at last they agreed to the 10 I had demanded. "But," they asked, "can you promise that nothing will happen to us, and no one will know we plundered the nearest forest? Will you tell us how, before you take our money?"

"Willingly," I replied. "We are in the month of November, and the snow is four feet thick. All the sledge trails are well

87

established. Every family must cut from the distant forest as many trees as they used for their new house, haul them to the vacant space in the nearby woods and fix them upright in the snow. They will fall, of course, when the thaw comes in May, but by that time the supervisor will have come and gone."

"That's a good idea," said the oldest peasant. "'Pon my word, it's very good."

"Then hand over my 10 roubles and set to work."

But they seemed in no hurry. "Now that we know," the old man went on thoughtfully, "what's to stop us doing it without paying you?"

"Why, in that case," I replied mildly, "when the supervisor comes I should stroll with him to the nearest tree and say to him . . ."

"Oh! Oh! I was only joking, monsieur le *stavanoi*. Here are your 10 roubles from each of us, and our thanks with them." Three weeks later, the pine trees were standing as dense and straight as ever. The supervisor came, saw that the wood by the village appeared intact, went to the distant forest, examined the space where the trees had been felled, and went away convinced that the rumour was false. No more was ever heard about it, as far as I know. Soon after I was promoted to the rank of *bailli* and was transferred from Saratof to Tver, where I am now."

"Do you still get similar bright ideas?"

"Ah! You want to know too much for one day," my companion retorted with the sly little smile peculiar to Russian jacks-in-office. "As a *bailli*, I've told you how a *stavanoi* does his job; you'd better ask a *stavanoi* if you want to hear about us *baillis*. But there, comrade, it's as broad as it's long. All peasants are arrant thieves! If I hadn't been sharper than they were, those tree-felling serfs would have done me out of my 2,000 roubles!"

I am afraid I must keep you waiting for an account of the activities of superintendents, for today I want to take you into one of the common prisons of St. Petersburg. Tomorrow the chain-gang leaves for Siberia, and I will let the condemned men speak for themselves. You may find a link between their crimes and the wrongs they are forced to endure.

When I applied to the Chief of Police for permission to visit the prison and talk with men sentenced to hard labour in the mines, he not only agreed but promised to send one of his staff to escort me, an officer who spoke fluent French and could act as my interpreter. A rendezvous was arranged for 10 o'clock this morning at the café I mentioned earlier, at the corner of the passage leading off the Prospekt Nevskiy. When I drove up in my *drojky* he was already waiting, and climbed in beside me. The prison is in one of the little streets behind the Prospekt Voznesenskiy, the "Ascension Prospect," and in a moment or two we were there.

My guide presented his credentials, handed over an official letter to the prison governor, and we were allotted a gaoler with a whole battery of keys. He led us along a corridor, unlocked a door on a spiral staircase, went down 20 steps and opened another door giving on to a second corridor whose walls seemed to be below ground level, for they streamed with damp.

"Do you want to see anyone in particular?" asked the turnkey.

"No," I replied. "It doesn't matter who, as long as he's one of those going to Siberia." The gaoler opened the first door. He was carrying a lantern while my guide and I both held candles, so the little cell was clearly lighted. I saw, on a wooden bench just big enough to serve as a bed by night and a seat by day, a little dried-up man with glittering eyes and a long beard, his head shaved at the back and his hair clipped short over the temples. A chain sealed into the wall ended in an iron ring encircling his leg just above the ankle. He looked up as we entered and said to my guide: "Is it today, then? I thought it was to be tomorrow."

"Tomorrow it is," my guide answered, "but this gentleman is visiting the prison and will give you two *kopeks* for a glass of vodka if you will tell him why you are being sent to the mines."

"He needn't pay me for that. I confessed to the judge and will tell Monsieur just what I said then. It is very simple and will not take long. Well, sir, I have a wife and four children, and just as we had eaten our last crust, in came the *stavanoi* to say our emperor needed money for a war and half a year's tax must be paid at once. My contribution was fixed at one rouble 75 kopeks. I told the *stavanoi* how things were with us, nothing in our *isba,* all of us half-naked, and asked for time to pay. 'The emperor cannot be kept waiting'," he answered.

" 'God! What can I do?' " I cried, clasping my hands in despair.

" 'I know what I can do! Have water poured on your head drop by drop till you pay!' "

" 'You can kill me, I know, but what good would that do? You would still not be paid, and my wife and children would die too'."

" 'On your knees, children,' sobbed my wife, 'and beg our lord the *stavanoi* for time. Perhaps your father can find work and pay the tax'."

"But," I broke in, seeking confirmation from my guide, "I thought that every landowner was compelled by law to allow the head of every family six arpents of arable land to grow food, and a share of the common grazing?"

"Yes, when the owner of the serfs owns land as well. But there are poor overlords who have no land. Then they hire out their serfs as *rabotchniks*, labourers. That is what happened in this case. Go on, my man," he added, turning to the prisoner.

"Well, the *stavanoi* wouldn't listen, and seized my collar to take me to prison. 'Stop,' I said to him. 'I would rather sell myself as a Volga boatman. That would bring me five or six roubles, enough to pay my tax and leave something over to be divided between my master, my wife and my children.' 'Listen,' he answered. 'I'll give you a week to pay. If you cannot get the money by then, it's not you I'll throw into prison, but your wife and children.'

"Out of the corner of my eye I could see my axe standing by the stove, and I was sorely tempted to seize it and split his skull. I might have done it, too, but luckily for him he went away. I kissed my wife and family goodbye, and as I went through the village I begged my neighbours to look after them, for it would take me two days to get to the government offices and two more to come back, and in four days they might die of hunger. Perhaps I should not be allowed to come back at all, so I told my friends I was going to sell myself on the Volga, and said my last farewells. All of them pitied me and cursed the *stavanoi*, but no one offered me a rouble and 75 kopeks to save me from having to go.

"Weeping bitterly, I tramped on for two or three hours. Then a man from my village, Onesim by name, overtook me, driving his little cart. We had never been friends so I did not speak to him, but he called out to ask me where I was going and why. I told him. I fancied I saw a flicker of hatred in his face, but perhaps I was wrong, for he smiled and said: 'Now that's an odd coincidence! I'm going to the government offices too, to buy vodka. For a rouble and 75 kopeks they'll fill this little barrel,' and he patted it affectionately. I sighed. 'What's on your mind?' he asked.

" 'I was thinking that if you would go without your vodka for four Sundays and lend me the money, I need not sell myself and my family would be saved.'

" 'What chance is there you'd pay me back? You're as poor as Job.'

" 'I swear I'd live on bread and water till I did.'

" 'I'd rather enjoy my vodka. That's much more certain. The best I can do for you is to give you a lift into town. Then you'll arrive fresh and get a better price for yourself.'

" 'No.' "

" 'Don't be a fool, man. Get in.' "

"The devil tempted me, sir. A kind of red mist swam before my eyes and I had to sit down by the roadside or I should have fallen. 'You see', he went on, 'you're not fit to walk another step. Get in, and when I've bought my vodka you shall have a dram of it to give you fresh heart.'

"So I got in. But when I sat by the roadside, my fingers had closed over a stone and I kept it in my hand. On we went through a forest. It was growing dark. I looked along the road ahead, then behind and on each side. Not a soul anywhere. I could see myself roped to a boat, hauling it upstream; I heard my dear ones crying for bread; and all the time, as though to badger me still more, my companion kept singing a little song about all the fine things he would bring his sweetheart from town. I was still clutching my stone—I swear the shape of my fingers must have been impressed on it—and suddenly with all my strength I hit him on the back of his head so that he fell forward between his horses' legs. I jumped down and dragged him into the wood. In his purse he had more than 25 roubles, but I took only one rouble and 75 kopeks and ran home without a backward glance, reaching my village at daybreak. I woke the *stavanoi*, paid him, took his receipt and then went to my *isba* where my wife and children flung their arms around me with tears of joy.

"When I could speak, I told them a friend had lent me the money. 'We must work harder than ever to pay him back quickly,' I said, pretending to be gay, but death was in my heart. Later that day I was arrested. Onesim, whom I thought I had killed, was only stunned, and when he recovered he straightway went to the police. I was thrown into prison and kept there five years before being brought to trial, but at last I stood before the judges and told them what had happened. I expected the death sentence, but because I had confessed they spared my life and are sending me to work in the mines—the copper mines, where no one stays alive for very long. It's tomorrow we go, isn't it, sir?"

I offered him a couple of roubles, but he shook his head. "It's no good giving me that now. The time I needed it was when the *stavanoi* was hounding me, before I tried to kill Onesim," and he curled up on his bench again. I laid the money beside him and went out.

The gaoler unlocked another door. The cell, the bench, the chain and iron fetters were the same as before, but the prisoner was a handsome young fellow of twenty-two or three. Like the other, he was quite ready to tell us his story. "My name is Gregory. My father and mother are both serfs, but rich, as peasants go, for our master, Count G——, gave them valuable privileges. I fell in love with a neighbour's daughter, and our families gladly agreed to plans for our wedding, but we had to wait till Count G——'s next visit to his estates, for we could not marry without his permission.

"Alas, that time the count did not come himself, but sent his superintendent. At first we were not troubled, for as the count's deputy he could sign the marriage permit. Indeed, when our parents waited upon him he promised to do so, but the days passed fruitlessly by. We asked him again, and he said: 'We shall have to see.' Still my love and I were not worried, for we thought his idea was to make us pay for the permit, and a hundred roubles would soon put the matter right. But he made no move, and Varvara grew pale and heavy-eyed, full of foreboding. Often I found her in tears.

"Then, one Sunday, he called all the villagers together and told us that, because of the war, the Czar needed fifteen more recruits from every hamlet in Russia. As the count's deputy, the superintendent would decide which of us must go, and would inform the *maire* of his choice next morning. That evening, Varvara threw her arms around me, sobbing that she knew my name would be on the list. How? She would not tell me, and when I persisted, all she replied was that a hare had crossed her path.

"She was right! My name was there! I ran home in desperation and found that my father had already offered the superintendent 500 roubles to release me, but in vain. I must be ready to leave with the others at dawn next day. Varvara and I took our last walk together through the fields where we had played as children, and paused on a little wooden bridge over a swift torrent to watch the whirlpool seething below us. There, at last, I made her tell me the secret she had locked in her heart till then. The superintendent was determined to make her his mistress. That was the price he demanded of her for his signature on our wedding permit. She had refused. His levy of recruits was a trick to get rid of me, grouped with other luckless fellows as a blind. Once I was gone . . .

"I had been working on the bridge, and knew where an axe lay hidden behind a beam. I felt for it, found it, swung it above my head and swore the blackguard should die by my hand. 'But, Gregory, they would kill you! Stop!' she called after me as I started to run towards the village.

" 'What does it matter whether I die here or in the war? I have sworn, and will keep my oath. You will find me waiting for you in the next world, if there is one.'

" 'Then farewell, my love. 'Tis I who will be waiting there for you!'

"I turned, and felt my hair rise in horror. The bridge was empty. I heard a sound like a last adieu, saw the flicker of her dress in the twilight as she fell, listened as her body struck the water. From that moment I knew nothing of what happened till I found myself in a prison cell, my clothes drenched in blood. I must have killed him. Oh, Varvara, you will not have long to wait." He broke into an anguished cry and hid his face. We crept away.

A third cell was opened and we went in. This prisoner was a giant of a man aged about 40, his eyes and beard a dense black, his hair—all I could see of it—white as though from grief or shock. At first he would tell us nothing, shouting to my guide that he had already faced his judges, once and for all, but when he understood that I was a visitor from France his manner changed, and to my amazement he addressed me in excellent French.

"That's different, sir. I'll gladly talk to you, and it won't take long."

"But," I interrupted him, "how does it happen that you speak my language, and with such a good accent?"

"It is very simple," he told me. "My master owned a factory, and used to send three boys at a time to Paris to learn our trade at the arts and crafts college there. I was ten when I left home. One of my group died in France, but the remaining two of us studied for eight years, my friend becoming a chemist and I a mechanic. We lived like other young students, all of us friends and equals, and it was easy to forget we were slaves, but once we were back in Russia it was soon brought home to us. My companion boxed the ears of a superintendent who insulted him. He was given a hundred lashes, and an hour later he put his head under a steam-hammer in the factory. I was more even-tempered and managed to escape anything more serious than reprimands. My dear mother was alive then, dependent on me, and for her sake I put up with more than I would have done had I been alone. She died five years ago, and then I could afford to marry my sweetheart. Ten months later our little daughter was born, my Caterina. How I adored that child!

"My master, too, had something to love—the pure-bred bitch he had sent for all the way from England, and a pretty penny she cost him, by all accounts. She was in whelp when she arrived and produced two pups, a male and a female. Our master hoped to naturalise the breed in Russia, but a day or two later, as he was driving up to his door, his pet dashed out to welcome him, he did not see her till it was too late, and she was killed by the wheels of his *drojky*.

"Her four-day-old pups were doubly precious, but how could they be reared? My master thought of a way. He knew my wife had a young baby, so he had the child taken away and ordered her to feed the puppies instead. My poor wife dared to protest that she had enough milk for all three, but our master thought the dogs might go short. The child must take her chance in the *messakina,* the communal kitchen.

"When I came home from the factory I went straight to Caterina's cradle, as I always did. It was empty! My wife told me everything and showed me her new nurselings, surfeited and fast asleep. I ran to the *messakina,* found my baby, carried her back to her mother, then I snatched up the puppies, one in each hand, and dashed their brains out against a wall. Next day I set fire to the château, but unluckily the flames spread to the village and 200 houses went up in smoke. I was arrested, thrown into prison, and have just been sentenced to the mines for life, for arson. That's my story, sir. And now, if you can bring yourself to touch a convict, will you shake hands? That would give me real pleasure. I was so happy in France."

I gave him my hand with all my heart, incendiary though he was. I would not have done as much for his master, though he is a prince. Now you have heard the stories of these three convicts, who, do you think, were the real criminals? The landed aristocrat —the superintendent—the *stavanoi,* or the poor wretches on their way to Siberia?

* * * *

8

PETERHOF, ORANIENBAUM, AND ROPCHA

On my return to Besborodko I found a Russian novelist waiting there to see me—Grégorovitch, author of *The Fishermen* and five or six other successful romances. He, Turgueniev and Tolstoi are the three most popular writers in Russia today, with the younger generation at all events. Gregorovitch wished to meet me as a brother novelist, and since he speaks French like a Parisian he offered me his services as guide and interpreter while I remained in St. Petersburg, a suggestion I gratefully accepted.

"Should you happen to be late any evening," said the count to Grégorovitch, "you are welcome to sleep in one of the rooms of M. Dumas's suite to save you the journey back to St. Petersburg." When a friend stays the night in a Russian house there is none of the fuss we make in France, where we always prepare a bed for him with mattress, blankets, sheets, pillows, coverlet, and so on. Oh, no! In Russia the master of the house, even when he has 80 servants like Count Kouchelef, simply says to his guest: "It is late. Stay here tonight." The guest bows, thanks him, and the matter is settled. The host has probably regaled his visitor with the best dinner his kitchen can provide, the choicest wines, endless cups of the finest tea brought from the East by caravan, music till one or two in the morning, and that's enough! The guest will be shown a room— not a bedroom, of course—where he glances round for a sofa or bench—whether upholstered or not is quite immaterial— failing which he will sleep on the floor with a rug over him and another rolled up for a pillow, and wake in the morning as bright and fresh as though he had rested on a spring mattress. To be sure, he cannot expect to wash night and morning, but twice a week he, like the rest of us, can have one of those steam baths that skin you alive.

Forthwith, Grégorovitch settled into the room next to mine,

Market scene in a provincial Russian town.

and before we went to sleep that night we had made plans—through our open doors—for our first excursion outside St. Petersburg. At eight o'clock next morning we would take the little steamer that plies across the Neva and catch the nine o'clock paddle-boat for Peterhof. We would lunch at Samson's, explore Peterhof and the country round, dine and spend the night with Panaef, a friend of Grégorovitch and editor of the *Contemporain,* at whose house we should meet Nikrassof, one of the most popular poets of young Russia. Next day we would visit the historic palace of Oranienbaum, where Peter III was seized by revolutionaries in July 1762, and return to St. Petersburg by rail so as to see as much of the country as possible.

Following out our programme, at 11 o'clock next day we stepped ashore at Peterhof on the quay where *drojkys* stand waiting to be hired. A man of my build needs one to himself, Grégorovitch took another, Moynet a third, and we were driven to the best restaurant in the town—Samson's. Its sign is a reproduction of the famous statue that stands in the great lake in the Royal Park, representing the Hebrew Hercules dislocating the jaws of the Philistine lion.

Unless you have seen one, you can have no idea of what a celebrated restaurant in this province is like. Russia prides herself on her national *cuisine,* particularly on those dishes that no other country can offer, depending as they do upon ingredients found within her mighty empire and nowhere else in the world—sterlet soup, for instance. Russians are passionately fond of it, but the only remarkable thing about it, to my mind, is its cost—fifty or sixty francs in summer, three or four hundred in winter. Yet the simple bouillabaisse one gets in Marseilles is much more to my liking. What makes stertlet soup so expensive? The transport charges!

The sterlet is found in certain rivers, chiefly the Volga and the Oka, and can live only in its native waters. The problem is to bring it, alive, the four or five hundred miles to St. Petersburg. (If it arrives dead, it is useless.) In summer there is no special difficulty. The fish travels in a tank of river water, shaded from the sun, extra supplies of the same water being carried in specially cooled jars. But in winter, with 30 degrees of frost, it's a very different matter, calling for a little furnace operated by a skilled man, to maintain the water always at the right temperature.

In the old days, before railways, great Russian lords kept special trucks, equipped with fish-tanks and slow ovens, to bring sterlet to St. Petersburg, for custom demands that the host shall show his guests the fish, alive and swimming, that, a quarter of an hour later, they will enjoy as soup. You may recall that the Romans did much the same, having their fish brought from Ostia to Rome by relays of swift slaves, changed every three miles, and the first delight of a real gourmet was to watch the rainbow colours change and fade from the scales of the fish as it died. The sterlet, however, has none of the iridescence of goldfish or mullet, for its skin is rough and spiky, like shagreen. Indeed, I maintain that the sterlet is simply a young sturgeon. Its flesh is insipid and greasy, and no Russian cook bothers to improve its flavour. A sauce that could do so has yet to be invented, and if one ever is, I predict it will be the creation of a French chef.

So, at Samson's we carefully avoided sterlet soup and asked instead for *Tchi*. This is a cabbage soup, infinitely inferior to anything our poorest farmer would send out to his field-workers for their mid-day meal, yet it is the staple fare of millions of Russian peasants and soldiers. Ours was served with the little lumps of beef or mutton it was made from, which were over-boiled, stringy and tasteless. The beefsteaks we ordered, the roast grouse and salad which followed, were all prepared, no doubt, from raw materials of the finest quality, but all spoiled in the cooking. As each dish was set before us we expressed our disapproval, and Grégorovitch, while not in the least understanding why we were not pleased—the poor man has never yet tasted anything but Russian cooking—faithfully translated our complaints to the waiter, thus giving as an opportunity of observing the friendly familiarity of Russian dialogue.

The Russian language has no ascending and descending scale of cordiality—only two extremes. If you are not addressed as *brate* (brother) or *galoubchik* (my little pigeon), you are *dourak* or *souk-insine*—terms that I shrink from explaining. It was marvellous to listen to the kindly tones Grégorovitch used when talking to the waiter on his own account, and the amusing contrast when he conveyed our displeasure. I have noticed that the common people refer to the emperor and empress as *batiouchka* and *matouchka*—"our father and mother"; when a poor old man paused beside us, Grégorovitch gave him a couple of kopeks and called him "uncle"; a woman who told us the way was "my aunt." When a man of high rank needs something from an inferior, his words are courteous and gentle—his deeds are harsh enough to outweigh them. If the Russian language is rich in terms of affection, it has an equally varied repertoire of abuse, used just as freely. Education has nothing to do with it, and the most polished aristocrat raps out his *soukinsines* and *yob-vachoumatts* as fluently as any *mougik*. I confess I could have wished for a similar command of invective and a chance to practise it on the chef of Samson's restaurant!

We strolled to the palace gardens of Peterhof, which seemed to me half French, half English. There were lovely shady clumps of trees like those I have admired in Windsor Great Park; there, too, were the vistas of ornamental lakes, the statues, even the carp, of Versailles. Some of these carp, the attendant told us, were there in the days of Catherine the Great, and when he rang a little bell we watched the fish poke their noses above the water to catch tit-bits thrown to them by visitors, just as the carp of François I still do at Fontainebleau. St. Petersburg's greatest fault is its imition of other places—its parks like those of Versailles, Fontainebleau and Rambouillet—its houses like those of Berlin. Even the Neva is something like the Thames. Still, St. Petersburg, as Pushkin said, is not the true Russia, but just a Russian window overlooking Europe.

We admired the statues, particularly one of a crouching nymph that had a certain originality, and the golden Samson lording it over the loveliest lake of all at the foot of the Cascade of the Gladiators, like the one at St. Cloud. The fountains and waterfalls were dry when we arrived, but a small tip to the attendant put that matter right, and produced a spectacle that would have cost twenty-five or thirty thousand francs at Versailles. One of the favourite diversions of Nicholas I was to make his pages and cadets climb up this cascade against the flow of the water while regimental drums sounded the "Charge!" We paid a special visit to a fountain shaped like a tree, every leaf a jet of water, and then mounted a fairly steep slope to the palace itself, an immense building daubed with yellow and white, surmounted by roofs of that pestilential green that Moynet dislikes so much. Passing through one of the vaulted arches we found ourselves in the upper garden where there is a magnificent stretch of water and a remarkable statue of Neptune with the air of a drum-major, wielding a trident instead of a gold-decked staff.

Having seen Peterhof itself, we went on a visit to the islands, driving along a very pleasant road cooled by little streams and shaded by great trees. The first and largest island, Tzaritzina, belongs to the Queen Mother, and on it she has built an exact replica of a typical Sicilian villa, even to the creeping ivy that covers it and has to be kept warm artificially in winter—like the sterlets—for frost would kill it. The next island, Banezzy, is owned by Princess Marie and, according to the custodian, it contains a masterpiece of sculpture, a sleeping Venus concealed beneath a catafalque. You lift the cover and Venus lies before your eyes. But marvels that are hidden, promised, anticipated, are invariably disappointing and this statue, remarkable though it is, failed to delight me. No! If the island does hold a masterpiece it is a work by Stavaser called *The Angler,* a bronze figure of a lad in water up to his knees, who has just felt a fish take the hook on his line. There is, of course, no line, no hook, no fish. You know it all from his tenseness, his right arm poised to take the strain, his keen glance, his lip trembling with excitement.

After the islands we visited the Belvedere, created by the Emperor Nicholas, whose all-powerful hand conjured up bronze and granite as readily as lesser men build with bricks and mortar. It testifies his omnipotence, not, alas, his good taste, but its site on the crest of a hill is delightful. Here Nicholas in his plainest uniform, with the empress and grand-duchesses dressed as shepherd-esses, would come to take tea and admire the view. (How like Louis XV at *le petit trianon*! To the extreme left lay Old Peterhof, and, far to the right, Poulkovo, the observatory built by Brulof, brother of the artist of that name, with 25 miles of plain between. We looked out across this plain, over the gulf with its leagues of open sea, to the far horizon where the misty-blue outline of Finland lay as though drawn with a rule; we could see the shining domes of St. Petersburg on our right, the broad English Park stretching away to the left, New Peterhof before us, and at our feet a field strewn with sad relics of Grecian art exiled here since the days of King Otho.

We went next to the Terrace of Montplaisir (another French name!) on the shore of the gulf, paved with marble and shaded by magnificent trees. Looking out across the water you can catch a glimpse of Kronstadt against the sky-line with its forest of masts and its ramparts bristling with cannon. This is where the dandies of Peterhof come to take the air on these translucent June nights, and we gladly lingered while Moynet sketched this glorious place. Then we settled ourselves in our *drojkys*, Grégorovitch gave detailed instructions to our *isvotschiks*, and off we started on our way to meet one of the most distinguished journalists in Russia today.

I need hardly tell you that journalism is still in its infancy in Russia, where hitherto censorship has done its best to prevent the growth of any ideas the land has tried to produce. Let us take a quick glance at the various periodicals—daily, weekly and monthly —published in St. Petersburg and Moscow.

St. Petersburg itself has only four, of which the most important is the *Sovremennik* (*The Contemporary*), with Panaef as editor-in-chief and Nikrassof—one of Russia's greatest living poets—as manager. It is a monthly journal, modelled on our *Revue des Deux Mondes*, and liberal in tone. It has between 3,500 and 4,000 regular subscribers and so can afford to pay its writers well. Next comes the *Otetchestwennjia* (*The National*), with M. Kraievsky as editor-manager. He chooses his contributors well and this publication, which has no political bias, is very successful from a literary view-point and financially sound, though it has fewer subscribers than the *Contemporary.*

The *Biblioteka dlia tchenia* was immensely successful as long as it was directed by Professor Senkovsky, who clearly understood the intellectual needs of the time, and whose concern was not to instruct his readers but simply to satisfy them. It professed liberal sympathies, but latterly its interest has declined until now it has more or less ceased publication.

The *Syn Otetchestva (The Young Patriot)* is an old-established paper, completely re-organised last year and now very well edited. It is small—each issue a couple of pages only, but its popularity is growing. It is published in Moscow. The *Ruski Viestnik (Russian Courier)*, founded in 1858 by M. Katlof, has been remarkably successful from its first issue. Within six months its output doubled and now it has eight or nine thousand regular subscribers and the best print in all Russia. It, too, is liberal in tone.

Besseda (Conversation) is the official organ of the Russian Slavs, a party which is strongly antagonistic to any infiltration of Western influences, urging that Russia should develop her own characteristics and refuse to borrow anything whatever from foreign sources. Not a popular periodical, yet its articles are sometimes well worth reading, especially on the question of the moment, the emancipation of the serfs. Its editor is a M. Kouchelef. The *Zemledelcheskiai Gaseta,* the journal of the landed aristocracy, is almost completely devoted to articles on emancipation, written from the liberal point of view. If there are any periodicals other than those I have listed, they are scarcely significant enough to mention.

Panaef and Nikrassof are close friends, sharing the same opinions on literature and politics, living and working together, in St. Petersburg in winter, and in summer in some country house or other outside the town. This year they chose a place between Peterhof and Oranienbaum, just below the German quarter. Our *drojkys* turned off the main road to the right, crossed a little bridge over a kind of moat, passed beneath the welcome shade of magnificent trees and halted in front of a delightful little chalet where seven people were gathered on the lawn around a beautifully laid table—Panaef, his wife, Nikrassof and four family friends. They all turned when they heard us arrive and gave a cry of pleasure on recognising Grégorovitch. When I was introduced, Panaef rushed forward with open arms. For him, as for me, it was love at first sight! We embraced like old friends, and were so from that moment. Mme. Panaef came forward, I kissed her hand and she returned my greeting with a kiss on my brow, a charming Russian custom. She is a woman of thirty or thirty-two with strongly marked features—her beauty is characteristically Russian—who has written several novels and short stories published under the pseudonym of Stanicky.

As she presented her guests to me, Nikrassof, quiet and undemonstrative, rose, bowed and shook my hand, apologising—through Panaef—for his inability to greet me in my own language. He knew no French, unfortunately. I wish we could have conversed, for I had often heard him described as a great poet and the only contemporary writer whose genius expresses the current trends of Russian thought. He is a man of 38 or 40, his face pale and profoundly sad, his temperament morose and cynical. He is a great hunter, chiefly, I think, because when hunting he can be alone, and, apart from Panaef and Grégorovitch, his closest companions are his dogs and his gun.

His latest volume is now very scarce and costly—the censor banned a second printing—but I managed to obtain a copy yesterday and sat up half the night over it, Grégorovitch explaining the meaning while I rendered three of his poems into French verse, though our tongue can but feebly convey his stark portrayal of the hopes, the despair, the cruel sufferings of Russia's serfs.

We spent the night at Panaef's house and next morning set off for Oranienbaum. The first thing I noticed as we entered the palace was the device surmounting the central lodge, the crown of a prince, yet not a prince of royal blood. My companion, knowing little of heraldry, insisted that it was the ancient crown of the czars, but the official guide intervened to explain that it was the crown of Prince Alexander Menschikov, to whom the palace originally belonged. The device was the crown of the duchy of Kosel, in Silesia, bestowed on Menschikov by Charles VI, with the title of Prince of the Roman Empire.

Menschikov came of peasant stock—tradition says his father was either a bargee or an ostler—and in his teens he earned his living selling meat pies in the streets of Moscow, where he chanced to be noticed by François Lefort, favourite of Peter I. Under the patronage of Lefort, Menschikov became an officer in the imperial army and rose to the rank of Commander-in-Chief. It was at his house that Peter the Great first saw and fell in love with the slave-girl, Catherine, whom later he married and publicly proclaimed as Czarina. Profiting from royal favour (and from mis-appropriating government funds) Menschikov amassed fantastic wealth, acquiring so many estates throughout the empire that it was said he could travel right across Russia from Riga, through Livonia as far as Derbent on the borders of Persia, spending every single night on his own land, in his own house. His rise to power was spectacular—so was his fall. When the accession of Peter II restored power to the old nobility in 1727, Menschikov was stripped of his titles, his wealth confiscated, and he with all his family was banished to Siberia where he died at Berezov in 1729. So the palace of Oranienbaum, where I had expected to find only the remembrance of Peter III, spoke to me even more vividly of Menschikov's meteoric career.

Still, we did not leave the palace without seeing the toy soldiers and wooden cannon that Peter III played with as a child, the room where, still a child in mind though a grown man of 34 and Czar of all the Russias, he waited in terror while rebel armies, commanded by his fiercely ambitious wife, the notorious Empress Catherine II, were marching on Oranienbaum in July 1762. There, faced by her envoy, General Ismailoff, and the alternatives of instant death or abdication, Peter III signed away his vast empire, asking only to be allowed to keep his dog, his negro servant, his violin and a few books, among them his German Bible.

When I tipped the old soldier who showed us round, he told me (as though it gave him a special claim on my bounty) that he had been to Paris—serving in one of the regiments that captured our capital in 1814! To prove it, he proudly showed me the inscription on a little silver medal he was wearing in his buttonhole. Before leaving the palace I had the pleasure of kissing the hand of Princess Helena, a delightful little girl of two. Her mother, the Grand-Duchess, could not receive me herself for reasons of protocol, so she sent her tiny daughter to greet me in her stead, just as an invisible god sometimes sends a cherub to console a mortal.

We felt we should like to see the royal residence at Ropcha where, a few days after his abdication, Peter III was savagely butchered. To do so we should have to return to Peterhof, a prospect that appealed to us since it would also give us an opportunity to see something of the country home of Countess Kouchelef, the aunt of our host at Bezborodko, and enable us to call on my old friends, M. and Mme. Naptal Arnault, who would certainly offer us lunch.

This time we travelled by train, alighting at the station nearest to the countess's estate, where she has gathered round her a whole colony of French men and women, many of them *artistes* belonging to the Paris theatre recently transported to St. Petersburg. A fellow-passenger, who left the train when we did, offered to walk with us to the French colony a mile or so away. He was a former stage-manager at the *Opéra Comique* in Paris, Josse by name, and reminded me that 20 years ago he had produced my verse-drama *Piquillo* in that theatre. How odd to find common ground with a chance acquaintance two thousand miles from Paris? In Russia, miracles like that happen every minute!

Moynet, Grégorovitch and I, almost dead of hunger, eagerly sought the home of Mme. Arnault, the talented actress who has graced so many performances of my plays. She and her husband had invited me to dine with them on the previous Saturday and had made splendid preparations for my entertainment—even to a display of fireworks consisting of two sunbursts and three roman candles! To my great disappointment I had been prevented at the last moment from keeping this engagement. Now, as we reached their door, we went straight in without being announced, as one does with real friends. Mme. Arnault, school-book in hand, was giving a lesson to her two elder daughters, while the youngest, still a baby, was peacefully asleep in her cradle. M. Arnault was out hunting, this being the opening day of the season.

Mme. Arnault and her daughters rose with a cry of joy to greet us, but I noted a certain hesitation in her voice as she enquired whether we would stay for lunch. "Thank you, indeed we will. We are starving," I replied, with more frankness than tact. It is not easy to improvise a meal for three hungry men in a country house where everything, even bread, has to be brought from St. Petersburg, six or seven miles away. Mme. Arnault and her cook had a consultation. All that their larder could produce was a duck and a dozen eggs, but an omelette and a salmi would hardly suffice. However, at a word from Madame the other French residents pooled their resources and we had a splendid lunch.

At table, we discussed means of transport to Ropcha, and learned that the only vehicle available was a *telega,* shaped like a boat on four wheels, with two planks resting on the axles on which passengers may sit, though normally it is used for transporting goods. Mme. Arnault, waving us goodbye, advised us to tighten our belts and we soon learned why. (In Russia, special body-belts are manufactured for sale to those unfortunates who travel by *telega.* Without such protection their internal organs are likely to be jolted out of place!) To this instrument of torture are harnessed three stout little horses. The middle one trots, the others gallop at full stretch; the road is a dusty track, full of holes and loose stones; the *mougik,* oblivious to the cries of the hapless passengers, apparently understands no human language, not even Russian; and we arrive at Ropcha bruised, battered, speechless, utterly exhausted.

Earlier that morning, however, we had a stroke of good luck. In Peterhof station, General Count T . . . . came over to me quite unexpectedly and reminded me that we were old acquaintances. I had not recognised him, but 25 years ago we had been fellow-guests at a dinner in Paris, when among the party were the Duke of Fitz-James, Count d'Orsay and Horace Vernet. In conversation we mentioned our proposed visit to Ropcha and he enquired whether we had a permit to view the castle. On hearing we had not, he kindly wrote a note to the governor on a page torn from my album.

The road to Ropcha is flat but well-wooded, crossing and re-crossing a winding stream full of trout. (Any trout offered to you in St. Petersburg are always described as "from Ropcha.") One always expects to find some analogy between places and the events that have occurred in them, and because of its tragic history I had imagined the Castle of Ropcha would be dark and sinister, like some stronghold in the days of Vladimir the Great. I found it a pleasant place built in the last century, set in a lovely shady garden with shining stretches of ornamental water. The castle itself was in a state of complete upheaval from top to bottom, with an army of workmen redecorating every room, including the suite forming the corner of the left wing that I had so much wished to see. It was there that Peter III, entrusted to the care of four "reliable" officers, was handed a glass of poisoned wine at dinner by his guest, Alexius Orlov. Soon the dying Czar was screaming in agony, and, to end his cries, Orlov forced him back on his bed and strangled him, while Teplof, his other guest, ran him through (it is said) with a ramrod made red-hot in the fire. The "official" announcement proclaimed that he had died of "an inflammation of the bowels" and his body was carried to St. Petersburg where it lay in state at the Convent of Nevsky. The face of the corpse was black with diffused blood, the throat was torn, but Catherine II cared little whether the people of Russia guessed how their Czar had died, as long as they realised he was dead.

As events turned out, I could not see these rooms, so instead I visited the greenhouses, the finest for miles around. The signature of Count T— produced a magical effect on the gardeners, who pressed me to taste their first peaches, apricots, grapes, cherries, and sent me away with a bouquet twice as big as my head, charming, no doubt, but not at all the sort of souvenir I had expected to carry away from Ropcha.

It was late when we reached St. Petersburg so we slept there and returned to Bezborodko at eight o'clock in the morning before anyone was about. I tiptoed silently to my apartment like a son of the family after a night out, to be met by exciting news. Home had regained his psychic powers, and his attendant spirits had returned in force! Scarcely had I reached my room when Millelotti staggered in, pale and trembling, to collapse in an armchair. It was some time before he managed to explain, in his broken French, the reasons for his terror.

He and Home shared a ground-floor apartment similar to my own, but some distance from it. (I always suspected that Home chose it to be as far away from me as possible. He openly maintained that my presence kept his spirits away.) At one o'clock that morning, said Millelotti, both men had been disturbed by loud rappings, and at last the maestro grew so alarmed that he ran into Home's room and sat on the foot of his bed. All through the night, Home, serene and happy, was in ceaseless communication with his spirit friends until, as dawn was breaking, a new spirit joined them asking to speak to Millelotti. "It was the spirit of my aunt who died nine months ago," the poor man faltered. "She entered into a little marble-topped bedside table that chased me all round the apartment and tried to throw itself round my neck!" At the cold touch of the marble against his cheek the maestro fainted and knew no more till he found himself lying, drenched with sweat, on his own bed, whereupon he had run to my apartment in panic.

Moynet and I rushed to Home's room, excited that his powers had returned and hoping to experience the same sort of contact with the psychic world that Millelotti had described. But all was peaceful. Was there any truth in the story? All I can say for certain is that both men seemed perfectly sincere, Home in his calm conviction, Millelotti in his agitation. If the spirits return I am to be told at once, but I rather fancy Home may be right, and that my presence is not congenial to his ghostly visitants.

*   *   *   *

9

EXPEDITION INTO FINLAND

I had already spent six weeks in St. Petersburg, taking advantage of Count Kouchelef's princely hospitality and seeing practically all there was to see in the town. Before leaving this part of Russia I very much wished to visit Finland, but where should I go in that vast country which is so thinly populated that it has only thirteen people for every square mile? Abo, the old capital? Helsingfors, the new one? Tornio, which used to be considered the most northerly town in the world until someone discovered that Kola in Archangel is three degrees nearer the Pole? Abo and Helsingfors I knew already, through my friend Marmier, and had heard something of Tornio from the English traveller who was making his second trip there to see the midnight sun. Besides, though I may have a gift for seeing things differently, I still prefer, when I travel, to visit places other people have not seen, so I decided on a trip to Lake Ladoga, via Schlusselburg, Konnevitz, Valamo and Serdobol.

The original inhabitants of this northern region were Huns who, in the time of Attila, strayed away from the main hordes that invaded Europe. The Germans were the first to give the name of Finland to this huge morass that its people, from habit rather than conviction, have come to regard as a country. Look at the map! Finland is just like a great sponge; all the holes are water, all the rest is mud. Still, sponge or not, this territory was vitally important to Russian Emperors in their centuries-long conflict with Sweden, and Finland suffered bitter vicissitudes before she was received into the imperial empire on terms that recognised her courage and independence of spirit.

Look at the map again. There are as many islands in the sea as there are lakes in the mainland, so that it is a puzzle to know where the sea ends and the land begins. All the dwellers in this archipelago are boatmen and fishermen. Summer and winter, communications between Sweden and Finland are maintained via

Grisel-Hamm and Abo. For five months in the summer the service is fairly regular, except when tempests prevent a crossing; for the five winter months when the sea is frozen, it is even better; but in the autumn when the ice is forming, and in spring when the thaw begins, there is real danger. Then the summer sailing boats and winter sledges are alike useless, and piraguas fitted with skids are brought into use. These light vessels of shallow draught can be hauled over the ice with great hooked poles, or, if the wind is right, they often glide over the floes for three or four miles to the edge of the open sea, where they may hoist another sail or take to the oars. Sometimes a gale blows up and the grinding slabs of ice threaten to crush the light craft. Sometimes dense fog closes down on them, concealing and intensifying the dangers all around. Seamen less skilled than the Finns, who are positive seals, would inevitably perish, but these hardy mariners know every inch of their course and every peril that may face them. The slightest chance circumstance—the look of the sky at dawn or sunset, the shape of a cloud, the flight of a sea-bird, holds a message of warning or of hope, and at last they come safe to land.

In summer, letters from Sweden reach Abo in three days, in winter when they can. The men who operate this postal service may be lost at sea in a blizzard for a week on end, hanging every moment between life and death, and all for a few kopeks a day. But none of them would live elsewhere, or leave their motherland for any other place on earth, not even Goethe's paradise of sunshine and orange groves. Such men have in their very nature a deep vein of poetic feeling that finds expression in their mythology and in their literature. The Finns have, indeed, two quite different types of poetry—their own primitive verse, robust and spontaneous, akin in spirit to their gushing springs, their torrents and crags; and a second kind acquired from their former conquerors, expressing unoriginal thought in civilised, indeed sophisticated manner—in a word, Swedish.

Hearing of my proposed cruise, Count Kouchelef at once offered to charter a vessel for our exclusive use—a princely gesture that we warmly appreciated—but for several reasons we preferred to take one of the two steamers that make this trip regularly every week in summer, starting from the Summer Garden. Accordingly Dandré, Moynet, Millelotti and I set out at eleven in the morning of July 20th, steaming up the Neva at a rate of six or seven knots. As we passed Bezborodko we could see a group of our friends gathered on the balcony to wave to us, some of them with field-glasses, for at that point the Neva is more than a mile wide and we were too far away to recognise individuals with the naked eye.

It was another hour before we finally found ourselves in open country, passing between two chains of low hills. There we noticed the ruins of two castles, one on the right bank, the other a short distance higher upstream on the left. Both of them were built by Catherine II, and after her death they were demolished by order of her son, Paul I. On the right bank, too, is a ruined factory that was founded by Prince Potemkin to make silk stockings for his own wear. He used a new pair every day, and gave any surplus to his friends. This factory (not the castle, oddly enough), is said to be haunted. Millelotti shuddered at the mere suggestion!

A quarter of an hour later we noticed a stone column rising behind the trees on the right bank. It marks the spot where Peter I stood during the battle for Notemburg, the fortress held by the Swedish army. After his victory Peter had the fort repaired and re-named it Schlusselburg, "the key to the city." (That was before he built St. Petersburg.) Soon, on both shores of the Neva we saw the first close-set fir trees of those immense forests that encircle Lake Ladoga like a wide dark-green belt. In summer, a strange phenomenon takes place in these woods—they catch fire for no apparent reason, and the resinuous pines burn fiercely and persistently. At one time, such outbursts were thought to be the work of incendiaries among the serfs, but now they are generally believed to be due to natural causes. During the fierce midsummer gales the pine trunks bend like reeds and rub against one another with such force that the friction makes them burst into flame. Whatever the cause may be, the result is an undisputable fact. During this expedition to Finland we saw only distant fires, but later, on our journey from St. Petersburg to Moscow, we literally passed between two walls of flame, so near to our train and so fierce that if the drivers had not doubled speed we should all have been roasted to a turn on both sides!

A mile or so further on we saw, to our left, a little village whose name I forget, which belongs almost entirely to the *scopsi,* a sect I spoke of earlier. There stands their Church of the Transfiguration, a suggestive and sinister name in view of their terrible rites of initiation—a sacrilege against nature and humanity. Soon we had our first glimpse of Schlusselburg with its gloomy citadel outlined against the silver waters of the lake. We landed on the quay with an hour for sightseeing, and Moynet quickly made a sketch of the fort—surreptitiously, for the Russian police are apt to deal sternly with any visitor caught making a drawing of a fortification. As it happened we were fortunate, for just as Moynet put away his album a soldier came up to us with a message. From Bezborodko I had written to the governor, telling him of my visit and asking permission to see something of the interior of the fortress. This was his reply, inviting us to come at once.

Millelotti declined, feeling that his nerves were hardly strong enough, but the rest of us instantly jumped into the waiting boat and were rowed across to the sombre stone ramparts whose jutting cannon command the head of the Neva and the entrance to the lake. We were well received and shown round the governor's quarters, then the barracks—features common to all fortresses. But Schlusselburg, as well I knew, also contains secret dungeons, and these we did not see. Indeed, judging from the available area it seemed impossible that they could exist, and a casual visitor would need to be very astute to guess where they are concealed. At last in an angle of the wall I caught sight of a low iron door, heavy and forbidding, well away from the buildings we had seen. Naturally I did not ask awkward questions or seek to probe the mysteries of Schlusselburg, but I made a sign to Moynet, who managed to sketch this door while Dandré and I directed the governor's attention elsewhere.

Our visit was short, for our boat was due to leave—not the one that had brought us up the Neva, but a stouter vessel capable of navigating Lake Ladoga, tempestuous as any ocean. Indeed, we thought it had left without us when we saw it steaming across the harbour with a plume of smoke trailing from its funnel, but abreast of the fortress it hove to and waited for us to come on board, greeted by frenzied wavings from Millelotti.

Ladoga is the largest lake in European Russia, a hundred miles long and seventy miles across, strewn with innumerable islands of which the best known, if not the largest, are Valamo and Konnevitz, whose famous monasteries are visited by thousands of devout pilgrims every year. Konnevitz was our first landing point and we were due to arrive there, all being well, at dawn next day. Dinner time had come and even gone while we waited expectantly for a gong to announce that a meal was served. Alas! On enquiry we found that not only was there no dinner prepared for the passengers, there were not even any provisions aboard! The poor pilgrims who use this steamer bring with them their frugal supplies for the journey—bread, tea and salt fish. Dandré had brought tea, naturally—being a Russian he could not live without it—but no bread, no salt fish. However, after much searching he managed to discover some black bread and a little cured bear-meat—rather like ham; in our *sac-de-voyage* we had knives and forks, plates and glasses; so by and by we sat down to a meal of sorts which Dandré enlivened with such hilarious stories that we were soon choking with laughter.

When we went on deck again we were far out on the lake, the shore of Olonetz just in sight on our right and Finland on our left. Both banks were covered with forests, whirlwinds of smoke billowing up from each of them in two or three different places, caused by the "spontaneous combustion" I mentioned just now. I tried to draw our captain into conversation on the subject, but I might as well have saved myself the trouble. He was a man like a fishing rod, very thin, long and yellow, buttoned up in a black overcoat that flapped around his ankles, his head engulfed in a great broad-brimmed hat with a high crown. Between it and his coat collar protruded the acute angle of his nose—the only part of his face that I could see. In reply to my question he gave his opinion that the smoke came from trees that were burning because they had caught fire—a remark so incontestable that it left me speechless.

Towards ten o'clock that night the boat began to roll ominously.

After a lovely sunset, dense clouds had piled up on the horizon until they formed a great wall of blackness where lightning flickered and thunder rumbled incessantly. Our compass—no one knew why—was playing crazy tricks, no longer able to tell north from south, and our captain frankly owned he had no idea where we were. I was not, however, unduly perturbed. These steamers can find their own way along their familiar route—like old posthorses—and I had no doubt we should arrive safely. We stayed chatting on deck till midnight, drank a last glass of tea to settle our digestions, then lay down to sleep on the nearest benches, my companions rolled in their cloaks, I as I was, for I have the excellent habit of always wearing the same amount of clothing, day or night, winter or summer.

Towards four in the morning I awoke to find that our boat, as I expected, had taken us straight to Konnevitz. Opening my eyes, I was rather intrigued to see, in the pale twilight of a northern dawn, the surface of the lake speckled with a host of black dots—sixty at least. They were the heads of monks standing up to their necks in water, holding open a vast fishing net. Nights in Russia usually retain a hint of winter, but this one had been exceptionally hot and stifling. We were about a hundred yards from the shore and everything on board was quiet, so without a word to anyone I took off my clothes, folded them neatly in a corner and dived over the side into the lake.

The monks of Konnevitz showed some surprise on seeing an inquisitive visitor, clad as Adam was before the Fall, coming out of the water to examine their catch. The great net was filled with thousands of little fishes—the size and shape of sardines—but what especially interested me was that each extremity of the crescent-shaped net was attached by a rope to a horse at the water's edge. All the monks had to do was to cast the net and keep it open. The harder work of hauling it in was done by the horses. I tried to convey my interest and approval to the monks by smiles, gestures and my limited stock of Russian, but they gave no sign of understanding. As a last resort I tried Latin—with the same result.

Russian clergy are in general incredibly ignorant. Priests are all of peasant stock, or the sons of priests (for a priest may marry

—once). A widower may become a monk, and a monk may rise to be a bishop. There are five grades in the heirarchy of the Russian church, the two lowest, *diatshek* and *diakon*, being known as "white clergy." Then come the "black clergy," the *jerei*, or parish priest; the *archjerei*, or bishop, and finally the *Mitropolit* or archbishop. The parish priest, with little or no education, teaches the children what he knows—usually nothing; a few such teachers may be able to read, write and do simple arithmetic; the really erudite know something of sacred history and can discourse upon it. A promising novice may win a place in a seminary, where he learns grammar, logic and swearing. A Russian priest has a more fluent command of profanity than a French sneak-thief, a German horse-faker or an English boxer!

The "black clergy" are notorious for drunkenness and gluttony, not to mention other more venial depravities, yet everyone seems to treat them with respect—outwardly at least. They all have long beards and wear on their heads a kind of brimless shako—always white—with a width of material hanging from it down their backs. In their hands they carry a staff like a long cane. Whether it is part of their regulation dress I do not know, but I never saw a Russian monk in the street without one. While fishing, however, the monks of Konnevitz were *en deshabillé*.

When the net was hauled in and the catch loaded into baskets, horses and fishermen went off to fish elsewhere, so I swam back to the ship and clambered on board, fortunately finding my clothes still where I had left them. When it was time for the passengers to go ashore, a rough plank was pushed out from the deck to a narrow jetty and across it we all in turn walked safely to land. Like all monasteries with any pretensions to popularity with visitors, this one maintained a hospice where pilgrims, both men and women, could obtain a meal. My frugal dinner of the night before, and my morning dip, had given me a ravenous appetite, so I joined the procession in search of breakfast. We were offered slices of raw cucumber well steeped in seasoned water, and black bread damp in the middle. (Though I had grown accustomed to the same sort of bread at Count Kouchelef's table, I still found it revolting.) The only eatable part of the meal was the fish I had seen caught an hour or two before, and with it everyone drank the inevitable tea.

After breakfast we enquired what there was to see on the island, and were recommended to visit the Horses' Stone. We gathered that there was some tradition attached to it so the idea appealed to us, and we set off accompanied by a guide. We passed beside the monastery burial ground, where the gravestones were half hidden by wild flowers, then across a clearing where a great Greek cross marked the tomb of Prince Nicholas-Ivanovitch Maurelof. (It shone so brightly that we thought it must be silver, but it was only tin.) On we went, between a field of grain gay with blue cornflowers and a freshly-mown meadow full of the sweet scent of hay, into a forest where suddenly the ground seemed cut from beneath our feet. We were on the brink of a ravine so deep, so full of green light and clear shadow, that for a moment I felt I must be in Switzerland, not Russia. A steep little wooden stair led us hundreds of feet down to the floor of the loveliest valley imaginable, where tall trees stood like cathedral columns and sunbeams piercing the vaulted roof of their spreading branches fell like a shower of golden rain all around us. In the midst of this valley stands an enormous crag on which, so our guide told us, the Finlanders of old used to sacrifice horses to their gods, before their conversion to Christianity. Now on its crest stands a tiny chapel sacred to Saint Anselm, of whom our guide knew nothing but imagined he was a holy martyr who had died there. In my opinion, any martyr dying in this valley was probably stung to death by gnats! Nowhere else in the world have I ever seen such a dense cloud of those abominable insects, and not until we had climbed out of their valley did they leave us in peace.

We spent the afternoon exploring the coast of Konnevitz in a rowing boat. I had been told it was the haunt of great seals, so lethargic that a man could come close enough to kill them with a club if he felt inclined, but the only ones we saw were like black cats. They looked at us with their great round eyes, and long before we came near them they slid into the water out of sight. At about five o'clock we returned to the monastery, where our dinner was on a par with the *déjeuner* I described to you just now. I had already become acquainted with Russian beds, and felt certain nothing could be harder or more uncomfortable than those in Count

Kouchelef's home at Bezborodko, but the beds at Konnevitz were infinitely worse. Yet we had to make the best of them, for we could not return to our steamer until the morning. Pilgrims were expected to need twenty-four hours to complete their devotions.

Such pilgrims, too! Of the very lowest class—if there are any classes among the common people of Russia. But for their beards, one can hardly tell men from women. They all look alike, dress alike (if you can call their rags "dress"), carry the same staffs, and bear the same heavy burdens on their backs. All of them are forever scratching themselves in a manner most alarming to anyone who normally has no need to scratch! There were a hundred or so grouped around us, and we did not spend a peaceful night.

At ten o'clock next morning we steamed away from Konnevitz en route for Valamo, but before we had gone more than four or five miles we were engulfed by a fog so thick, so black, that it was impossible to see more than a few yards. Claps of thunder roared and reverberated all around us and the surface of the lake began to shudder like water coming to the boil in a saucepan, as though the storm was not in the atmosphere but raging in the depths beneath our keel. For hours we pitched and rolled at the mercy of giant waves while the pilgrims lay prostrate in rows on the deck, beating their foreheads on the planking and wailing prayers. I have lived through five or six tempests, but never another like that. Even the captain had given up hope and was rushing madly from stem to stern crying that all was lost.

At last there came a sound like a troop of galloping horsemen. It was the wind sweeping across the lake, tearing the fog into shreds and rolling them away. The whole surface was white with foam as far as eye could see, but gradually we began to glimpse the distant horizons, then the island of Valamo ahead of us. A mile or so before reaching it we passed a sea-girt crag still known as Nuns' Island, though the nuns who once lived there all died long ago and only the ruin of their convent still remains. Valamo itself has a narrow firth guarding an estuary that reaches far into the heart of the island, and as we entered it we saw a little church, all gold and silver, bright as a jewel, set upon velvet turf in a bower of trees. It was designed by Gornestoef, Russia's finest architect in my opinion, and the precious metals, though used in profusion, were employed with such sublime artistry that they could not offend the most exacting taste. It was the first piece of architecture I had seen in Russia that I found completely satisfying.

The entrance to Valamo was so narrow that our boat almost brushed against the trees on the bank as we went through, then it suddenly broadened into a gulf sprinkled with little islands full of shade and freshness. After skirting them, we saw on the mountain-side to our left the monastery of Valamo, a huge building with no architectural distinction but imposing by its very mass. A gigantic flight of steps led up to it, broad as the stairway to the Orangery at Versailles, but three times as high, and so thronged with people passing up and down that it made me think of the ladder in Jacob's dream.

The moment our steamer pulled in beside the little quay we jumped ashore and joined the ascending crowd. We had heard that the Abbot was a man of culture, so we hoped it might be possible to see him and pay our respects. We were met at the top of the steps by a young novice with long hair, delicate features and a pale complexion, who had been leaning against the convent door in a pose full of grace and melancholy. From a distance of twenty yards we could have sworn he was a woman, and even after speaking with him we were not sure that he was really a man. I told him my name, with no great hope that an echo of it might perhaps have reached this lost island of Lake Ladoga, and he went to inform the Superior of our arrival. Five minutes later he returned and invited us to enter. To my great astonishment, the Abbot knew of me, and spoke of *Monte-Cristo* and *The Three Musketeers,* not as having read them himself, but as having heard them praised by others who had. He offered us a collation of fruit and tea, then suggested we might like to see over the monastery with the young novice as our guide.

No one knows for certain when the monastery of Valamo was founded, but it was undoubtedly already in existence in the 16th century. Today it has nothing of artistic or scientific interest; no paintings, no library, no written or oral records of its history. It is eloquent merely of the prosaic squalor of monastic life. The

Abbot was waiting for us on our return. Since the steamer would not leave until the evening of the next day, he enquired how we should like to spend the morning and afternoon. "Exploring the island and perhaps shooting a few rabbits," I replied, for I had heard that rabbits were plentiful on Valamo. The Abbot graciously gave us permission to do both, and since the island is best seen from the water he promised to send his own boat for our use, but when I ventured to ask if he would allow the novice to come with us I evidently went a little too far. My request was refused, the gleam of animation dawning on the face of the novice died away, he resumed his customary air of detached melancholy, and our interview was over.

When we made our appearance at the hospice that evening we found that the Abbot had kindly sent down for us a lavish supply of fish (perch, a foot and a half long, weighing more than eight pounds—finer than I ever saw in France and wonderfully succulent), salad and root vegetables, a great loaf of black bread and an immense flagon of *qvass*—Russian beer—holding four or five gallons. In addition, we had procured a chicken and some eggs, and with this wealth of ingredients for a feast at our disposal I declared I would not entrust them to any Russian chef, especially one who was a monk. Dandré, the only member of our party who spoke the language fluently and so could establish friendly relations between myself and the natives, procured me the use of a corner of the kitchen, made sure the chicken was plucked without being first immersed in boiling water, and foiled an attempt by the monastery cook to put flour in my omelette. Dandré, who had retained a grateful memory of French cooking, swore that this was the first dinner worthy of the name that he had tasted since he left Paris. I had succeeded in producing for us an excellent meal, but—alas! —it was beyond my powers to make the beds any softer! Never did I discover what Russians use to stuff their mattresses! I have heard of French beds stuffed with peach kernels or plum stones, but those would be as down compared with the beds we had in Russia!

The Abbot's boat was to be ready for us at six in the morning, but long before that, as the first streaks of dawn lightened the sky,

I jumped out of bed. (Sheets are completely unknown in Russia and one goes to bed fully dressed, so that getting up is a simple matter.) Confident that my companions would find me when they were ready, I went down Jacob's ladder and sat under a clump of trees to watch the infinitely subtle variations of colour between dusk and daylight that can be found only in these northern altitudes, so different from the rapid change from dark to bright sunrise that we are accustomed to in the south.

At six my friends came down to join me, and we found the boat duly waiting for us with four sturdy oarsmen. One of the monastic virtues is implicit obedience to an order. The discipline of the cloister is even more rigid than in the army, and one can always count on a monk's submission to any duty laid upon him—though his intelligence may remain open to doubt. We tried to question them about any traditions or history the island might possess, but could not get two words out of them. On more commonplace subjects we were more successful, and learned that the monks of Valamo go to bed at nine, rise at five, have two meals a day of fish and vegetables, and rarely eat meat except on feast days. All the manual tasks of the convent are performed by the brothers themselves, who each learn a trade. One of our oarsmen was a tailor, another a shoemaker, a third a carpenter. The very boat we were in had been made by the monks.

We began by following the shores of the gulf, putting in to all the little creeks where trees, bright green and full of vigour from the short but fierce Russian summer, trailed their lower branches in the water. One purpose of our excursion was to find a spot where Moynet, and Millelotti, too, could sketch the beautiful little church we had seen as we entered the bay. Leaving them happily busy with their pencils and sketch-books on the shore, Dandré and I explored further along the coast, hoping to find a place where we could land and hunt rabbits, but not one of those usually prolific little animals did we see. (I remembered, too late, that the man who told me there were rabbits on Valamo was the same one who said there were tame grey seals on Konnevitz!)

I noticed there were practically no birds, either, in spite of the magnificent foliage all around, as though they had given up trying to rear nestlings in a place where summer lasts only a few weeks. Hence the absence of any sounds of life and gaiety in these woods, whose air of solitude is doubled by their silence. We had brought the food left over from our evening meal to serve us for lunch, and later in the morning we returned to share it with our artist friends. They had both made excellent sketches, and Moynet's was outstanding, the best he has ever done, though he was very much out-of-sorts from a feverish cold.

At five p.m. our steamer cast off, and at six we waved goodbye for ever to Gornestaef's little masterpiece of red, gold and silver, for one cannot hope to make the pilgrimage to Valamo twice in a single lifetime. At dawn next morning we were in sight of Serdobol and the end of our sea-trip, for we planned to return to St. Petersburg by land. After skirting a whole archipelago of small islands, almost completely uninhabited, we landed at eight o'clock on the waterfront of this poor little Finnish town built between two mountains. Every town, even in Finland, has its main street where hungry travellers go in search of food, and there we came across a group of German students who, like ourselves and the lion of the Scriptures, were going about seeking that they might devour. Dandré, who speaks German like a native, fell into conversation with them and introduced us, whereupon they enthusiastically joined our party. Our joint researches produced a fowl, some fish and plenty of eggs, so we contrived a satisfying meal. True, there was no butter to cook with, but wherever there are fowls there are sure to be pigs, and we had no difficulty in obtaining lard, which served very well.

There was nothing to attract us in Serdobol itself, but I had been strongly advised to visit the marble quarries of Ruskiala, some twenty miles outside the town. I confess that in my travels I usually avoid such utilitarian places as factories, mines and quarries—all very important, no doubt, but their products are quite sufficient to satisfy my curiosity. In this case, however, I felt I had no option. My friends in St. Petersburg had said so much about these quarries, which had provided most of the material for the Cathedral of St. Isaac, and would certainly want to know what I thought of them when I got back, so we hired a *telega*, that instrument of torture-by-locomotion I have already described, and said goodbye to our student friends, who gave us their traditional three cheers as we set off at a gallop behind five strong horses.

The road was said to be excellent (Russians always think their roads are good), and though in Serdobol itself the surface was so rough that we all had to hang on grimly, once we were outside the town the going was smoother and very flat, so that we could give some attention to the countryside, which was most picturesque. In a patch of shade at the foot of a high rock a group of gypsies were cooking their dinner in the open air, while a donkey, the sole motive force of a cart piled with all the tribe's possessions, was steadily munching the soft green moss and tender shoots of grass among the boulders. Beyond question, the ass fed better than his masters, but then, servants generally do.

At about half-past two in the afternoon we came to a post-house, such as one can see beside every main road in Russia, all exactly alike, each a regulation number of miles from the next. In them, travellers are sure of finding the bare necessities for a night's rest—shelter from the weather, two benches and four stools (made of deal painted to look like oak), and the inevitable *samovar*, always on the boil. All this is free and yours by right, since by stopping at a post-house you automatically become a guest of the government. But do not expect more! If you want to eat you must bring your own food. If you need a bed, carry a mattress with you. Otherwise you must be content to sleep on one of the wooden benches, which are even harder than convent beds, but a great deal cleaner.

The man in charge of this particular post-house was most obliging, and not only undertook to obtain supplies for our evening meal, but also offered to guide us to the quarries, which lay half a mile or so away across fields. (I should add that the house stood on rising ground and commanded a delightful view—a rare sight in this part of Russia, where the land is usually flat.) A few moments' walk brought us in sight of a conical hill so white and dazzling that one would have sworn it was snow. It consisted entirely of debris from the marble workings, and beyond it we found ourselves in a wide flat space strewn with immense square blocks of marble ready to be carted away. What dynamic power, I wondered, could transport such huge masses of stone? Our guide explained that they would not be moved till the depth of winter, when close-packed snow lay several feet thick on the frozen ground. Then with cranes and levers each block was hoisted on to a sledge and hauled down to Lake Ladoga where specially constructed sailing barges were waiting to convey them to St. Petersburg.

I was examining one of these blocks with half-hearted interest when I suddenly realised that I was practically alone. The last of my companions was just disappearing into a narrow vertical cleft that I had not noticed until then in the face of the marble mountain. I ran across the quarry floor and followed him for fifty yards along a fissure, my shoulders brushing the rock on each side, until all at once we found ourselves in a vast square cavern with glistening white walls a hundred feet long and forty feet high. After pointing out its beauties, our guide added that now he would take us to a quarry of green marble a mile or two away, the most extraordinary sight in the world, on no account to be missed. We compromised. Moynet and Dandré wished to visit this phenomenon, while I preferred to go back to the post-house to prepare dinner, hastening my departure when I heard the post-master telling Dandré of yet another quarry, this time of yellow marble, now derelict and consequently even more picturesque. Millelotti, no great lover of quarries, asked to come with me, and by the time our friends rejoined us our evening meal was ready on the stove.

After dinner, presided over by our genial guide, we converted the main room into a dormitory where we spent half the night talking and drinking tea before we fell asleep. One fact I learned on this trip is that while Russians are fanatical lovers of tea, Finns are just as devoted to coffee. It is by no means unusual for a Finnish peasant to go 25 or 30 miles into town and back to buy a pound or two of coffee, possibly on behalf of a group of neighbours. Even in poor hotels in Finland we were served with perfect coffee enriched by delicious cream from their lush dairy farms.

Next morning we returned to Serdobol, where we stopped to change horses, then drove on to Otsois along a road winding between the shore of Lake Ladoga and a range of granite cliffs weathered into columns, but I am no geologist, and I confess I was more interested in the excellent strawberries offered to us in hand-woven baskets by country-women on the roadside. Beyond Otsois, we soon lost sight of Lake Ladoga and began to climb a steep winding road hewn out between the granite mountains, so narrow that our *telega* filled the whole width. If we had met another vehicle, leapfrog would have been the only solution! We feasted our eyes on the grandeur of the mountain crests, and I particularly recall one looking so exactly like a ruined castle that not until we were close up to it could we believe its formation was natural. The whole range was covered with magnificent forests, and at one place we were able to study at close quarters the effect of a fire such as I mentioned earlier. The wind had driven it northward into the densest part of the forest, where in all probability it would burn for a considerable time. We noticed a rather strange thing. The fire did not spread from one tree to the next, but along the ground between them, creeping like molten lava over the resinous carpet of pine needles and cones, encircling the base of the trunk, then flowing on. It was not until some moments later that the tree began to quiver, its bark burst open, and flames climbed its trunk to devour its branches. Sometimes the charred stump had remained standing, but at a touch from my walking stick it would collapse in a heap of black dust.

We slept that night at Mansilda and travelled on to Kronnberg in the morning along a pleasant but rather dull road. Once past Kronnberg we came to another granite range where the fantastic crags, deep ravines and two or three lakes shining like polished steel in their dark green frames reminded me irresistibly of Switzerland. Beyond Poksouilalka we found ourselves once more beside Ladoga and crossed a bridge to the little islet on which the town of Keholm is built. Keholm, like Schlusselburg, was formerly a Swedish fortress, and to enter it you must cross a wide moat commanded by a fortified rampart, an interesting piece of military architecture that today stands in mournful ruins. We drove through the fortress from end to end, but it had no historical traditions to claim our interest, so we did not stop until we reached the postern overlooking the lake, where we spent the night. (The gate-house is now an inn, and I confess the beds there made me long for the wooden benches at Ruskiala!)

In the morning we strolled around the town and were pleasantly impressed by its clean streets, most of them bordered with neat little single-storey wooden houses, the streets themselves so crowded with strawberry-sellers that we seemed in the midst of a conference of fruit-growers. Our route out of Keholm lay on the far side of a whole series of lagoons and I had been wondering rather anxiously how we and our *telega* could cross this stretch of water. My anxiety on that score was soon settled, or, rather, it gave way to dismay. At the water's edge a sort of raft was bobbing up and down, and from it six men jumped ashore as we approached. Four of them went to our horses' heads, the other two pushed at the back of our seat, ignoring our protests and giving us no chance to dismount, and in an instant the *telega* slid forward bodily on to the floating planks. The raft lurched and almost capsized, but our bargemen quickly flung their weight to restore our equilibrium, then, pushing with long poles against the sandy bottom, they drove us along at a fair speed, despite a strong adverse current. This place is a maze of intersecting waterways and could with a minimum of effort be made into a northern Venice. Many of the islands in the lagoons already contain houses, shops, even their own churches; on others stand castles like fortresses, flanked by turrets and crowned with battlements. Fifteen or twenty minutes later our *telega* was hauled ashore on the opposite side of the lake, still without our being allowed to leave our seats. The crossing, which remains in my mind like a dream, cost us one rouble.

Leaving the lagoons behind us, we came to a region where the land, cleared of trees by forest fires, was being cultivated and proving highly productive. We noticed remarkably good crops of wheat and rye almost ready for harvesting. When we reached Naiderma we had our first real opportunity of observing the traditional national costume worn by the women of Finland—a blue skirt with a broad scarlet band around the hem, a voluminous white bodice tightened in at the waist and a red kerchief knotted under the chin to frame the face, very becoming to a pretty girl but far from kind to those who were plain.

The next stage of our journey brought us to the River Vuoksi, which higher in its course forms the celebrated Imatra Falls, the finest, if not the only, waterfalls in Russia. Whether it was in flood when we saw it I do not know, but it certainly covered the floor of the valleys through which it flowed. The country continued mountainous and well-wooded, but as we approached Magra we began to notice that the region seemed infested with droves of pigs, running wild. At first sight I took them for wild boars and had already stopped the *telega* to get a shot at their leader when I realised that he had a triangle of wood fixed to his forelegs and coming to a point above his neck—presumably to prevent his breaking into any enclosures. A few miles further on they were so numerous and so tame that whole herds of them lay in the road, sleeping in the sunshine, and our driver was forced to get down and use his whip to persuade them to move out of our way.

After Koutiatkina the road divides, the right fork leading to Viborg, the left to St. Petersburg, and soon we were crossing the Bolchaia-Nevka by the monumental bridge built by our compatriot Bethancourt in 1811. We drove through Apothecaries' Island, cut across the little River Karpovka, entered the capital by the Ostrov road and shortly afterwards we were back at Bezborodko after an absence of ten eventful days. That evening, which as usual we spent singing and playing music until four in the morning, it suddenly occurred to me that I had passed the fifty-sixth anniversary of my birth between Valamo and Serdobol.

IO

MOSCOW: THE ROAD TO JELPATIEVO

Once the wedding festivities were over,[1] our stay in St. Petersburg ended too, and at eight o'clock next morning we set out for Moscow,

(1) The wedding of Daniel Dunglas Home and Alexandrina, took place in the cathedral of St. Petersburg on August 1st.

400 miles away—a dull journey across endless steppes and inter-minable forests, all the more tedious since Russian trains are so slow. Still, we did have a little excitement in the form of a forest fire. Suddenly we heard our engine whistle with the full force of its brazen lungs; our speed quickened as though the train had gone mad and bolted; then we felt the heat, and when we looked out the whole countryside was a mass of flames as far as eye could see —a magnificent spectacle, especially since night was falling. We tore through the very heart of the conflagration at something over fifty miles an hour—double our normal speed—and so I survived my baptism of fire, a baptism that, as you will see, was ratified a couple of days later by my confirmation in the art of incombusti-bility. Now I am qualified to face Hell itself, should the necessity arise, without taking any further examination.

Halfway between St. Petersburg and Moscow we passed through Vyshniy-Volochok, a town notorious as the traditional rendez-vous of thieves and receivers of stolen goods from both capitals, and at ten o'clock next morning, after 26 hours of travelling, we reached our journey's end. In response to my telegram, Jenny had sent Didier Delange, Narychkine's confidential secretary, to meet us at the station with a carriage driven by an elegant Russian coachman who wore a little hat with a turned-up brim and a peacock's feather, a long black caftan tightly buttoned from top to bottom, a silk shirt, wide trousers stuffed into the tops of his high boots and a broad eastern-looking sash around his waist.

Now we were in the heart of old Russia—the true Russia, not the pale counterpart we had known in St. Petersburg. Next to Con-stantinople, Moscow is the largest city in Europe, or, rather, the largest village, for Moscow, with its parks and little wooden huts, its lakes and market-gardens, its flocks of crows feeding among the hens, its birds of prey sailing over the rooftops, seemed to me far more like a village than a town. Its origins are lost in legend, and a legendary city it has always remained, from the days of Yuri-Dolgoruki in the 12th century until Napoleon, at the turning point in his victorious campaigns, left his mark on the ruins of the Kremlin. Small wonder that my heart beat high with excitement as we drove through, and not only at the thought of seeing my old friends again.

Jenny was waiting to welcome us at the door of their villa in Petrovsky Park. Narychkine was on the steps leading up to the entrance, occupied, as he is every morning, in inspecting the horses that are his pride and joy. (He owns the finest stud-farm in all Russia, the only one with bloodstock descended from the famous stallion that belonged to Gregory Orloff—I forget his Russian name, but it means "the brave one.") They both greeted us with cries of joy, Narychkine leaving his string of horses for a moment or two until Jenny carried us off to a charming pavilion arranged for our exclusive use, separated from the main building by a lilac hedge and a garden full of flowers. It had been completely refurnished in our honour—we even had a bed each, an unheard-of luxury in Moscow!—with everything a charming hostess could devise to surround us with comfort and induce us to prolong our stay. But, alas! my days in Moscow were already numbered, for I particularly wished to be in Nijni-Novgorod for the opening of their famous Trade Fair.

Our exclamations of thanks and appreciation were cut short by the gong for lunch, which was served in the villa and was a far better meal than I had come to expect from a Russian chef. Without the slightest reservation I can praise one of Russia's national dishes—a lightly boiled sturgeon seasoned only with horse-radish and served cold. After lunch, my host offered to drive me to any place I cared to choose. (Whether Narychkine proposes going out or not, a carriage is always kept in readiness for him, fifty yards from the entrance steps, with four horses harnessed to it in a marvellously impressive fan-shaped formation.) However, I wished my first excursion to be to see the Kremlin by moonlight that evening, so Narychkine drove off to his club while my companions and I threw ourselves down like children on the new-mown hay in the park, revelling in its scent, the golden sunshine, the warm friendliness that had made this relaxation possible. That afternoon in Petrovsky Park is one of the most cherished memories of my life! Another is the sight of the Kremlin that night, swathed in floating mist and bathed in soft moonlight, its spires shooting up towards the stars, a fairy palace that filled me with rapture beyond my power to describe.

Narychkine invited a guest to meet me at lunch next day—the Moscow Chief of Police, Schetchinsky by name. Before we had been more than 10 minutes at table a wild-looking police officer rushed in unannounced and uttered one word—*"Pajare!"*—"Quick!" The Chief of Police sprang from his seat while Narychkine and Jenny, with one voice, exclaimed: "A fire! Where? A fire is no rare event in Moscow and is always a serious matter, for of the 11,000 houses in the centre of Moscow only 3,500 are of stone, the rest are of wood. Just as St. Petersburg counts its disasters in floods, Moscow numbers the fires that have reduced great stretches of the city to ashes, the most terrible being, of course, the one in 1812, when barely 6,000 buildings remained standing.

I was seized with a sudden urge to see this fire for myself. "Can I come with you?" I begged the Chief of Police.

"If you promise not to delay me a single second."

I seized my hat as we ran together to the door. His *troika,* with its three mettlesome black horses, was waiting. We jumped in and shot off like lightning while the messenger, already in the saddle, spurred his own mount and led the way. I had no conception of how fast a *troika* can move behind three galloping horses, and for a moment I could not even draw breath. Dust from the macadamised country road billowed up in clouds above our heads; then, as we skimmed over the pointed cobbles of Moscow's streets, sparks struck by our flying hooves fell around us like rain and I clung desperately to the iron strut while the Chief of Police yelled: "Faster! Faster!"

As soon as we left Petrovsky Park we could see smoke hanging like an umbrella—fortunately there was no wind. In the town there were dense crowds, but the messenger, riding a horse's length ahead, cleared a path for us, using his knout on any bystanders who did not move fast enough to please him, and we passed between ranks of people like lightning between clouds. Every moment I feared that someone would be run over, but by some miracle no one was even touched and five minutes later we were facing the fire, our horses trembling, their legs folding beneath then. A

E

whole island of houses was burning fiercely. By good fortune the road in front of it was fifteen or twenty yards wide, but on every other side only narrow alleys separated it from neighbouring dwellings. Into one of these alleys rushed M. Schetchinsky, I at his heels. He urged me back—in vain. "Then hold fast to my sword-belt," he cried, "and don't let go!" For several seconds I was in the midst of flames and thought I should suffocate. My very lungs seemed on fire as I gasped for breath. Luckily another alley led off to our right. The Chief of Police ran into it, I followed and we both sank exhausted on a baulk of timber. "You've lost your hat," he laughed. "D'you feel inclined to go back for it?"

"God! No! Let it lie! All I want is a drink."

At a gesture from my companion a woman standing by went back into her house and brought out a pitcher of water. Never did the finest wine taste so good! As I drank, we heard a rumble like thunder. The fire-engines had arrived!

Moscow's Fire Service is very well organised, and each of the 21 districts has its own engines. A man is stationed on the highest tower in the area, on the watch day and night, and at the first sign of fire he sets in motion a system of globes to indicate exactly where smoke is rising. So the engines arrive without losing a second, as they did on this occasion, but the fire was quicker still. It had started in the courtyard of an inn, where a carter had carelessly lit his cigar near a heap of straw. I looked into that courtyard. It was an inferno!

To my amazement, M. Schetchinsky directed the hoses not on the fire itself but on the roofs of the nearby houses. He explained that there could be no hope of saving the houses that were actually burning, but if the sheets of iron on neighbouring rooftops could be prevented from getting red hot there might be a chance of saving the homes they covered.

The only source of water in the district was 300 yards away, and soon the engines were racing to it to refill their tanks. "Why don't the people make a chain?" I asked.

"What is that?"

"In France, everyone in the street would volunteer to pass along buckets of water so that the engines could go on pumping."

"That's a very good idea! I can see how useful that would be. But we have no law to make people do that."

"Nor have we, but everyone rushes to lend a hand. When the *Théâtre Italien* caught fire I saw princes working in the chain."

"My dear M. Dumas," said the Chief of Police, "that's your French fraternity in action. The people of Russia haven't reached that stage yet."

"What about the firemen?"

"They are under orders. Go and see how they are working and tell me what you think of them."

They were indeed working desperately hard. They had climbed into the attics of the nearby houses and with hatchets and levers, their left hands protected by gloves, they were trying to dislodge the metal roofing sheets, but they were too late. Smoke was already pouring from the top storey of the corner house and its roof glowed red. Still the men persisted like soldiers attacking an enemy position. They were really wonderful, quite unlike our French firemen who attack the destructive element on their own initiative, each finding his own way to conquer the flames. No! Theirs was a passive obedience, complete and unquestioning. If their chief had said "Jump in the fire!" they would have done so with the same devotion to duty, though they well knew that it meant certain death to no purpose. Brave? Yes, indeed, and bravery in action is always inspiring to see. But I was the only one to appreciate it. Three or four thousand people stood there watching, but they showed not the slightest concern at this great devastation, no sign of admiration for the courage of the firemen. In France there would have been cries of horror, encouragement, applause, pity, despair, but here— nothing! Complete silence, not of consternation but of utter indifference, and I realised the profound truth of M. Schetchinsky's comment that as yet the Russians have no conception of fraternity as we know it, no idea of brotherhood between a man and his fellows. God! How many revolutions must a people endure before they can reach our level of understanding?

This callous apathy seemed to me even more terrible than the fire itself, and sick at heart I turned away. When I was clear of the crowd I hired a *drojky* and was driven back to Petrovsky Park, where I found my charming hostess waiting to take me to see the famous Convent of the Virgins, *Novo-Dyevichy*. I begged a few moments grace, changed my clothes and brushed my badly singed hair, then ran to join Jenny in her carriage. This was a place I had longed to visit, not only because of its long and colourful history—it dates from 1524 and was built by the great Prince Vasili Ivanovitch, father of Ivan the Terrible; its tombs of Russia's illustrious dead—among them those tragic royal ladies who led revolts against Peter the Great, his sister, Princess Sophia, and his first wife, the Czarina Eudoxia; but even more because it is one of the loveliest buildings in Russia, a masterpiece of architecture, a rich treasure house so vast that it contains eight churches. It stands in a great loop of the river Moskova, and even Moynet—no lover of Russian architecture—thought it so lovely that he went back next day and made it the subject of a superb painting.

During my first fortnight in Moscow, Narychkine's famous carriage did nothing but take me sight-seeing, several times to the Kremlin, which always spoke to me of Napoleon and 1812, once to the Foreigners' Cemetery, where so many thousand French soldiers who died in that campaign lie buried. I grew familiar with Red Square—in Russian, "Red" does not necessarily mean "scarlet," but is a synonym for "fine," "grand," "beautiful"—where the first thing that impressed me was an unusually democratic monument to Minin, representing the people—he kept a butcher's shop in Nijni-Novgorod—and General Prince Pozharsky—representing the aristocracy and the army. Both stand in a masterly group on the same pedestal—one of those strange anomalies one comes across in Russia. France, the home of liberty and equality, has nothing like it.

A few yards away from the monument is the entrance to the bazaar known as the Golden Line, occupied almost exclusively by goldsmiths and vendors of precious stones, thronged by collectors of old gold and silver in search of chalices, goblets, bracelets, belts, rings, all sold by weight, irrespective of their craftsmanship. That is where you may find turquoises, always eagerly sought after by Russians and consequently rare. The vendors are Persians or Chinese and the stones are usually unmounted. If mounted, they are generally set in silver. The value of a turquoise depends on its colour, and between two stones of the same weight an almost imperceptibly deeper shade of blue may add 500 francs to the cost. To a Russian, a turquoise is more than a jewel. It is a talisman, an object of superstitious veneration, a token given by one friend to another, or by a lover to his mistress. If, while they are apart, the stone changes colour or grows pale, the giver must be ill or unfaithful, possibly even dead, so they believe.

Russians are as fond of jewellery as any Eastern potentate, and their hands are often loaded with rings, but you will always find that the stones are mostly turquoises. At the Nijni Fair I saw turquoises, rubies and emeralds sold by weight like nuts, turquoises fetching twice the price, in Russia, that they would be worth elsewhere.

In this commercial quarter, the *Kitay-Gorod*, near the Spaskiya Gate, stands the *Vasili Blazhennyi*, the fantastic Polrovsky Cathedral, which to me looked like a nightmare dreamed by a disordered brain, translated into stone by a lunatic architect. Ivan the Terrible had it built in 1554 as a thanksgiving for his capture of Kasan, and urged the architect to make it a supreme masterpiece of his art. When it was finished, Ivan had its creator's eyes put out to ensure that he could never build a similar *chef-d'oeuvre* for any other patron. The whole church, surmounted by heaven knows how many bulbous cupolas, is painted in vivid clashing colours, chiefly bright red and pale green. I made several enemies in Moscow because I failed to share the universal admiration for the *Vasili-Blazhennyi*, but I made amends by my unstinted praise for the Treasury of the Czars, a wonderful display of historical relics, from the walnut throne used by Vladimir Monomaque in 1113 down to the litter on which Charles XII, sorely wounded, was borne from his last battle. There is a vast room filled with thrones that, of themselves, portray the entire pageant of Russian history; there are crowns her monarchs wore, their jewels and robes, their household furniture, the objects they handled as they ate and drank, played with when at leisure or clutched in their dying grasp.

I visited *Tzaritzina*, the ruins of a palace that was never completed, for Catherine, for whom it was planned, refused to set foot in it, protesting that its long rectangular shape and six turrets made her think of a tomb flanked by six candles; Kolomenskoye, a country palace which still holds souvenirs of Peter the Great as a boy—the mews where he used to feed his falcons; and the four oak trees in whose shade he did lessons with his tutor Zotof; Ismailoi, where he had his first little boat and studied navigation with Master Brandt. I went to Sparrow Mountain and enjoyed a magnificent view of Moscow; visited monasteries, churches, museums, until even the most enthusiastic local archaeologists could think of no-where else to send me. Then I decided to make a pilgrimage to Borodino, where Napoleon fought one of the bloodiest battles of his Russian campaign.

Narychkine very kindly placed a travelling coach at our disposal and sent Didier Delange with us to act as interpreter. We drove out of Moscow across the broad Katinka plain, where horse races and military reviews are held, and took the Dorogomilof road. It was in this suburb that Napoleon spent the night before marching on to occupy the Kremlin. The inn, built of stone, survived the fire that swept the town and the room where he lodged is still shown to visitors. Our road lay over the crest of Salutation Hill, where the French army had its first view of Moscow, then on to Veslaina, a village that was once the property of Boris Godounof. The church and its extraordinary bell tower were built to his design. We passed through Narra, and as we approached Koubenskoye we came upon a flock of sheep quietly making its way homeward, without a shepherd, from the pastures where it had spent the day. It was a communal flock, each villager owning two or three, and at nightfall every animal returned to its master's shed. (I saw a herd of cows do exactly the same in Moscow! Do you wonder that I called it a village? Can you imagine cows wandering home alone through the streets of London or Paris?) At Mozhaisk we had to wait for fresh horses, and took the opportunity to climb the crag where the ruins of the old fortress still stand, and to visit the Church of Saint Nicholas the Miraculous with its effigy of the saint holding his church in one hand and a sword in the other.

It was three o'clock in the morning when our horses appeared, and at daybreak we were passing the Convent of Feraponte, which served as a hospital after the battle. Soon we reached Gorky—a village that belongs to the crown, crossed a little stream called the Kolochia (one of five that water the plain), and so came to Borodino, a quiet little place that gave its name to the battle. One evening at Narychkine's villa in Petrovsky Park I had told a fellow guest that I hoped to visit the site of Napoleon's victory, and he had at once written to a friend of his, Colonel Constantin Vargenevsky, who lived in a charming house a mile or two from the battlefield, telling him of my intention. A week later I received a cordial letter from the colonel, placing his home and his services at my disposal whenever I cared to come. He had not known when to expect us, or even whether we should come at all, but he welcomed us warmly, improvised a dinner and put us up for the night. In the morning we set out in the colonel's own carriage to explore the terrain, a groom following with two saddle horses so that if we chose we could leave the road and ride over the open country where, on that never-to-be-forgotten September day in 1812, great masses of French cavalry charged to annihilate the Russian forces in the gorge of the great redoubt. We spent all day discussing the ebb and flow of the battle, the tactics of both commanders, the fearful slaughter—for 75,000 men fell in that epic fight. Now all that remains to mark the site is the convent of *Borodino-du-Sauveur;* a memorial column raised by the Russians at the centre of the great redoubt; several long mounds like a range of low hills, tumuli raised over the piled dead; and an enclosure showing the position of Napoleon's tent. The convent was built by the widow of the Russian General Touchkof to enshrine the only relic of her husband's body she could discover on the battlefield—his hand, severed just above the wrist, which she recognised by a turquoise ring she had given him. We visited this convent and were received by the present Abbess herself, who in the world was Princess Ouroussof.

On leaving the convent, we crossed a potato field where the crop had been killed by frost the night before—August 9th—and I recalled that as we left Moscow on the 7th I had noticed the leaves were beginning to fall as they do in October, at home. At nine in the evening we began our journey back to Petrovsky Park, where we arrived late the next day to find Narychkine somewhat disturbed. He had just been informed that one of his villages had been burned to ashes, and the flames, driven by the wind, had crossed a river by a wooden bridge and partly consumed a second.

If you are interested to know what a Russian *boyar* of the old aristocracy is like, Narychkine is a typical example. His property includes estates and mansions all over Russia—in Moscow, Jelpatievo, Kasan and a dozen other places for all I know. He himself has no idea how many villages he owns, or how many serfs. To keep count of such matters is his steward's concern (in between lining his own pocket from his master's revenues to the tune of a hundred thousand francs a year). Narychkine's household is a veritable apotheosis of casual inconsequence, a total lack of good management. One day Jenny expressed a fancy for some pineapples, and Narychkine ordered some. Next day I happened to notice a *moujik* with a load of magnificent pineapples disappearing in the direction of the store-rooms, but apparently no-one else saw him, for a week or more passed without a sign of pineapple at table. One evening, Narychkine complained of the dessert and I reminded him of the fruit.

"That's true," he exclaimed. "I did order some."

"And they arrived," said I. "Perhaps they have been forgotten, or, more probably, someone else in the house took a fancy to them."

All the servants were summoned, from Koutaisof, the chef, down to Carmouchka, the coachman, but not one of them had seen any pineapples.

"Let us go and look for them ourselves, Jenny," I suggested, and after a long search we found them, neatly stacked in a corner of a little cellar used for storing game and butcher's meat. There were 40 of them, and they could not have cost less than a couple of hundred roubles.

Every week a gamekeeper on one of Narychkine's estates brought baskets filled with wild duck, woodcock, hares, and if Jenny had not distributed most of this game among her friends, three-quarters of it would have been wasted. One day the gamekeeper arrived with a very fine greyhound at heel and I asked Narychkine if he bred them.

"I rather think so," he replied. "I know I had a pair of champions sent over from London three or four years ago."

"Would you have one of their pups saved for me, when they have any?"

"There may be some already. Call Simeon." The gamekeeper duly presented himself. "How many greyhounds have I at Jelpatievo?"

"Twenty-two, Your Excellency."

"What?"

"Your Excellency gave no orders, so I kept all the pups, except for a few that died. As I have just had the honour to inform Your Excellency, there are now twenty-two, all in good health."

"You see," observed Narychkine, turning to me, "you won't be robbing me if you take one. Have two, if you like."

I have already mentioned his stud farm—his greatest interest in life—where he has a hundred pure-bred horses and never sells a single one. They are his famous trotters that win half the races in Russia. Every morning, in his cashmere dressing gown, he sits on the terrace of his villa watching each horse being led past the foot of the steps—a marvellous sight to see. He never uses these splendid animals to draw his carriage—but hires horses for that purpose at fantastic expense. The only exception is in Jenny's honour. Her *calèche* with its two trotters is well-known even in St. Petersburg, where highborn Russian ladies seethe with fury and despair because she—a mere actress—can travel twice as fast as they can.

It had been decided that, when we left Moscow, Narychkine and Jenny would take us to visit the Convent of Troitza and then on to Jelpatievo, where we would open the shooting season with two or three days sport before I continued my journey towards Astrakhan via Nijni-Novgorod, Kasan and Saratov. Narychkine had not seen this particular house of his more than twice in his life, and could not recall whether it was fully furnished or even whether there were any beds! (Like all true *boyars*, Narychkine is a connoisseur of luxury but can live like a Spartan when he chooses.) Didier Delange was therefore despatched post-haste to inspect the place, and came back four days later with a long list of the bare necessities to make it habitable—mattresses, blankets, bedlinen, cooking utensils to the tune of several hundred pounds. Everything was bought, loaded on to three great waggons and driven off in Didier's charge to refurbish the house for our visit. Yet we proposed staying there only three days at the most. How can any fortune, however vast, keep pace with living on that scale, especially when expenses are doubled by a steward or two?

Before leaving Moscow, Moynet and I made sure we had adequate supplies of winter clothing, for when the snows came we should be on the steppes of Kalmuck or among the mountains of the Caucasus, exposed to fifteen or twenty degrees of frost. We each had a warm suit made, and one of those sheepskin overcoats that rich *moujiks* wear, called *touloupes*. We added fur-lined boots and slippers, sheepskin hoods, the very sight of which sent us into fits of laughter, and a portable stove, complete with a samovar for making tea. The only remaining essential was an interpreter, and the rector of the university chose one of his best students to accompany us in that capacity, a young fellow with the pleasant-sounding name of Kalino.

On the morning of September 7th we set out for Troitza, Narychkine, Jenny and I in a carriage with Didier Delange—his master's shadow—on the box. Kalino and Moynet chose to travel in a *telega* and started off at five in the morning, as excited as schoolboys on holiday; we followed at a more reasonable hour, after a good breakfast. It is a magnificent road from Moscow to Troitza, bordered with trees and made doubly interesting by its view of the aqueduct of Mytishchi, built by Catherine to provide a water supply for the city. Every hundred yards or so we saw pilgrims plodding on foot towards the convent or returning to their homes.

The sun was setting as we had our first view of this immense shrine, the slanting rays striking fire from its spires and golden cupolas. It is as large as a town, and has given rise to a village outside its gates where I counted a thousand houses and six churches. Most Russian towns are built on flat land, but Troitza stands on a height overlooking a range of low hills. Inside its thick stone walls guarded by eight towers, lie nine churches, the palace of the Czar, the residence of the Archimandrite and the cells of the monks. It is the Middle Ages, still living on unchanged.

We could not enter it until the morning, so we sought the rooms reserved for us in the hostel attached to the convent. Warned by my account of the fare provided at Konnevitz and Valamo, Didier had brought from Moscow an excellent supper already cooked, relieving us of all anxiety except as to our rooms and beds. The rooms were dirty and the beds hard, but with good tea and good conversation one can easily stay awake till two in the morning, and by rising at six one has only four hours of martyrdom.

Next morning I was waiting to go in as soon as the convent gates opened, for I was hoping to find some verification of a legend I had heard of Peter the Great. Narychkine had scoffed at the tale I told him as we drank our tea the night before, laughing when I said I expected to find, to the left of the Great Door of Ouspensky Cathedral, a tomb covered by a stone slab six feet long, with a saw cut through it at the place where the neck of the corpse would be. Quickly I passed under the vaulted entrance and hurried down a tree-lined path to the Cathedral. It is surrounded by a railing enclosing the monks' burial ground. I took four or five steps to the left inside that railing and uttered a cry of joy. There was the stone, sawn through as the legend said, and though I am not very familiar with Russian letters I managed to make out the inscription: Abraham Lapuchine. I was so excited that I ran back to the hostel, woke up Narychkine and made him come to see it as a penance for doubting me. (It never ceases to amaze him that I know more Russian history than the Russians themselves!) Here is the legend.

After the ill-fated conspiracy of Euxoxia-Alexievna Lapuchine against her husband, Peter I, in favour of her son Alexis, the Czar sentenced the four military ringleaders to be beheaded, their heads to be displayed on poles at the four corners of the execution platform. When the day came, three of the conspirators died on the block, but the fourth pole, bearing the name Abraham Lapuchine, was empty. Lapuchine had fled, and all Peter's efforts to trace him failed. The fugitive had taken refuge in the convent of Troitza, where he became a monk and died three or four years later from natural causes. After he was buried, the Abbot himself sent to inform the Czar. Peter's first intention was to exhume the body and decapitate it, but, yielding to the Abbot's protest that such an act would be sacrilege, he had the stone "severed at the neck" instead. There it still lies, a mute testimony to the inflexible code— and the barbarity—of Peter the Great.

My prestige as a student of history thus restored, I went on to explore the inside of the cathedral. I particularly wished to see the altar where Peter himself, as a child, was hidden by his mother, Nathalia, from the *Strelitz* who had sworn to kill him. I found it without much difficulty—a double-headed eagle now marks the spot—and nearby I discovered the tomb of Boris Godounof, who usurped the throne of Russia at the end of the 16th century. Boris always had a special veneration for Troitza and loaded it with treasures in honour of Sergius, its patron saint, following in this respect the example of Ivan the Terrible, whose father, Vasili-Ivanovich, dedicated him to St. Sergius on the day he was born, placing him on the shrine of that saint in the Cathedral of the Trinity in Moscow. (Later, the Empress Anna enriched this shrine with columns and a canopy of solid silver weighing half a ton. Dissolute queens and bloodthirsty kings have always been the most lavish patrons of the saints.)

Sergius was born at Rostov in 1315, and when he became a hermit he begged Prince Andrew of Radonega to give him a few square feet of land on which to build a cell. The prince gave him a square mile, and in recognition of his munificence he was buried near the saint in the little Church of the Holy Trinity that Sergius built beside his cell. The present monastery surrounds this hallowed ground, and its name, Troitza, is derived from Trinity.

Unless you have seen the treasures stored here, you can have no conception of the riches a Russian convent may possess. There are 10 vast rooms crammed with gold and silver chalices and crosses of exquisite workmanship and priceless value; missals, offertories, altar cloths and ecclesiastical robes sewn with jewels. The eye is dazzled by the diamonds and precious stones of every kind covering each object with a shimmering veil of radiance. One of the greatest treasures shown to visitors is an onyx found in Siberia and presented to Archbishop Plato by Potemkin. It carries a natural marking of a cross with a figure kneeling in prayer at its foot. Finally, in striking contrast to all this worldly wealth, we were shown the simple, tattered robe and cowl worn by Saint Sergius, who certainly never dreamed that his successor, Archbishop Nikon, would parade in a tunic loaded with fifty pounds weight of fabulous jewels.

Once there were 300 monks at Troitza, but now there are barely one hundred. The monastery owns various properties outside its walls, and one of the most surprising is the Troitza Restaurant in Moscow, much frequented for its celebrated sterlet soup. There one can eat and drink—even get drunk—as in other cabarets, and the only indication of its monastic ownership is the rule that the doors of private rooms must not be shut. (If the same rule were observed at the hostelry attached to the monastery, I fancy there would be a marked falling off in the numbers of men and women pilgrims visiting Troitza. Many of them make the journey, not from religious motives, but for the novelty of enjoying human passions in an atmosphere of sanctity.)

I was copying an inscription from a particularly ugly obélisque erected in the courtyard by the Metropolitan Plato, when Kalino brought to me a young monk who could speak a little French, though no one in the monastery knew this. He earnestly begged me to keep his secret, otherwise his desire to meet me would involve him in painful consequences. He told me that, two months ago, the monks had been told of my arrival in St. Petersburg, and warned that I was to be treated with grave suspicion if I presented myself at Troitza. Why, I never managed to discover.

I wanted to visit the Convent of Bethany, where the father and mother of St. Sergius were born, a mile or two from Troitza. The road was far from good, so to avoid any risk of damage to his master's carriage, Didier Delange hired for me a vehicle called a *tarantass*, very popular in Russia though quite new to me. Imagine the boiler of a railway engine mounted on four wheels, with a little window at the front and a door in the side, reached by means of a little portable ladder. The *tarantass* has no springs and no seats, the floor being covered with straw that a fussy traveller can have renewed if he insists. When a family party makes a long journey by *tarantass*, two or three mattresses are placed on the floor instead of straw, which saves the expense of an inn and enables the travellers—15 or 20 on an average—to keep on the move by night as well as by day. When they set eyes on this abominable contraption, Moynet and Kalino declared they would rather walk. As for Narychkine, watching us from the balcony with his slanting, Slavonic eyes and his air of mockery, he wished us every pleasure on our journey. " 'Pon my soul," said I to Jenny as I helped her climb into the *tarantass*, "it would serve him right if we took him at his word."

The road was execrable, though the countryside was charming, and it took us three-quarters of an hour to reach Bethany where we found Moynet and Kalino, who had walked up in half the time. In the church we saw the coffin in which St. Sergius was buried—before his body was transported to the vermilion shrine in Moscow Cathedral where he now lies under his silver canopy; and the tomb of Archbishop Plato, whom modern Russians seem to regard as greater than his namesake of ancient Greece. We saw his house, a simple dwelling with a prayer carved on the lintel: "God bless all who enter here." Apart from an engraving, the gift of Louis XVI, and some curtains embroidered by Catherine II, the furnishings were severely plain, and the worthy cleric's straw hat was still hanging on a nail beside his bed.

Next morning, having seen all there was to see at Troitza, we set out for Jelpatievo. There were two possible routes, and it was decided that Narychkine, Jenny and I, in the carriage, would take the better road (if such tracks can be dignified by that name), while Moynet and Kalino would take the other in a *telega*—a vehicle that can get through anywhere. Their route led past a lake that was said to be full of herrings exactly like those in the sea, and I made Moynet promise to taste some and tell me whether this was so. (It was no use asking Kalino. As a native of Little Russia he had never tasted any salt-water fish, not even herrings.)

Our road brought to my notice something I had never seen

before, a kind of pontoon made of innumerable pine-logs lashed together side by side, lying over the surface of a quagmire. It was about 30 feet wide and more than half a mile long. As we drove over it, it swayed and quivered alarmingly under our wheels and the horses' hooves, but Narychkine assured me that such "roads" were quite common in this part of the country, and when I compared notes with Moynet, later, I found he had made a sketch of an exactly similar track that he and Kalino had crossed.

Didier Delange warned us that we should soon come to a much more difficult patch of road—he called it a "mountain of sand"— where we should sigh in vain for a track of pine logs like the one I had been thankless enough to criticize. The next time we stopped to change horses, eight were harnessed to the carriage instead of the usual four, and we skimmed over the ground with truly regal speed—for a while. After half an hour we saw that the road ahead lay through a yellow cutting over the crest of a little hill. "Is that your 'mountain of sand,' Didier?" I asked. "That molehill?"

"That's it."

"Goodness! I was expecting something at least as steep as Montmartre! Don't tell me you had eight horses put in just to pull us over a little pimple like that!"

"Indeed I did, sir. God grant we may not need another eight before we're through."

This was before I had seen the coach of an English ambassador being pulled by sixty-two oxen in Persia, and sixteen horses for four passengers seemed to me altogether too lavish. "Bah!" I replied with more than a hint of sarcasm, "let's hope twelve will be enough!"

"Get on, there," shouted Narychkine, and the postilion plied his whip. The horses redoubled their speed, but as they breasted the first slope their pace slackened from a gallop to a trot, then to a walk, and the carriage lurched to a standstill. "Well?" I asked.

"Well," replied Didier, "now we're in it."

I leaned out to look. The horses were in sand up to their bellies and the coach was engulfed beyond its axles. "The devil," said I. "We must lighten the load instantly," and I jumped down. A second later I gave a cry of alarm. "What is it?" Jenny called in terror.

Clutching the step, I shouted: "Quick! Give me a hand or I shall be swallowed in this quicksand like another Edgar of Ravenswood." Narychkine stretched out an arm to me, Jenny offered both hers, and with their help I managed to climb onto the step where I clung, breathless.

"What's your opinion of my mountain of sand now?" asked Didier.

"It must be hollow, and deeper than it is high," I returned. "But the point now is to lighten the sinking ship and get all passengers safe to land."

"How?" Jenny's voice was anxious.

"Don't worry," I reassured her. "You shall hop to terra firma like a bird. Jump up and pass me your cushions. You, too, Narychkine, you lazy lout. Good! Now the padded seats. Didier, pass down the ones from your box." Narychkine stared at me, utterly bewildered. I placed the first cushion squarely beside the step, threw another a few feet away and a third further on.

"Ah! Now I see," Jenny exclaimed in delight and relief. "It's no wonder you can write novels! Such imagination!"

Carrying the rest of the cushions in my arms I jumped to the furthest, threw the others ahead, one at a time, until they reached firm ground. Then I returned to the carriage. "Ladies first. Come along, Jenny!" I called, and watched her as she jumped from each cushion to the next, as lightly as a wagtail hopping from stone to stone. "Now the aged. It's your turn, Narychkine."

"Old man, indeed," he grumbled. "I'm two years younger than you!"

"And you don't think that's old? What about it, Jenny?"

She laughed gently, and stretched out her arms to welcome Narychkine as he reached the edge of the sand. Then came Didier, who managed to gather up the cushions as he crossed.

"Now what are we to do?" asked Narychkine. "Didier, you're a fool! Why didn't you take the other road?"

"Stop grumbling, *boyard,* and sit down. Here are three cushions for you, two for Jenny and one for me. See what deference we pay to your rank!"

"That won't help us to get home for dinner."

"Never mind. We'll call it supper. Didier, my friend, you said we could get eight more horses, didn't you?"

"I think four might be enough."

"Ride back and get them. Bring two men as well, and a long plank."

"I'll do as you say, sir, but I don't understand," and Didier, with the postilion's help, busied himself manoeuvring one of the leading horses back across the sand.

"What do you want a plank for?" asked Narychkine.

"You'll see! Leave it all to me. I'm in charge of the rescue work!"

As soon as the horse's legs had stopped trembling, Didier jumped on its back and galloped off. "Bring back some good strong ropes, too," I called after him. "The longest you can get."

By and by we saw him coming back with his four horses, his ropes, two men and a plank. I rose to meet him. "Lay that plank over the sand from the firm ground to the carriage step," I ordered. "Then space your men along it to form a chain, so that our luggage can be passed back to us here."

"Ah!" said Didier as he passed on my instructions. "Now I begin to understand." Soon all our trunks and bags stood safely beside us, and the carriage was a quarter of a ton lighter. "Now unhitch the horses."

"What? All of them?" asked Narychkine. "Do you think you can pull the coach out yourself?"

"Maybe," I returned, and he gave a shrug of perplexity. I turned to Didier. "Do you think you can get them out, now that they have nothing behind them?" Freed from their load and encouraged by a touch of the whip, they soon extricated themselves and joined us on the hard ground. "Good!" said I. "Now, Didier, pay attention. With the long ropes, hitch your four fresh horses to the coach, and harness the eight tired ones on in front. Then, a good strong pull, all together, should do the trick."

"Your Excellency," said Didier to Narychkine as he ran to do my bidding, "I really believe this idea will work." It did! Those horses could have moved an 80-pounder cannon, and at their first attempt they pulled the carriage clear.

"And a very pretty little trick, too," said Narychkine. "So simple."

"Yes," I agreed, "like the egg of Christopher Columbus!" Turning to Didier, I went on: "Now get your men to carry all this luggage round to the far side of the hill, skirting the quicksand. Hitch your twelve horses, two abreast, to the empty carriage and climb back on your box. The strip of sand is not so wide that you can't get across it, and you will always have at least four horses on hard ground to help the others through."

"What about us?" Narychkine said, petulantly. "Are we to walk?"

"A couple of hundred yards won't overtire you, will it?"

"I suppose I could manage it. But it seems to me when one owns a carriage, one should not have to walk."

"You're wrong, there, my friend! Never have I done as much walking as when I've had carriages." My plan worked well. The coach skimmed over the bad spot as if on castors, and by the time we had walked round to it the luggage was all loaded up ready for us to take our seats. "Now, Narychkine," I suggested, "give these good fellows a couple of roubles apiece."

"Not a sou! They should keep their roads in better condition."

"Nonsense! The quicksand is no fault of theirs. If you won't hand over four roubles, I'll give them eight myself. Then they'll take me for a great lord, though I'm sure they'll never take you for a poet!"

"Delange," roared Narychkine, "give them twelve roubles and tell them to go to the devil!"

"Delange," I amended the instruction, "give them twelve roubles and tell them your master sends his thanks and good wishes."

"They'll take me for a prince! On second thoughts, they won't. A prince would have given them a good thrashing, and nothing else."

"That's the first sensible thing you have said all day! Give him a kiss to thank him, Jenny!"

"A fine thing! So I have to pay him for being such a cross-patch!"

146

"Pay him twice over! The more a woman pays with that sort of coin, the more she has left!" I doubt if there is in the whole world a man more haughty and morose on the surface, nobler and more generous at heart, more a true aristocrat, than Narychkine. A *boyar* of the old school—all the better for having a French mistress to keep him in order.

We continued our journey through country that seemed to me unusually lovely in the moonlight. I remember we crossed a bridge over a river, climbed a steep mountainside and passed through an entrance gate into a park, where we bowled smoothly along for a quarter of an hour before arriving at the castle at nine o'clock. We had been expected at six, and all that time Koutaisof, Carmouchka and Simeon had been standing waiting, with a dozen *moujiks* from the estate who had come to pay their respects and enquire after their master's health. Their master was well, but starving and in no mood to receive the homage of his humble vassals with even a show of patience. He brushed past them and stalked indoors, but Jenny paused long enough to say a word or two to each, and I have no doubt they all went away happy, satisfied that their long wait was appreciated and well worth while.

II

TRAVELLING DOWN THE VOLGA: NIJNI-NOVGOROD AND KAZAN

Delange had excelled himself, and in this remote province, in a castle uninhabited for 20 years, he had contrived to surround us not only with comfort but with absolute luxury. All the furnishings of my room in Petrovsky Park had been brought here for me and all my personal belongings, down to my tooth-brush, silver spoon and the little drinking glass I have carried everywhere on my travels. (At this very moment, on the evening of July 16th, 1860, as I sit writing these memoirs on the terrace of the Palace of Chiatamonte,

I am sipping iced *sanbuco* from the self-same glass that was so often filled with Russian *hydromel* in Moscow and Jelpatievo.)

Jenny and I were up at dawn, strolling in the park surrounded by the 22 greyhounds whose very existence had been unknown to their owner. After breakfast, a hunting brake was waiting to take Narychkine and myself for a day's sport with the guns, a most convenient vehicle that I have not seen elsewhere. It is long and narrow, so low that it cannot possibly overturn, no matter how rough the ground. The passengers sit back to back on a seat that runs the whole length and may take any number from four to eight or more, though on this occasion there were only two of us. A hundred beaters did their best to put up game for our guns, but sport was very poor. I have mentioned earlier that birds are scarce in Russia, and those we did see, mostly wild duck, were so unused to human beings that they showed no fear and could hardly be induced to rise. True, there were hares, but they already had their winter coats and looked so like white persian cats that I could hardly bring myself to shoot. Indeed, I missed the first three or four I aimed at, to Narychkine's great amusement, and after four or five hours we had bagged only a score. (Though on this occasion we did not see any, Russia is infested with one kind of game—wolves. A few years ago, during an unusually hard winter, packs of starving wolves attacked so many villages in this area that the government offered a reward of five roubles for every tail handed in. After a while, having paid out two and a half million roubles and thereby acquiring half a million tails, the authorities grew suspicious, and found that a factory in Moscow had netted a fortune by buying wolf-skins for next to nothing and using them to make counterfeit tails.)

I was amazed to see that practically none of Narychkine's estate at Jelpatievo was under cultivation, yet the land was good, and when a crop was sown the yield was excellent. It was the same, he told me, on his other estates, which were largely given over to bracken. The few acres that had been cleared grew merely hay worth a couple of kopeks for a dozen trusses. The difficulty is labour, for no other part of the world, except actual deserts, is so thinly populated. It seemed wrong to me that all this land should be so neglected, and I suggested to Narychkine that he could at least use it as pasturage. The idea was coldly received. "Would you have me become known as 'Narychkine, the pig-breeder'?" he asked scornfully.

Time was flying, as it always does, and it was already a month since I arrived in Moscow, where I had planned to spend a fortnight. The Fair at Nijni-Novgorod had already opened and would close on September 25th, so if I meant to see it and carry out my plans for the rest of my journey, I could not delay any longer. It was imperative for us to catch the boat plying between Tver and Nijni when it called at Kaliasin on Sunday morning, which meant leaving Jelpatievo on the evening of Saturday, September 13th. Although the weather was still fine and clear it was getting much colder, and if the Volga froze I should have to stay here until the spring.

Two days before we were due to leave, Didier Delange disappeared. He returned a couple of hours before our departure, carrying a magnificent fur cloak that he delivered to Narychkine. I found it spread out in my *drojky*, a parting gift from my host. When I thanked him and protested at such lavish generosity he retorted: "Did you really imagine I should let you go to the Caucasus wearing a *moujik's touloupe*? If anyone who saw you in that garb knew that you had been my guest, I should be quite disgraced!" What could I do but accept?

It was hard to leave these dear friends of mine, not knowing when, if ever, we should meet again. Indeed, if Carmouchka, the coachman, had not taken things into his own hands and whipped up his horses, we might never have got away. It was two in the morning when we set out, and I have never seen a more beautiful night, clear and starlit, though the horizon glowed red with yet another huge forest fire. Two hours later we stopped to give the horses a breather at a little village called Troiski-Nerli, a 'free village', the landlord of the inn announced proudly. How had it gained its freedom? By purchase from the government? From its former overlord? He did not know. All he could say for certain was that it was now free. Beyond question it was cleaner and looked more prosperous than any other village I had seen in Russia. The inn itself was very pleasant, its kitchen gay with porcelain. When I say 'kitchen', I should add that it was also the communal dining room, drawing room and bedroom. It could even become a ball-room if necessary, for it boasted a gigantic Barbary organ that the host pointed out to us with pride. While we enjoyed a glass of his vodka, he entertained us with its repertoire of Russian melodies. Then, realising our nationality, he quickly changed the cylinder and played us a whole series of French tunes. He even refused to let me pay for the vodka, exclaiming that we were his guests, so I put my rouble back in my pocket and thanked him with a warm handshake. Another thing pleased me about this good fellow's house—it was pleasantly warm but not too hot, and the air was fresh. Often, since I came to Russia, I have been invited to visit the *isbas* of villagers but have been driven back at the very door by the heat and the stench.

We reached Kaliasin at seven, with five hours to fill in before the boat was due at noon. Very obviously, Kaliasin was not a 'free' town, and never have I seen a more sordid hovel than the so-called inn where we had to stable our horses. We tried to make ourselves comfortable in a sort of loft from which we had to dislodge a dozen crows, but after a minute or two our legs itched so unbearably that we hastily sought refuge somewhere else. At the entrance to a very muddy yard I paused to watch a dozen young Russian girls preparing something that looked to me like sauerkraut, and singing one of those sad, haunting melodies that express the essential melancholy of the Russian character.

I was eager for my first glimpse of the Volga, the greatest river in Europe, that rises in Tver and flows more than two thousand miles before pouring itself into the Caspian Sea, the very Queen of Rivers. A kind of hollow led us towards it, a channel made by the torrential rains rushing down to join it in certain seasons of the year. From a distance we could see its banks, but the river itself was out of sight until we reached the edge and looked over. What a disappointment! We have a dozen wider rivers in France, wider, that is, than the Volga was then. In the spring, when the snow melts, the river may rise twenty or even forty feet, sometimes overflowing the banks that now towered above it, but in the autumn, the Volga is, to use a mathematical phrase, reduced to its lowest terms.

At Jelpatievo we had met the army surgeon attached to the regiment stationed at Kaliasin and had promised to call on him as we passed through the town. He invited us to a meal at his house, and we accepted all the more readily because Narychkine's cook and butler had loaded our carriage with food and wines that we were delighted to share. The spread was so bounteous that our surgeon suggested asking some of his friends to join us, and we gladly agreed. Every officer in the regiment, from the lieutenant-colonel down to the youngest lieutenant, was soon laughing and talking with us in the surgeon's vast drawing room. Shortly after, the regimental band struck up under the windows. We had reached the coffee stage when Didier warned us that the boat was arriving. Hastily draining our glasses we all hurried down to the quay, arm in arm like friends of twenty years standing, followed by the band in full blast, while the whole population of Kaliasin, who had never in their lives seen such festivities, brought up the rear.

Once on board, I was glad to spend an hour or two in quiet relaxation, translating into French verse (with the help of my Russian friends) some of the poems of Lermontov. I consider him somewhat akin, in spirit and quality, to our own Alfred de Musset. His work is particularly popular with the ladies, and his songs set to music, are sung in every salon in Russia. This distraction was all the more enjoyable to me because the journey itself was uninteresting, with nothing to see but the edge of the flat, bare banks until we reached Uglich. This little town, a veritable forest of spires, stands on the right bank of the Volga at a point where the terrain forms a small plateau, and its chief interest, for me, lies in the legends that surround it.

Demetrius, son of Ivan the Terrible, lived here with his mother until he was murdered in the palace garden on 15th May, 1591, at the age of ten. (Or, if you prefer the alternative version, the son of a serf was murdered in his stead and Demetrius escaped to claim the throne of Russia some years later.) Vengeance fell on everyone in the palace that day, guilty or innocent. The very bell in the Cathedral tower that rang to sound the alarm was charged with complicity and banished to Siberia; one of its ears was torn off, it was thrashed with knouts and formally deprived of its civil rights, forbidden, that is, ever to let its voice be heard again.

In 1847, the inhabitants of Uglich petitioned the reigning Czar to pardon their bell and allow it to return to its native city after its 256 long years of banishment. Their request was granted, word was sent to the governor of Siberia in Irkoutsh, where the bell lay, and great festivities were arranged to start it on its homeward way. But the worthy men of Uglich had overlooked one thing—the cost of transporting their bell over eight hundred leagues of open country, a matter of ten or twelve thousand roubles. This was beyond their power to pay, so the bell has remained in exile ever since, but now, with its civil rights restored, its voice is heard whenever a prisoner in Siberia is pardoned.

Towards noon next day we paused for a quarter of an hour at Mologa, the most northerly point of the Volga, went on to Romanof—famous for the superlative quality of the *touloupes* made there from the skins of a special breed of sheep introduced by Peter the Great—and spent the night anchored off Somino. (These Volga boats do not travel by night at this season of the year, for the river bed is shifting sand and the water is very shallow, so that there is real risk of running aground.)

Nothing could be duller or more depressing than the stretches of the Volga we had seen so far, shut in between high, flat brown banks with never a country house to break the monotony, never an island, not even another boat. However, I had other, more pleasant things to look at, for Moynet took the opportunity of showing me some of the very fine sketches he had made during our journey, including those he had done on his trip to Kletchino—the herring lake—and the little town of Pereslavi-Zaleskoi on its banks. Anyone wishing to gain an accurate impression of the wealth and power of the Church in Russia should visit this little place. Its population is small—only two thousand, but it contains twenty-five churches of which one—the Church of the Transfiguration—is remarkable for its style of architecture and the shrine where the body of Saint Nicholas Stylite lies buried in the chains he wore during his lifetime.

We halted at Yaroslavl, notable for its lyceum, (there are only six others in the whole of Russia), and its Hotel Pastoukov, said to be the best outside the capital and the only one in the provinces with real beds. Two ladies came aboard here, and the captain brought them to the saloon where I was working to introduce me, Princess Anna Dolgorouky and her companion. The princess, a relative of the Princess Dolgorouky I had met on my way to Russia, is about thirty years of age, extremely intelligent and well-informed. Like many other Russian ladies of high degree she speaks French fluently and also reads a good deal of what is currently published in Paris. It surprised me, at first, that men of similar rank are far less conversant with our language and literature. Probably their wives and daughters, not being in the least concerned with politics, have more time to devote to culture.

On the other hand, their natural curiosity may stimulate the ladies to take a wider interest in other countries as well as in their own. Or it may be that, in Russia, education for men is directed into other channels. Kalino, for example, who does speak French and was chosen as the most promising student at Moscow where, presumably, he has received a typical university education, knows absolutely nothing of the history of his own land. The princess has the whole pageant of Muscovite history and legend at her finger tips, and when she advised us to go ashore at our next stopping place, Kostroma, to see the Convent of Saint Ipatiyev, Romanov's house and the Susanin Monument, we gladly acted on her sugges-tion, jumping into a dinghy the moment our boat slowed down and making for the shore with all speed. (One good thing in Russia is that passengers do not have to show their passports or health certi-ficates before they are allowed to land. No one asks who you are or what you want.)

In a *drojky* we were driven up the steep gradient from the river bank to see something of the town itself, one of the oldest in Russia, and its cathedral in the heart of its citadel, the Kreml. I found the convent interesting but not unlike others I have already spoken of—one cannot describe them all! The house of Romanov appealed to me more strongly because of its historical associations. In 1612, at a moment when Russia's state seemed hopeless, three men arose to save her: Minin, who spoke for the people: Pozharsky, for the nobility; (we have already seen the monument to these patriots in Moscow); and Archbishop Romanov, for the Church. He was twice taken prisoner by invading Polish armies, thrown into dungeons, loaded with chains, tortured, but nothing could shake his steadfast faith in his religion and his country's cause. He so typified the spirit of Russia that he became the focal point round which his countrymen rallied, and it was from his family that Russia chose her next sovereign.

The monument to Susanin expresses Russia's gratitude to a man of the people, a humble peasant. In 1669, during the Polish invasion, Ivan Susanin was forced to act as guide to a detachment of some 3,000 enemy troops seeking a cross-country route to Moscow. Instead, he led them deep into the immense trackless forests until even he no longer knew any way out. The soldiers battered him to death and so lost their last hope of escape, for not one of them ever left the forest alive. By order of the grateful Czar, Michael Romanov, since that day no taxes have been collected or men conscripted from Karabanovo, the village where Susanin was born. (Rumour says that as a result of this indulgence Karabanovo is now the most dissolute village in Russia.) The monument is a column of pink granite from Finland, surmounted by the figure of Michael Romanov, and the bas-reliefs around the pedestal portray the whole story of Susanin's devotion.

We made our way back towards the quay with considerable misgiving, for we had over-stayed the agreed hour by at least another three-quarters, but as we came in sight of the shore we heaved a sigh of relief. The boat was still waiting for us, with Princess Anna on deck, chatting with the captain and calming his impatience as they both watched for our return. The instant we set foot on deck he cast off and shot away at a rate of knots, trying to catch up his lost three-quarters of an hour. How charming such shipboard friendships can be! So kindly, so brief that not the slightest cloud can intervene, and they live on in the memory like a patch of clear blue sky, as does my memory of Princess Anna.

Twenty or twenty-five passengers had joined the boat at Kostroma, thirty more came aboard at Kineshma, and at Balakhna, where we anchored for the night, so many crowded on that our boat settled a foot deeper in the water. The captain was really worried, for even earlier our keel had occasionally scraped the bottom, but fortunately no mishap occurred. Towards ten o'clock we began to grow aware of a great noise like distant thunder or the rumbling that precedes an earthquake—the roar of two hundred thousand human voices at Nijni-Novgorod. Then we rounded a bend and the river itself seemed to vanish under a forest of masts flying flags of every size and colour. These were the cargo boats that had brought all the merchandise to the fair, and only with the greatest difficulty did we succeed in worming our way between them to tie up at the Siberian Quay. The scene on shore was like a great overturned ant-hill, and on the landing stage at least a thousand *drojkys* and *telegas* were drawn up in line waiting to be hired. We took a *drojky* and moved off through the surging crowds at a walking pace, passing the Hippodrome, where, I noticed, two celebrated Moscow artists, Samarin and Givotchine, were on the bill, eventually finding ourselves in a long queue waiting to cross the bridge of boats, which is erected and taken to pieces every year. The bridge is 1500 yards long and it took us a quarter of an hour to reach the far end, where we found ourselves at the quay called Nijni-Bazaar, on the edge of a low, sandy island formed where the Oka joins the Volga. Still forced onward by the crowd, we passed between rows of little shops, built on piles and crammed with all sorts of articles in common use— boots, gloves, *touloupes,* caps, every conceivable kind of headgear.

Pressing on, we at last reached *terra firma* at the foot of a steep slope called St. George's Hill, a magnificent causeway more than half a mile long, a gift made to the town by the Czar Nicholas. I had been in touch, by correspondence, with a M. Grass of Nijni-Novgorod and also with M. Nicholas Brilkine, editor of the local paper, *The Mercury*. I decided my first call should be at the office of *The Mercury*, and without the slightest exaggeration we had to push our way through at least 300 people waiting there, before we at last stood face to face with M. Brilkine. I had no need to tell him my name, or even to open my mouth. He knew me at once, and wasted no time in preliminaries.

"You're rather later than we expected," said he, " but never mind.

There will still be plenty to show you. First I'll take you to Grass. You're staying with him, I think? Anyway, I know he has rooms ready for you. Then you had better call on the Governor and leave a card. He knows you are coming and will expect to see you. As a matter of fact, he's planning a little surprise for you."

"For me?" I exclaimed. "Whatever can it be?"

"Ah ha! That I cannot tell you, but you certainly will be surprised."

"What is your Governor's name?"

"Alexander Mouravief."

"The only Alexander Mouravief I know of was banished to Siberia."

"That's the man. You know, I expect, that the Emperor proclaimed a general amnesty? Since he was sent to Siberia on rather flimsy evidence, he was offered the governorship of Nijni-Novgorod as compensation."

"But wasn't he involved in the conspiracy of 1825?"

"Yes. You wrote a novel on the subject. You'll be able to talk to him about it."

M. Brilkine called his subordinates, gave orders to ensure that all would go well in his absence, put on his hat and took me off to meet his friend, M. Grass. We left his office by a back door, and I exclaimed delightedly at the spectacle that lay before me. Far below lay the junction of the Oka and the Volga, and the whole area covered by the fair, five square miles of it, was spread out before my eyes, crowded with shops and booths, with people of every nation thronging the narrow spaces between them. Seen thus, from the terrace of *The Mercury* in the high town, the fair was clearly divided into four separate zones. The first is on the island between the two mouths of the Oka; the second lies between Lake Bagrontosovo and the nearer of the two canals of Lake Motscherskoe; the third between those canals, and the fourth between the further canal and the forest. This last area is occupied by women—prostitutes, in point of fact, seven or eight thousand of them, come from every part of European and Asiatic Russia for the six weeks of the Fair. Unless one has seen this vast hive of commerce and entertainment from above, as I did, one can have no conception of the size of it, or of the teeming multitudes it holds.

"Come along!" exclaimed M. Briltine, taking me by the arm. "You'll have a week to look at all that, while I . . . "

"You're a very busy man, and I'm keeping you from your work. Let us go and find M. Grass."

M. Grass was expecting us and had prepared rooms for us in his own house. He had more time to spare than M. Brilkine and readily offered to show us the town and the Fair, while the editor of *The Mercury* hurried back to his office after reminding me to be sure to call on the Governor as soon as possible. After settling into our rooms—three days on the steamer had left us in need of a wash and change—we set out with our guide to explore the town. First we went back down the hill towards the river, and halfway down M. Grass paused in front of the Strogonof Church to tell us an interesting detail. It was really two separate churches, one for use in winter, a long, low building heated by four huge stoves, and a summer church, three times as high as the other and surmounted by an immense cupola decorated by an ikon as tall as itself.

Then we went on down to the Fair. Dominating its entrance is the church of Saint Macaire, (Macaire is the patron saint of this great annual enterprise), with an Armenian church on the right and a Mohammedan mosque on the left, all looking out over the central section constructed on piles over the busy canal, consisting of 2,500 shops built of stone and roofed with sheet metal. Immediately in front of Saint-Macaire are two diagonal rows of booths reserved for Chinese merchants and covered with fantastic ornaments that no other nation can produce—embroideries, hangings, banners covered with serpents, dragons, brilliant birds of scarlet, blue, orange. The roofs of these shops are built out with fretted strips of wood shaped to look like pagodas and painted with dazzling colours that yet never seem to clash. Tea, too, is sold here, 32,000 cases already since the Fair was opened, we were told.

Millions of pounds worth of merchandise changes hands—precious stones as plentiful as nuts, carpets and rugs, caviare, silks, leather work, damascened swords and firearms of every conceivable variety. Even France has her stalls here—a few dress shops, jewellers, drapers offering cloth from Sedan and Elbeuf, but I must confess they can hardly have given Asiatic visitors a good impression of our taste or quality. The vendors are as fascinating as the goods they offer—Hindus displaying fine shawls, yellow-skinned men from Turkey unrolling silks and gauze, craftsmen with sensitive fingers proffering saddles, bridles, belts set with turquoises, and all deals are completed solely by word of mouth,—no written contracts, no bits of stamped paper. It is impossible to describe the magnificence, the squalor, the noise. It was like a story from the Thousand and One Nights, and we had all the difficulty in the world to convince ourselves it was real. The hubbub was absolutely deafening and we were completely bewildered by the milling crowds, the hawkers pestering us to buy their wares, which were mostly rubbish.

Toward five in the afternoon. M. Grass suggested we should make our way back towards his home, where dinner would be ready at six. We had only half a mile to go, but it took us more than an hour to get there. As we passed the Governor's residence I left my card, or, rather, since I had exhausted my supply of that sort of projectile, I wrote my name on a piece of paper and entrusted it to a servant who solemnly promised to convey it to his master. He must have done so without delay, for before we had finished dinner an official despatch arrived inviting us to take tea at the palace that evening and to dine there next day. M. Grass was able to tell us that the approved hour for drinking tea was from ten to eleven in the evening, so we hastily unpacked our trunks and donned the starched shirts, black trousers, tail coats and patent leather shoes that had last seen the light of day at St. Petersburg.

As we walked to the Governor's Palace in the falling dusk, we had the pleasure of seeing the whole Fair being lighted up with torches, flares, every variety of illumination, and the prettiest sight of all was to see the little boats darting hither and thither on the canals, weaving a magic, ever-changing pattern, like dancing fireflies.

At precisely ten o'clock we presented ourselves at the palace and were received by the Governor, Alexander Mouravief, and his niece, Mademoiselle de Gallinsky, who introduced us to their guests, the Princesses Scherkaskoi and a few close friends, among them M. Karamsino, son of the historian. Scarcely had I joined the circle when, as I sat wondering what the promised surprise would be, the door opened and the footman announced: "The Count and Countess Annenkof."

The name struck a cord in my memory, and I found myself trembling. As I rose, the Governor took me by the hand and led me towards the newcomers. "May I," he said, "present the hero and heroine of your novel *Le Maître d'Armes?*"[1] I uttered a cry of amazement and they both threw their arms around me. They were, indeed, the same Alexis and Pauline whose adventures I had heard from Grisier and used as the plot of my novel. (The book, incidentally, was banned in Russia, and read there all the more eagerly for that, even in the palace itself. Madame Troubetskoi told me that she and the Empress were enjoying it in a private boudoir of the royal apartments when the Czar came in unexpectedly. Hastily they thrust it out of sight under some cushions, but Nicholas noticed their action and observed: "I'll wager you were reading *Le Maître d'Armes*, the book I have just banned!" It became so well known in Russia that, at the Fair, I found haberdashers selling handkerchiefs printed with a scene from the story, showing Pauline's *telega* attacked by a pack of wolves.)

Needless to say, my heroine, her husband and I talked the whole evening, and I heard the sequel to the adventures I had described. It was in 1825 that Alexis was banished to Siberia and Pauline chose to share his exile. They came to like the life and the company, for the majority of their fellow exiles were thinking men, the flower of Russia's culture and intelligence, two hundred years in advance of the rest of the country. The Count and Countess Annenkof stayed there for 27 years and fully expected to spend the rest of their lives in exile, but when they were sent an official pardon in 1853 they felt it was their duty to return to Russia.

We spent three days at Nijni. We had hoped to remain longer, but we could not have absorbed all the excitements of the Fair if we had stayed the whole time it was open, and we still had much to see elsewhere in Russia. As it happened, M. Grass had business to

_____

(1) Published in 1840.—Ed.

see to in Kasan, so we all travelled there together aboard a small steamer called the *Lotsman*. It took all the pilot's skill to win clear of the thousands of boats covering the whole breadth of the Volga, below as well as above Nijni-Novgorod, but at last we had the open river ahead of us and could make good progress. Towards evening we dropped anchor off Liscovo, a village that once belonged to a Georgian prince, Knias Grousinsky, dethroned by the Russians at the end of the last century. Here he spent the remaining years of his life, and acquired a reputation for eccentricity that is still the talk of the countryside for twenty miles around. I have made a collection of tales of his escapades, his fantastic whims, his erratic moods, now being published under the title of *Jacquot Sans Oreilles*.[1] It is not for me to discuss the merit or otherwise of that little work, but it does at least give an accurate picture of the customs of Old Russia.

Next day at dawn we went on down the river, and I was interested to notice that we were now among people of a type I had not seen before, gypsies, apparently, speaking a language of their own, quite unlike Russian. There is a little colony of them between Nijni and Kasam, and they toil at hauling loaded barges up and down this stretch of the Volga. The heavier the boat, the more men are harnessed to it, and I counted 40 of these *tchouvachs* pulling a craft upstream, past our own. They wear a simple tunic of coarse grey sailcloth, sometimes trimmed with red, and knee-length trousers below which their legs and feet are bare. I was told they originally came from Finland to settle here, an inoffensive tribe that does not mix with other inhabitants of the region, and the only work they will do is towing barges twelve hours a day for a wage of a few pence.

Towards noon we passed, but could not see, the town of Makharief where the Fair used to be held before it was transferred to Nijni-Novgorod. When Napoleon was marching on Moscow, all the Frenchmen in that town were rounded up and interned here at Makharief, and one of them, M. Armand Domergues, a former stage-manager of the Theatre-Français, wrote an account of the harsh treatment they suffered. (It was published in Paris in 1835.)

(1) In 1860.—Ed.

At about six, through the gathering dusk, we had our first sight of the minarets and spires of Kazan, that old Tatar stronghold built on a hill some three miles from the Volga, and it was already dark when we went ashore, landing on a slippery embankment with deep clefts here and there. Fortunately we had no need to get to the town itself that night, for M. Grass owned a kind of large shop or warehouse a few hundred yards from the Volga bank, where there were plenty of planks for us to sleep on. (We said goodbye to beds at Jelpatievo, and shall be lucky if we see another before we reach Tiflis.)

Sleeping on a plank has one advantage—it encourages early rising, and the light of dawn was still in the sky when Moynet and I went out to explore Kazan. I already knew that, in spite of its links with the East and its period under Moslem domination, it is now entirely Russian, a town with 980 streets, 10 bridges, 4,300 houses, 68 churches, 4 convents, 10 mosques, 2 hotels for travellers and a population of 50,280 inhabitants—Mohammedans, Christians, orthodox Russians, *raskolniks* and protestants. In its population, its customs, the dress of those who throng its streets, Kazan is the point where Europe merges into Asia.

From the alluvial plain where we stood, a great sea-wall, some 25 yards wide and high enough to overtop the Volga's periodic floods, ran straight as an arrow to the town, three miles away. Following this thoroughfare, we entered Kazan across a bridge that spans an immense ravine with the Arab name of *Boulak*. The suburb on the far side of this ravine is inhabited mainly by Tatars, although many Christian Russians live there too, and it pleased me to see the Mohammedan mosque surmounted by its crescent, and a Christian Church with its cross, standing side by side like friendly neighbours. I doubt whether such an example of religious amity exists outside Kazan!

There is a touch of broadminded tolerance, too, in a local custom I thought rather quaint. The Mohammedan religion, as everyone knows, forbids wine or any strong drink as a beverage. However, medicinal doses are permitted as a remedy in cases of illness. In Kazan, the sign over a wine-seller's shop is '*Balzam*'—'Pharmacist' —and any Tatar who happens to be suffering the tortures of thirst

F

can go in, drink his medicine—a bottle of wine—and come out cured. Mahomet will not frown, for he was a sick man, not a drunkard.

The most striking feature we noticed on entering the town was a monument raised to the Russian soldiers who died when Ivan the Terrible captured the town from the Tatars, a massive, sombre structure in keeping with its purpose. On each of its four façades, a flight of steps leads up to the interior chapel, in the midst of which stands an immense tomb where the skulls of the fallen lie buried. (Their other bones are piled in an immense catacomb below the chapel, and the sacristan who showed us round mentioned that, in his opinion, the bones of a good many Tatars had been included by mistake.)

Having visited this gloomy memorial, we went on towards the Kreml, or citadel. I knew no-one in Kazan, but I had with me a letter of introduction to the officer in charge of the quarter-master's stores, a M. Jablonovsky, authorising me to purchase a tent for my use when crossing the steppes. On our way to the Kreml I took the opportunity of calling on M. Jablonovsky, and found him a charming man who at once offered to show us the town.

We began, naturally, with the Kreml. Tradition says that its highest tower, shaped like a pyramid, was built by Ivan with the debris of the mosques he destroyed when he captured the town. Another tower, somewhat lower, is venerated by the Tatars as the burial-place of their saint and queen, Suyumbeka. The cathedral, inside the walls of the Kreml, contains the miracle-working image famous throughout Russia as "Our Lady of Kazan."[1] (All Russian churches are built to the same pattern and have five cupolas, a small one at each corner and a big one in the middle. Some are larger than others, or more brightly gilded, but that is the only difference.)

On leaving the Kreml we went to look at the shops. Kazan is justly famous for beautiful leatherwork—I brought back some wonderful examples of craftsmanship—and for every variety of fur, from bearskins to marten, squirrel and silver fox. It takes a clever marksman to hunt the smaller animals, for he must shoot them

---

(1) Sometimes called "The Black Virgin of Kazan."—Ed.

through the eye with a bullet as small as a pea, to avoid damaging the skin. Larger creatures, bears, for example, can be trapped or killed in whatever way the hunter prefers. One shopkeeper told us that the keenest bear-hunter he knew was a woman, who had brought him 53 fine skins in the last five years. The same man added, (I repeat his statement without vouching for its accuracy), that a popular method of trapping bears was to place, near a den, a globe-shaped copper jar with a fairly narrow neck, baited with some tasty morsel such as honey. The bear forces his pointed muzzle in to lick the honey, cannot withdraw his head from the jar, and so is easily captured.

While strolling past the shops we met the Rector of Kazan University, (founded by Alexander in 1804), who insisted on taking us to look over this seat of learning. It contains, (like most other universities), a library of 27,000 books that nobody reads, 124 students doing as little work as possible, and a Natural History Museum visited only by foreigners, though one of the countless exhibits displayed there is unique in the whole world—the foetus of a monster with a human head and the body of a goat. In the Medical Museum, set up in a central position, are the skeletons of two men who died under the knout, showing the resulting contortion of their bones. The tall one was Spaikin, an escaped galley-slave, the short one a sturdy peasant named Bekof, and these partners in crime kept Kazan in constant terror for ten years till they murdered a saintly and well-loved monk in the chapel of the famous monastery.

In Russia, capital punishment, as such, does not exist. Instead, a convicted criminal is sentenced to receive 'corrective treatment', five hundred, a thousand, two thousand or more lashes, according to his misdeeds. The strongest constitution cannot survive more than a couple of thousand, but the judge's conscience is clear. The patient's death is obviously due to his own weakness, his inability to suffer correction. Regrettable, no doubt, but no fault of the authorities. Spaikin, tall, thin, overcome with remorse for his last crime, died as the knout fell for the 2,221st time; sturdy little Bekof, tough and defiant, lasted until the 2,400th.

At the University, the Supreme Chief of Police joined our party, and offered us every assistance in his power. Travelling in Russia is made so easy, so delightful, (provided one is not exactly unknown), and I am deeply grateful to all the officials, soldiers, merchants, who, everywhere I went, so generously placed their time, their homes, tables, carriages and every conceivable convenience at my service. And their generosity! After leaving Nijni, for instance, I found three or four additional parcels among my luggage—thirty or forty pounds of the finest tea in the world, a joint gift from the friends I had met there. In Kazan, which I entered that morning without knowing a soul, I received at least twenty invitations to dine that same evening.

However, I was anxious to return to M. Grass, who had promised to make enquiries, during the day, about possible means of transport for the next stage of my journey. All he had been able to discover was that a vessel from Astrakhan, the *Nakimof,* had gone upstream five or six days ago and was expected back at any moment, on its homeward voyage. Such a chance would be a godsend for me. It would have been possible to travel overland—some of the roads were still open, though the season was far advanced—but my purse was hardly equal to the expense of hiring a carriage, or even a *tarantass,* and relays of posthorses. Travelling by boat costs so much less!

At dinner with M. Jablonovsky, next evening, I mentioned my plans, and the company at table warmly protested at the shortness of my stay in Kazan. General Lahn and his brother, the colonel, who claimed to have met me in Paris, had already arranged a day's hunting for me. "In any case," they insisted, "the *Nakimof* will stay here long enough to load up her supply of fuel. She burns wood, you know, and has to restock every few days."

The colonel exchanged a word or two with the Chief of Police, who readily promised that the *Nakimof's* papers would not be in order. She could not leave Kazan until the day after our proposed excursion. Despotism may have its disadvantages, but on occasion it can be a great convenience! So it was arranged. Twelve of us enjoyed a good day's sport in the woods some twenty miles from Kazan, a *battue* with all the usual shouting, the continuous beating of the undergrowth, the incessant fusillade from our guns. Our total bag was 45 hares, of which I shot a dozen, and we returned to Kazan in triumph.

There, good news awaited me. The *Nakimof* had arrived, and would leave next day for Astrakhan. With all speed I arranged our passage with the captain—a mere 200 francs for ourselves and our luggage—we exchanged last goodbyes with our friends in Kazan, and settled ourselves on board for the night, wondering what fresh excitements we should encounter on the next stage of our travels.

12

ON TO ASTRAKHAN

The Volga, as you know, rises in Tver, and since Russia is one vast plain the river meanders quietly along for the two thousand odd miles of its course to the Caspian Sea. Beyond Kazan it bends sharply southward, as we perceived when we awoke next morning, for the sun, which, on our journey from Nijni to Kazan had risen directly ahead, now rose well to our left. When we went on deck the view was magnificent. We were at the point where the Kama, rushing down from Siberia, pours itself into the Volga with such force that it changes the colour of the water from brown to white. The small, snow-covered lumps of ice swirling along on its surface looked to us like a multitude of swans.

The Kama teems with fish of every kind, from trout to the great beluga—white sturgeon that may weigh 400 pounds, and the dreaded catfish that no-one will buy without first inspecting it closely, for human remains are often found in its stomach. After being joined by this important tributary the Volga broadens, with here and there an island. The left bank is still low and flat, but the right is some 400 feet high, though the soil is mostly clay or chalk, without a single rock. Simbirsk, capital of the government of the same name, is the first town of the slightest importance in this stretch of the river, and it lies 154 miles below Kazan. What strikes a visitor most forcibly in Russia, once he leaves the few large towns behind, the thing he finds almost unbearably depressing, is the loneliness. The land is so empty, even along the banks of the Volga, Russia's chief artery! In more remote areas the solitude must be terrifying!

At Stavropol the river makes a great elbow-bend towards Samara, then swings back to its former line at Sizran, but we passed these places during the night. (The *Nakimof*, more venture-some than the boats higher up the Volga, pressed on her course throughout the hours of darkness, for her captain was frankly anxious to be clear of this stretch of the river before the October frosts gripped the Volga in a sheet of ice.) Every time the boat stopped to renew her stock of firewood we went ashore, but the hamlets were all exactly alike, a few wooden *isbas* and a handful of peasants in red shirts and *touloupes*.

Three days after leaving Kazan we reached Saratov, where the captain told us we should have 36 or 48 hours to spend on shore, while he unloaded part of his cargo and took on more. What were we to do? I asked Kalino, who at once informed me that Saratov had thirty thousand inhabitants, six churches, two convents and a gymnasium—the fellow is a born statistician—but he had no idea how we might amuse ourselves. It was freezing as we went ashore, and we wandered around till mid-day, by which time the sun had thawed the streets into a welter of mud. Then my eyes fell upon a little lingerie shop, where the sign over the door gave the owner's name: Adelaide Servieux. "Moynet," I cried, "we are saved! Here is a Frenchwoman," and pushing open the door I led my party into the shop.

At the sound of our entrance a young woman, obviously a *Parisienne*, came from an inner room with a business-like smile of greeting. "Good-day, my dear," said I. "Like yourself, I am French. Can you suggest how a man might while away a day or two in Saratov?"

"That rather depends," said she, looking at me attentively and breaking into a laugh, "on the sort of man. A wandering friar could spend the time preaching; a travelling salesman could peddle his wares, but M. Alexandre Dumas has only to find a French family!

166

With them and their friends, the time will pass all too quickly!"

"Kalino," I exclaimed, turning to him, "you may travel the world over, but you will never hear anything like that, save from a French heart!"

M. Servieux had by now come from the inner room to join his wife, and shaking me warmly by the hand he said: "You'll all stay and dine with us, I hope?"

"Gladly, on condition that you allow me to provide the meal." I would willingly have cooked it, too, to save Madame the trouble, but I was over-ruled. Until dinner time we talked. During dinner, and afterwards we went on talking! Some friends of theirs joined the party—Madame Zenaida, a plump, talkative little woman with bright eyes, who wrote poetry; the Chief of Police, a M. Posniak, who invited us to spend the next day with him; and a young man of about twenty-six, Prince Labanof, who was amazed when I told him I had met his aunt and cousins in Florence!

I sent Kalino to fetch some of my famous tea from the boat, and we sat enjoying it for hours, still talking. At last, M. Servieux said: "Stay the night! We can give you a room each—no beds, of course, but since you've been in Russia for five months I'm sure you will be used to that!" So it was arranged. Next day, M. Posniak showed us the town; in the evening we all dined together again, this time at his house; and at eight o'clock my new friends, whom I shall always remember, as I think they will remember me, escorted us back to the *Nakimof* by torchlight.

Our next stop was at Nikolaevsk, a little village on the left bank of the Volga, opposite Kamyshin, where we arrived at nine in the morning, and this time I knew in advance what we should be doing. I had planned a trip by *telega* into the Kirghis Steppes, hoping to see something of the nomad tribes who live there, the Kuzaks, and the curious salt lakes to be found in that part of the country. The trip, some 175 miles would take us three days, and we would rejoin the *Nakimof* at Tsaritsyn, where the Volga runs nearest to the Don.

Accordingly, we landed at Nikolaevak with the minimum of hand-luggage and made our way to the post-house to hire horses and a *telega*. Before anyone can hire horses in Russia he must have a special permit, a *padarojny*, issued by a government office, which he must show to the chief ostler or 'postmaster'. This functionary is in duty bound to have at least nine horses ready for hiring at any time of the day or night, sufficient for three *troikas*, and in his office is a record book in which he must enter the names of all customers and the horses supplied to them. (This book hangs from a string fixed to his desk by a large wax seal bearing the stamp of the local authority, and if that seal—or even the string—were ever broken, he would lose his licence.)

As likely as not, however, the postmaster will tell you that he has just hired out the last horses in his stable, but, if you wish, he could obtain some from a neighbour—at an increased price, of course. If once you fall into that trap, you are lost! The postillions will pass the word along, and your journey will cost you three or four times the regular tariff. That is why most Russian travellers carry a whip, called a *nagaika*, which they buy when they apply for their permit, not, as yet, from the same office, though that will doubtless come in time. In 1858 they are still sold separately. Travellers use them to persuade a postmaster to produce horses at the proper charge, or to encourage postillions to improve the speed of their mounts. You can wear out a *nagaika* every hundred miles or so, without ever touching a horse!

A *padarojny* states the name of the bearer and, even more important his rank or *tchine*, which determines his precedence. If, for example, a captain were about to drive away with fresh horses and a colonel came along with a similar request, the horses would at once be taken from the captain's carriage and harnessed to the colonel's; a colonel would give way to a general, and so on. My own permit was issued in Moscow by the Governor, Count Zagrevsky, who thoroughly disapproved of my presence in the town and was anxious to encourage me to travel on. Consequently it was a most princely and impressive document. In it I was described as a *littérateur français,* a term that no post-master we encountered had ever seen before. Kalino explained that my status was at least equal to that of a general, so I was accorded every possible facility.

Nothing could be more depressing than these flat, interminable Russian plains covered with grey heath, so utterly desolate that it was quite an event to catch sight of a horseman silhouetted against the distant skyline, and we sometimes travelled fifteen or twenty miles without seeing a single bird flying overhead. After our first change of horses we began to notice, here and there, small groups of Kirghiz tents made of skins and shaped like pyramids about twelve feet square, with a vent hole at the top to let out the smoke.

The Kirghiz, who came to Russia via Turkey and are probably of Chinese origin, are Mohammedans, now divided into three groups, the Great Horde, Middle and Little Hordes. Unlike their neighbours, the Kalmucks, who are a placid, law-abiding race of lama-buddhists, the Kirghiz are incorrigible thieves, and we were warned to be on our guard against them. We Frenchmen well remembered seeing some of them over-running our homeland in 1814, the lost legion of the Russian army, with their lances or bows and arrows, their shaggy little horses and rope stirrups. Nowadays, except among the poorest, muskets have replaced the bows and arrows.

Once or twice we passed these tents close enough to see women and children clustering round the opening. Each dwelling contains a pallet of skins or a few sleeping mats, a storage chest and a few cooking pots. It takes four camels or eight horses to transport each of these families, with their belongings. Kirghiz horses are small, swift and tireless, finding their own forage on the open steppes. Their owner does no more than remove their bit and bridle after the day's work and turn them loose.

We proposed travelling day and night, for there was nothing of interest to see on the steppes, and since we knew we should find absolutely nothing to eat on the way we had brought supplies of bread, hard-boiled eggs and wine. We found great difficulty, however, in obtaining fresh relays of horses after nightfall, for the post-masters feared we might be attacked *en route* by Kirghiz. We ourselves were not in the least apprehensive, for we had our guns and we knew that a strong force of Cossacks was stationed at Lake Elton to maintain law and order in the country through which we should pass. We were not held up during the night, except once, by the cold, for on these windswept plains the temperature sometimes drops to six or seven degrees below zero.

The post-house where we stopped to warm ourselves a little

169

was exactly like those we had seen elsewhere in Russia, simply four white-washed walls, a couple of benches and stools, a table, a stove and a samovar. The only difference here was that the water was so brackish that our tea was undrinkable. Still, the stove was warm, and rolling ourselves in our cloaks we slept comfortably enough for a couple of hours, until dawn, when we resumed our journey.

All day we pressed on across a veritable desert of flat land that may have been a green carpet gay with flowers in spring or summer, but in October was merely a dull grey-brown. It was not until three o'clock in the afternoon that we saw before us the first objective of our trip, Lake Elton, a vast silver mirror stretching away to the horizon, one of the largest of Russia's salt lakes. These lakes are a natural phenomenon, so far from the sea, yet so rich in salt that thick white deposits are formed on their banks. There are at least 135 of them, and less than a quarter have so far been exploited commercially by the government. From that small proportion about 300,000 tons of salt are extracted annually, chiefly from Lake Baskunchak and Lake Elton. Gangs of workmen dig it out with picks and shovels and load it on to carts to be conveyed to every part of Russia, and in Tiflis we saw great blocks of it piled up for sale in the market-place. Some of the smaller lakes dry up completely in summer, but fill again when the snows melt in spring.

Lake Elton, some 45 miles round, never dries, and on its southern shore stands the administrative office controlling the workings. It is not a hotel, and nearby wooden houses are, at best, of doubtful cleanliness, so we pitched our tent a short distance away, surmounted by a little French flag given to us by the ladies we had met at Saratov. I was busily preparing to cook our evening meal when I heard a troop of horses coming to a halt outside our tent, and saw, coming towards me, a Russian officer wearing the severely-cut uniform of a Cossack.

"Pardon my intrusion, Monsieur," said he to me in excellent French, "but would you by any chance be the M. Alexandre Dumas we have been expecting in Astrakhan for the last month?"

I bowed, acknowledged my identity, and added: "General Beklemichef, I presume?"

"What!" he cried. "You know my name?"

"General Lahn, whom I met in Kazan, told me of you, and even gave me a letter of introduction to Madame Beklemichef."

"You shall deliver it in person, tomorrow," he replied with a smile. "Meanwhile, would you like me to take you around the lake? We who are stationed here find it extremely dull, but since you have come on purpose to see it . . ."

"Half-way round will be quite enough!"

"Then I'll bring horses here for you at ten in the morning and we will all ride along the shore. You can send your conveyance to meet you at the far side."

"Alas! Our conveyance is already on its way back to the last post-house we passed. All we have here is our tent and our overnight bags."

"So much the better," replied the general. "We will ride as far as Bestouchef-Bogbo. My *tarantass* can then take you on to Tsaritsyn. Leave it there, and I will pick it up when I next go that way. As for your tent and other luggage, I'll have it sent over to Bestouchef-Bogbo for you."

Moynet and I looked at each other and laughed. This was real Russian hospitality! "Thank you very much, General," said I, shaking him warmly by the hand.

"Have you everything you want for tonight? Can I send you anything from the cook-house? Where will you sleep?" Not until he was fully assured that we had everything we needed did he finally leave us, repeating his promise to see us in the morning.

We had pitched our tent to face away from the wind, so that when we lit a great fire of bracken opposite the entrance only the heat reached us, the smoke being wafted away towards Astrakhan in a dense black cloud. Our tent had a round table fixed to the central pole, and I spent the evening writing. For the first time since I left France I felt free and at ease, no longer pent up between the walls of houses, railway carriages, coaches. It was the hardest thing in the world to convince myself that I was so far from home, camping between the Ural and the Volga, with Tatar tribes to my left and Kalmouks to my right.

I was just about to roll myself in my *touloupe* and settle down for the night (on the bare ground) when a Cossack brought me a note from General Beklemichef. and a magnificent white *papak* "to keep me warm during the night." A *papak* is a sheepskin hat like a hussar's busby, but not so stiff. I had not been able to help giving an admiring glance or two at the one the general was wearing when he called, so he had sent me one like it. (Never look twice at anything belonging to a Russian, or he will surely offer it to you!) Thanks to the general's kindness I was able to put into practice the rules of hygiene observed in Eastern countries. The *papak* kept my head warm and the wind whistling through the tent ensured that my feet stayed cold.

At nine next morning word reached us that breakfast was ready in the mess, and an hour later we left the general's table to find our horses saddled and bridled, our tent packed and loaded, our escort waiting. It took us three hours to skirt one side of the immense lake, through country that never varied, except that the bracken grew redder, the nearer it was to the salt, looking at first glance as though it were in flower. Every five or six miles we came to a tiny Cossack outpost manned by three soldiers and their mounts, an adequate guard for the lake, since the Kirghiz never make an open attack. Those sneak thieves prefer to work singly and in the dark, awaiting their chance to slip unseen behind a patrolling ranger, scoop up a bag or two of salt and vanish like shadows.

Towards two o'clock in the afternoon we halted for a meal beside a second lake—nameless, though it is twelve miles round— then pressing on through the remaining few hours of daylight to the little village of Stafka-Karaiskaia, where we were to spend the night. Of its 40 houses, six or eight are occupied by government officials and most of the rest belong to Armenians who provide furnished lodgings for the officers of the Cossack regiment stationed in the area. I was given a typical room there, and the sum total of its furniture was a wicker chair, a wooden bench, a small table covered with oilcloth, and on the wall a portrait of the Czar Alexander II with his family.

The general entertained us to supper in the one restaurant the place possessed, where, later, we watched a game of billiards—

the only means of relaxation in this god-forsaken spot where the heather has no birds and the lakes no fish. No wonder the billiards-table is booked for days in advance! Even so, I was offered a game —someone was willing to make a great sacrifice in the name of hospitality—but I declined. Courtesy must not be abused!

Next day we explored the salt-workings, then climbed the only high ground in the whole of this vast expanse of open country, whence Bestouchef derives its suffix of Bogbo, meaning "by the hill." Looking eastward from its summit we had the Volga behind us, the great lake on our left, a little Cossack fort directly ahead, and to our right a long stretch of salt pasture-land covered with grazing sheep. So we had completed our project; travelled two hundred miles across the steppes and seen Kirghiz and Cossacks in their native land. More, we had made the acquaintance of one of the finest officers in the Russian Army, and been offered a *tarantass* when we least expected it.

At eleven we climbed into it and said goodbye to General Beklemichef. Two hours later we were being ferried across the Actouba, and by five we had reached Tsaritsyn, where we were very relieved to see, by the last glimmer of daylight, the *Nakimof* swinging gently at her moorings. We had been away a day and a half longer than we had intended, and would have had no just cause for complaint if she had sailed without us.

We left the *tarantass* as arranged, and without losing a moment jumped into a boat that took us out to the *Nakimof,* where Captain Pastoukof gave us a cordial welcome. When we thanked him for waiting for us he laughed, and explained that after dropping us at Kamyshin he had been ordered back to Saratov, where a boat loaded with twenty cannon and gun-carriages had grounded on a sandbank. He had towed her off, the guns were now well on their way to Astrakhan, and the *Nakimof* had arrived back at Tsaritsyn only a couple of hours before we did. It was our turn to be kept waiting, for he had agreed to tow another boat, loaded with grain, downstream to our next port of call. Actually, she was not yet loaded, but would be ready the next afternoon.

I had a bright idea! If, instead of the afternoon, the captain would wait until the evening, Moynet and I could hire horses and ride over to see the Don, which is only forty miles away from the Volga at this point! A wonderful way to spend the day! But no! He would not risk further delay, and soon after mid-day we were on the move. Behind us, the Volga had already begun to freeze and we watched lumps of ice floating down beside the *Nakimof,* but we were running south, and they gradually melted in the warmer water. The air had lost the biting cold of a day or two ago; overhead we saw wild geese flying in geometric formation, and the sky was a clearer blue.

This is the country of Stenka Razin, that hero of a thousand tales of adventure, a Cossack bandit as famous as Robin Hood or Fra Diavolo, who plundered the rich, defied the law, and led a revolt that almost freed this part of Russia from the power of the Czar. He was vanquished and captured in 1671. Being merely a Cossack of humble birth, he was broken on the wheel. (Had he been born a prince he would have been hailed as a mighty conqueror.) Stenka Razin was a born leader, with a brigand's audacity, a general's grasp of strategy, the cunning of a master of intrigue. Above all, he was handsome, impulsive, generous and unpredictable—as every popular outlaw is.

At Vodianoia we saw our first green tree, a leafy willow in a hollow by a brook. (For six weeks we had seen no leaves at all!) A dozen miles further south, below Silver Island—where, says tradition, Stenka Razin divided with his men the booty from their raids—trees stood in little groups, with cows lying in their shade, chewing the cud, just like a picture by Paul Potter. Here the Volga is much broader than before, but no more interesting, and I remember Sunday, 24th October, as a very dull day, except for two things that delighted me: the sight of our first eagle, sailing majestically over the steppes down to the river bank, where it stood motionless to watch us pass; and a magnificent sunset, with an orange-red glow that I had not seen since my travels in Africa.

Next morning we saw our first Kalmuck tents, and towards eleven we counted a horde of 30 Kalmucks who had just watered their camels at the river bank. The sky above them was literally darkened by flocks of migrating birds, geese, ducks and cranes.

174

Later the same day we were very interested in two unusual buildings near the left bank, a Chinese pagoda and a castle in a strange architectural style I did not recognise. Around them stood a ring of Kalmouk tents. From our captain we learned that the pagoda was sacred to the Dalai-Lama, and the castle was the residence of the reigning prince of the Kalmucks.

At ten that night we saw a thousand shining lights, nosed our way between innumerable boats and heard the roar of human voices. We had reached the port of Astrakhan.

13

FESTIVITIES IN ASTRAKHAN

I had been in touch with a M. Sapojnikof, a merchant of the town, who had placed his house at my service for as long as I cared to stay, but it would have been most inconsiderate to disturb him at such an hour, so we spent one more night aboard the *Nakimof*.

In the morning we (and all our luggage) went ashore and were conveyed by *drojky* and *telega* to M. Sapojnikof's address, where I found that the phrase in his invitation was to be taken quite literally. The whole house, in charge of a steward, was ready for us to use as our own. My host and his family were out of town. Meals would be ready at any hour we cared to name. There was even a fine carriage with two pure-bred horses to take us wherever we wished to go! There's hospitality for you!

Lunch was served in the dining room, and we found it excellent, except for the wines. Though magnificent grapes are cultivated in Astrakhan, thanks to the irrigation system, the wine made from them is poor, or so I thought. Later, I revised my opinion a little, when I found that the flavour I disliked in the wines of Kislar and Kaketia came from the goatskins in which they are stored.

We were finishing our meal when the steward announced the

Chief of Police. By now we fully realised that, no matter how disconcerting a visit from such an official might be at home, in Russia it was a kind of civic welcome to the town and the first link in a chain of pleasant relationships, so we greeted him cordially and offered him a glass of wine. As he sat sipping it with obvious enjoyment, I concluded that the flavour of goat was very much to his taste, and probably regarded locally as a sign of excellence, just as a strong tang of resin in their wines is prized by the gourmets of Athens.

The Chief of Police had called to place his services at our disposal, and to tell us he had sent word of our arrival to the Civil Governor, a M. Strouvé, and to the Military Governor, who, oddly enough (as it seemed to me), was Admiral Machine. M. Strouvé hoped for the pleasure of our company at dinner that evening, and Admiral Machine would expect us on whatever day best suited our convenience. I accepted M. Strouvé's invitation with our warm thanks, and the Chief of Police rose to convey this message, but before he left I asked him to come round the house with me.

Something was beginning to worry me. When the steward had taken me on his tour of inspection I had seen many rooms, large and small; plenty of cupboards, cabinets, writing desks; but nowhere had I seen a bed. When I asked the steward where we were to sleep, "Anywhere you wish," he replied with expansive courtesy. I explained to him what I was hoping to find and his eyes grew round with amazement. Either he did not understand, or he thought me extremely difficult to please. Fortunately, the Chief of Police, thanks probably to his contact with foreigners, knew at once what I wanted, and agreed to search the bazaars for sheets and pillows or cushions, to supplement the mattresses and rugs Moynet and I had brought with us. As for Kalino, being a Russian he was quite happy to sleep anywhere and anyhow.

While on the subject, I will add that he was as good as his word, and before nightfall we had two pairs of sheets and two pillows. I did my best to explain to the servant how to make a bed, not entirely satisfactorily. One sheet he could understand— doubtless I should roll myself up in it—but the second he considered utterly superfluous and every night I found it folded like a handkerchief and placed neatly on the table.

With the Chief of Police we drove through the town to call on M. Strouvé, who proved to be a charming man of 32 or so, of French descent and therefore speaking the language like a Parisian. His 25-year-old wife and two children completed the family circle. He begged me to call on him for any help or information, and I enquired about the pagoda and castle that had so intrigued me as we came down the Volga.

"Ah!" he said. "That is where Prince Toumaine lives. We must let him know you are here. One of my Kalmucks shall ride over this afternoon and tell him. Undoubtedly he will want to meet you. It wouldn't surprise me if he arranges all sorts of festivities in your honour."

Dinner would be at six, so we had four hours in which to explore the town. The Chief of Police had gone off to search for the bedding we wanted, so I asked M. Strouvé if he could spare one of his clerks to be our guide. "I have one waiting," he replied. "He speaks French, and says his father was a friend of yours in Paris years ago."

This seemed incredible! Pure magic! "What is his name?" I asked. "Cournaud." Then it's perfectly true," I gasped, as my memory took me back over thirty years, and I recalled a man about ten years my senior, whom I had often met at parties. One day he disappeared, and gossip said he had lost all his money at the gaming tables. All I could discover then was that he had gone to Russia, hoping to earn a living teaching French. So this was his son! Warmly I shook his hand, as happy to meet him as he was to be my guide, and for a week I had his company everywhere I went.

In ancient days, Astrakhan was fabulously rich and prosperous, the Tatar "Star of the Desert," "Treasury of the Golden Horde," but that was before Ivan the Terrible seized the land. Now it is merely the capital of the province of the same name, which has an area of 90,000 square miles and a population so scanty, so scattered, that outside the towns you will hardly find one man in ten square miles. The people are mainly of Russian blood, freely mixed with that of Armenians, Persians, Tatars and Kalmucks. The Tatars, some 5,000 of them, live by breeding particularly fine sheep whose fleece, of almost every colour, but chiefly white, black and greyish-brown, is famous all over the world. One curious breed has tails so large and heavy that little two-wheeled carts have to be tied behind the sheep to carry them. We did not see any of these carts, but we certainly saw the sheep and their phenomenal tails. We even ate one of them when we dined beside Lake Bestouchef-Bogbo, and though it consisted entirely of fat (except for the bone, of course), it was delicate eating and quite delicious.

Once there were Indian tribes in Astrakhan but these have now disappeared, leaving, from their intercourse with Kalmuck women, a race of half-breeds called *metis,* very strong and active, with a zest for hard manual work. These are all porters, carters, sailors, and I thought them remarkably good-looking, for their mixed blood has given them a skin fairer than that of their fathers, and eyes less oblique than those of their Kalmuck mothers. The Armenians have preserved their purity of race, and their women never leave their homes until nightfall, when they look like phantoms or Grecian statues in their long white robes.

Pavements are unknown in Astrakhan and the roads are mere tracks deep in sand or mud. In the hot weather they are completely deserted from ten in the morning until four in the afternoon. Between four and five the shops open, the streets fill with chattering crowds, and every door and window is crowded with heads looking out to watch the passers-by. Water is scarce and of poor quality. The Russians once tried to remedy this by sinking an artesian well, but 130 yards down they struck, not water, but a layer of gas that shot up through the bore-hole fifty feet into the air. They lit it, and it burned like a great funeral pyre until dawn.

If water is scarce, water-melons are plentiful and particularly good; they are so cheap that we were constantly refused them as being beneath our notice. (We finally bought some surreptitiously, and found them most refreshing.) Nothing so simple as water-melon was served at dinner that evening, for M. Strouvé and his French chef had devised a superb meal for us and the dozen other guests he had invited to meet us. Once the doors were closed I could have believed myself back in France, for we talked of poetry, novels, current literary trends, the theatre, music, even fashions, which interested the ladies intensely. What an influence France exerts on the whole civilised world!

The Chief of Police offered to take us, next morning, to see inside the homes of Tatar and Armenian families. (He had made tactful enquiries beforehand to ensure that our visit would be acceptable. Some of the stricter sects had refused, on the grounds of national or religious prejudices, but others, more civilised and broad-minded, had replied they would receive us with pleasure.) Our first hosts were Armenian, father, mother, one son and two daughters, and they had gone to considerable trouble to welcome us hospitably. The son was roasting a fillet of mutton over red-hot charcoal, while the mother had covered the table with preserves of every kind—made from roseleaves, pumpkins, walnuts—and at least three sorts of grapes. (I am told that 42 different varieties are cultivated in Astrakhan.) I tried them all, expressed my pleasure, and was at once offered the recipes for a dozen Armenian dishes that will delight my friends in Paris. (The only change I shall make is to use less cinnamon, which Armenians relish as much as we do mustard!)

To arrange a visit to a Tatar home had been far more difficult, and we found less to interest us. This Tatar had four wives, as his religion permits, and as we entered they all stood stiffly in a row, dressed in such finery as they possessed, with their joint husband one pace ahead, like a corporal with his platoon. One wife was a negress, and her babies were clearly recognisable among the eight or ten young children scrambling over the floor and furniture (two or three wooden chests), jumping on all fours like frogs, doing their best to get as far from us as possible, which was no great distance in a hut twelve feet square. A stay of a few minutes was enough to bring home to us the joys of polygamy, and we hurriedly escaped in search of air less heavily charged with ammonia and carbon-dioxide!

At M. Strouvé's house a messenger from Prince Toumaine was waiting, bringing an invitation for us and our friends to visit him the day after tomorrow, October 29th, when he would arrange a special feast in our honour. Naturally we accepted with pleasure, and watched the messenger gallop off into the distance as we walked to the house of Admiral Machine, our host for that evening.

Early next morning we went pheasant shooting (with no great success but a good deal of pleasure), returning in time for a ceremony at noon to inaugurate the building of a new breakwater. An altar had been erected on the bank at the point where the work would start, and round it stood the Russian clergy of the town in their magnificent robes; then came the local officials in full uniform, Moynet and I standing with them as instructed; next came a ring of soldiers, and beyond them the whole population of Astrakhan—Kalmucks, Tatars and Russians. The Russians, mild-looking men with long hair and beards, a fresh colour and white teeth, wore their traditional costume—*touloupes*, red shirts, wide trousers stuffed into high boots. The Tatars have beautiful eyes, shaven heads (covered by their *papaks*), bristling moustaches, and bandoliers across their chests, worn over their long military over-coats. The Kalmucks are yellow-skinned, their sparse hair grows in little tufts on their heads and chins, their eyes turn upwards at the corners, and you would recognise them anywhere by their manner. Russian peasants are humble enough, God knows, but the Kalmucks positively cringe! Their usual garb consists of a flat yellow cap, long tight tunic and wide trousers. (They attended on this occasion purely out of curiosity, taking no part in the religious ceremony, since they are followers of the Dalai Lama.)

At noon a gun was fired and the service began. When mass was over the band struck up, the Admiral walked down the bank and with a ceremonial mallet struck the first pile; M. Strouvé did the same with the second, and I was given the honour of striking the third. At the sound of each blow the guns fired a salvo and in the intervals the band played with gusto. The inauguration thus completed, gifts of bread, wine and salt fish were distributed to the crowd. At once they sat down on the ground to enjoy this vast picnic, and I was interested to note that the Tatars, true to their religion, left their wine untouched and slaked their thirst in the waters of the Volga.

My friends and I walked to the quay where a boat was waiting to take us to the sturgeon fisheries. The flesh of this great fish is very tasty, and almost like meat, well worth the attention of a gourmet, but it is prized even more highly as the source of caviare, *visigha* (its spinal marrow, greatly prized as a delicacy throughout Russia and the Near East), and gelatine, so much in demand for making jelly, that standby of second-rate cooks. The flesh, salted down, is a staple article of diet everywhere in Russia.

There are three separate fishing seasons. The first runs from the end of March to May 15th, when the ice breaks up and the water level is at its highest. This is the time when the eggs are abundant and of finest quality, providing the choicest caviare. The second season is in July and August, when the fish, having spawned, return towards the sea. The third, the one we were to see something of, is from September to November, when the catch includes *belonga* and *sevriouga* (*Accipenser stellatus*).

Half-way through the afternoon we arrived at one of the largest fishing stations on the Volga, with no fewer than a hundred huts used by the fishermen. They had been advised of our coming, and had awaited our arrival before taking the day's catch. An immense barrier of vertical beams, driven into the river bed a foot or so apart, prevented the fish from swimming back up the river, their instinctive urge at this time of the year. Every three yards across the river a rope is fixed, and from it hang iron chains of varying lengths, ending in very sharp hooks, not baited. Boats move up and down along the ropes, and the men can easily tell, when they lift the chains, whether a fish has been hooked. If so, it is a simple matter to heave it to the surface, but then the struggle begins. To deal with a *belonga* weighing seven or eight hundred pounds will tax the strength of eight or ten men. In less than an hour and a half we watched them take 120 or 130 fish, which were then towed to a slaughtering pen where the caviare and *visigha* are harvested. Never have I seen such a hideous spectacle!

As everyone knows, these great fish are extremely tenacious of life. Some of them, eight or ten feet long, were still leaping and writhing after their bellies had been split and their caviare removed. They made one last supreme effort when their spines were laid open and the marrow scraped away—the *visigha* that Russians value so highly and make into little pies. They then lay still, though their hearts continued beating for half an hour or more. Each operation on every one of these great creatures takes fifteen minutes, terrible and utterly revolting to watch.

The caviare from the largest sturgeon taken that day was presented to me as a trophy, half of it salted and the remainder fresh. It filled eight 10 lb. barrels, and even the unsalted remained in perfect condition until we reached Tiflis, three months later.

It had been an exhausting day, and once we reached Astrakhan we declined all invitations in favour of an early bed, to restore our energies for our visit to Prince Toumaine next morning. At eight o'clock on the 29th we embarked in the *Verblioud* and moved slowly upstream against the current, reaching our destination at about half past ten. The left bank of the Volga was crowded with Kalmucks to greet us, the landing stage was gay with flags, and as we hove in sight the prince's artillery saluted us, our boat replying with its two little cannon.

It was easy to distinguish the figure of the prince, waiting for us on the landing stage, wearing national costume—a white coat, very tight and fastened from top to bottom with tiny buttons, a kind of flat Polish *chapska* on his head, loose trousers and boots of Morocco leather. I had taken care to make sure of the correct procedure beforehand, and followed it precisely. Since the feast was being given in my honour, I duly went straight up to the prince, threw my arms around him, and rubbed his nose with mine, a gesture which expresses every good wish. (I was rather proud of carrying out this manoeuvre as successfully as though I had been doing it all my life, for a Kalmuck's nose is by no means prominent, and is, moreover, deeply entrenched between his jutting cheekbones.) Prince Toumaine was a man of 30 or 32, fairly tall and rather fat, with very small hands and feet. (The average Kalmuck lives in the saddle from early childhood, so his feet do not grow in the usual way. The continual pressure on the stirrup broadens them until they are almost square.)

After returning my greeting, the prince stood aside to let me pass, welcomed M. Strouvé with a simple hand-shake, and the rest of the party with a bow. The castle was 200 yards from the river bank and a guard of honour escorted us to the open front door, where we were received by the major-domo. He conducted us through the palace until we reached a closed door on which he gave a ceremonial knock. Instantly it was flung open by some invisible means, and we were in the presence of the Princess of the Kalmucks.

She was seated on a kind of throne. Her maids of honour, six to the right and six to the left, were squatting on their heels, all as motionless as statues in a pagoda. The Princess was arrayed in a robe of Persian silk embroidered in gold, open at the front to reveal the bodice of her dress, gleaming with pearls and diamonds. Around her neck she wore a plain linen collar, like a man's, fastened in front with two huge pearls. Her head-dress was square, the upper part consisting of ostrich feathers dyed red, the lower part divided and turned back to reveal her brow. On one side it reached the base of her neck, on the other it was raised to the level of her ear, which gave her a delightfully inconsequential air.

She was not quite twenty, and the Chinese slant of her eyes was vastly becoming; her nose was a fraction less pointed than our European taste would consider perfect, and her red lips were parted over her pearly teeth. I thought her as pretty as any Kalmuck princess could be. I approached her to make my bow, but she smiled and gave me her hand to kiss—a signal favour, as I learned later. I sank to one knee without the least idea whether etiquette allowed this, and respectfully placed my lips on her little hand, a trifle brown, perhaps, but beautifully shaped. (How I wished the ceremonial was the same for women as for men! I should have thoroughly enjoyed rubbing noses with this princess!)

As she rose to greet her other guests, her maids of honour shot upright as though impelled by some hidden spring. Turning towards me the prince asked if we would care to attend a service to celebrate our visit. He had ordered the High Priest to arrange it with special prayers to the Dalai-Lama for our well-being and happiness. We replied that we should be delighted, whereupon the prince added in in a conversational aside: "It won't take long. Then we can enjoy a meal."

The assembled company began to move towards the door, the princess followed by her ladies in waiting, walking in pairs with short stiff steps in a kind of ritual march. At the palace gate two fine carriages were waiting, and a score of horses with the traditional Kalmuck saddles raised a foot or so above the animal's spine so that the rider is standing rather than sitting. I was accorded the honour of riding with the princess, my friends entered the second carriage, and the prince mounted his horse. Scarcely had we taken our seats when, at a word from their mistress, the court ladies instantly relaxed their rigidity, hitched their robes between their legs as high as possible, and, without using the stirrups, leapt astride the first horse they could reach. Then, bare to the knees and shrieking with excitement, their head-dresses (copies of the one worn by the princess herself) slipping this way and that until they looked positively tipsy, they galloped off towards the pagoda a few hundred yards away. I was struck dumb with amazement—then with delight: I had encountered the unexpected—a traveller's highest ambition!

The doors of the pagoda stood wide open, the temple itself silent until the moment when the prince and princess, leading their guests, set foot on the threshold. Then there burst forth an incredible din like some cacophony from the underworld. Twenty musicians faced each other across the broad aisle leading to the altar, some beating drums, cymbals, tomtoms, others blowing with distended cheeks into trumpets, conches, or great tubes ten feet long. (A trumpet-player lasts six years, the prince told me later, a conch-blower four, more or less, but performers on the long tubes never more than two. After those periods of service they start spitting blood. They are pensioned off and put on a special diet of mares' milk, but only a few ever recover.) None of the performers understands a note of music, that much is instantly obvious. Their function is to bang or blow as hard as possible. The greater the noise, the more they are glorifying the Dalai Lama, or so they believe.

Waiting at the door to receive us was the master of ceremonies, clad in a long crimson robe, with a yellow hood covering his head and a white staff in his hand. He led us between the ranks of musicians towards the High Altar where the priest, robed in yellow, was kneeling on a Persian carpet. As we approached he rose, turned, and conducted the service of thanksgiving while the musicians redoubled their efforts. After a quarter of an hour they fell to the ground exhausted, and a welcome silence fell like balm upon our tortured ears. Even so, after the deafening noise, it was several minutes before we could hear one another speak, and meanwhile we followed our guide around the temple. What struck me as even more remarkable than the statues of porcelain, bronze, silver and gold, or the floating banners bright with serpents and fabulous monsters, was a kind of cylinder two feet high and four feet across, its rim decorated with religious emblems like the signs of the zodiac. It was a prayer mill. Not, of course, for the use of commoners, but ready in case the prince should be too busy or too forgetful to say his prayers. Then someone turns the handle of the prayer-mill once or twice and the Dalai-Lama is just as well satisfied.

On returning to the castle we found the courtyard crowded with Kalmucks, three hundred or more, assembled to enjoy the feast that the prince was providing in my honour, for which his servants had slaughtered a horse, two cows and twenty sheep. The choicer portions of horsemeat, minced with onion, pepper and salt, are eaten raw as an appetiser, a national dish that the prince asked us to taste. We each managed to swallow a piece the size of a nut, and though I would hardly recommend it to our French gourmets it was nicer than some of the dishes offered me at the tables of Russian noblemen. Before we sat down ourselves, the prince made sure that his Kalmucks had all that they could want, and, as if he felt the need to apologise for the slight delay, he explained: "Those are the people on whom my way of life depends. It is only right that I should give them a little pleasure on an occasion like this." He is a real humanitarian and very rich, though his wealth lies chiefly in flocks and herds—fifty thousand horses, thirty thousand camels and more sheep than can be counted—eleven or twelve millions—which are sold in thousands at the Fairs held annually at Kasan, Tsaritsyn and Derbend.

For his visitors, Prince Toumaine had provided the choicest delicacies at his command, meat from a young camel and a six-months-old colt, lambs, chicken, game in overwhelming abundance. When at last we reached the dessert stage, the prince asked me to come to the window, glass in hand, to receive a toast from the Kalmucks still feasting outside. As I appeared they all rose to their feet, each with his wooden drinking vessel in one hand and a half-gnawed bone in the other, gave me a cheer and drank my health. The prince decided that my glass was too small for an adequate response, so he handed me a great horn bound with silver, poured into it a whole bottle of champagne, and though I am no drinker I managed to drain it in honour of his subjects, the 300 in the court-yard and their 11,000 fellow-serfs throughout his realm.

After that Homeric repast we were informed that the races were about to begin, and we all walked across the courtyard between rows of wildly cheering Kalmucks to a dais that had been erected while we feasted. The princess and her maids of honour took their places, we grouped ourselves in a semicircle of chairs and watched the competitors lining up on our left. The course was about seven miles over open country, and the finishing line was on our right. There were 100 starters, ridden by men or women, for in this part of the world women enjoy an equality with men to which their French sisters still vainly aspire. The prize for the winner was a calico robe and a yearling colt.

The horses made a whirlwind start and soon vanished behind a low hill. Half an hour later we could hear their galloping hooves again, long before we could see them, then the first rider came in sight, followed by a second, with the rest of the field spread over a mile or more. A boy of 13 kept the lead and passed the winning post fifty yards ahead of his nearest rival while the crowd shouted his name: Bouka. Shyly he came forward to receive his robe from the hand of the princess, putting it on without losing an instant. (It was much too long for him and he clutched up the front as best he could, letting the back sweep the ground like a sort of train.) Then the prince presented him with a colt which he mounted at once and rode off in triumph.

"Now," said the prince, "you shall see how a Kalmuck moves house." Four camels, laden with a tent and everything needed by a nomad family, were led forward by the father, mother and two sons. At a word of command the great creatures kneeled while their loads were removed, then wandered off to graze while their owners erected the *kebitka*. Ten minutes later, everything was in place. One of the sons came to the dais, bowed low in oriental fashion, offering us the hospitality of his father's tent, and soon I was sitting crosslegged on a carpet beside the prince and princess, accepting a cup of Kalmuck tea. Full of confidence I raised it to my lips, and instantly felt certain I had been poisoned! It was the most abominable beverage that ever turned a Christian stomach! (I found that it was made from a piece of tea-brick from China, boiled in a saucepan with milk, butter and salt.) However, the prince drank two or three cups with obvious enjoyment, and the princess sipped hers without the faintest grimace, so I overcame my qualms. Next we were offered fermented mares' milk, but this time I was more cautious, and after passing it across my firmly closed mouth, murmuring appreciation to please my host, I placed my glass on the ground and took the first opportunity of upsetting it.

Like all pastoral peoples, Kalmucks live with the utmost frugality. Milk is their staple diet and bread is almost unknown. They drink quantities of tea, and *eau-de-vie* made from mares' milk is their idea of luxury. Without a compass or any other contrivance they find their way straight across these immense solitudes with complete accuracy. Their sight is incredibly keen, and even after sunset they can distinguish a rider on the horizon, can say whether his mount is a horse or a camel, and, more amazing, whether he is armed with a lance or a rifle.

Our visit over, we thanked our host, and returned to our former seats by the dais. The same instant the nomads began to take down their tent, piled their chattels in a pyramid on their camels, seated themselves on the apex of the load, the father on the first, the mother on the second, followed by their sons. They filed before us, crossing their hands on their breasts and bowing, then galloped off, silhouetted for a moment against the skyline before disappearing behind a hillock.

Scarcely had they vanished when two horsemen, each with a hooded falcon on his wrist, rode side by side from the courtyard, followed by two carriages and twelve or fifteen horses ready saddled. Word had reached the prince that a flight of swans had just landed on the river-bank a mile or two away, so once more we climbed into the carriages and were driven over the open steppe—smooth as a carpet—while to my great delight the court ladies mounted their horses with the same swift, unconscious grace as before—beaded slippers, bare legs, brocade robes tucked up as high as possible—but this time in complete silence to avoid disturbing the game.

Suddenly a dozen swans rose not twenty yards away, and at the same instant the falconers let slip their hawks, urging them on with excited cries. In a few seconds the two birds of prey, mere black specks compared with their massive quarry, were in the midst of the flock which dispersed, screaming wildly. Each falcon hovered a moment, chose its victim and swooped down. The doomed swans strove in vain to fly above their attackers, but the falcons, with their long pointed wings, fan-shaped tails and slim bodies, easily soared over them and dropped like plummets. Instantly the swans folded their wings and swept down towards the water, but half-way there the falcons were upon them, gripping their necks. From that moment the swans knew death was near, and made no attempt to escape. One fell to the ground, the other in the water where it plunged below the surface, but the falcon hovered over the spot and renewed the attack each time it came up for air. Terrified, streaming with blood and in its death throes, the swan tried to beat off the hawk with its mighty wings, but in vain, and a moment later the victor pounced with a scream of triumph on its lifeless prey, riding downstream on the white body as on a floating island, until two Kalmucks and the falconer put out in a boat to retrieve the great bird.

Each hawk flew back to its trainer's wrist to be rewarded with the customary titbit from a pouch hanging at his waist. Prince Toumaine has a passion for falconry and always has ten or twelve fully-trained adult birds in his mews and as many young ones still being taught. These freedom-loving creatures will not breed in captivity, so nomad tribesmen search for eyries and bring in the nestlings before they are fledged. As we drove back along the river bank towards the castle, where dinner awaited us, the falcons were flown at another quarry, a magnificent grey heron. Attacked by two enemies at once, it had no chance of escape, but, unlike the swans, it fought fiercely to drive them off with its long stabbing beak, a fearsome weapon. One falcon, swooping down from a great height, brought it plunging senseless to the ground not far from our path. Quickly the triumphant hawks were whistled back to their trainers, fed and re-hooded, then the heron, which proved to be unhurt, was carried back to the castle to live the rest of its life in peace as a household pet.

The hospitable profusion at dinner transcended even the meal served at mid-day, with more courses than I can list and a bewildering variety of wines, followed by excellent coffee with the princess in her "private suite"—three luxurious intercommunicating tents standing a short distance outside the castle walls. Then one of the court ladies began to play a balalaika while her companion entertained us with a Russian dance. I use that word for want of a better, for the "dance" consisted only of body movements and a series of languishing gestures with her arms and hands, all executed with no voluptuous grace and no sign of pleasure. After ten minutes she flung wide her arms, sank to her knees as though to invoke some invisible genie, then rose to her feet again and touched the next lady-in-waiting, who at once proceeded to follow her.

I began to fear that all twelve of them would do the same, in turn, but after the third one retired the princess asked if we would show them some of our French dances in the main hall of the castle, where (believe it or not) stood a grand piano, imported from Europe at some time in the past but never opened until that evening, when Mme Strouvé and the two ladies with her played waltzes, quadrilles, gavottes, minuets, indeed every piece of dance music they could remember.

Many times I have done my best to describe the indescribable, but never could I hope to convey to you the uproarious merriment that followed. Everyone joined in with the utmost enthusiasm, and if they confused left with right, moved the wrong way round and bumped into one another, what did it matter? They clapped their hands to mark the rhythm, stamped their feet, laughed, shrieked with delight while tears of joy and excitement streamed down their cheeks. At last, breathless, I climbed on an armchair, clutching a curtain as I surveyed the scene. The prince stood holding his sides, helpless with laughter; most of the others seemed on the verge of hysterics; and the princess herself, instead of returning to her seat with her usual decorum, flung her arms impulsively round her husband and in a voice warm with enthusiasm uttered a phrase that I was indiscreet enough to ask Kalino to translate for me. It was: "Dear friend of my heart, never have I enjoyed myself so much!"

There was no question of our returning to Astrakhan that night. Where my friends slept I never knew, but the prince insisted on giving me his private room. (When I protested he assured me he would not in any case be using it, since he proposed visiting the princess's apartment.) After the dusty day and the evening's exertion, I longed for water to cool and freshen my body, and seeing the royal dressing table bearing an impressive array of bowls, ewers, bottles of every conceivable size and shape, I hurried thankfully towards it. Alas! Not a drop of water anywhere! The porcelain was wonderfully beautiful, a delight to the eye, but not put to practical use. I seized a bottle, hoping to find eau-de-cologne, but the first contained Kirsch, the second *anisette,* the next *kummel,* the fourth gin. Evidently the prince had assumed that the elegant bottles gracing his dressing table were intended for liqueurs or spirits. Hope revived as I saw a bed in an alcove, for crisp linen sheets are almost as refreshing as a bath, but when I threw back the eiderdown (a thing I loathe), I found no sheets, no blankets, only a feather bed by no means as virgin as the piano in the hall. In the end I changed my clothes and lay down on a leather-covered couch, full of amazement (before I fell asleep) that a prince so rich in luxuries, should be so poorly provided with the simple necessities of life.

Though it was quite late when I went to bed, and the others were still later, at seven in the morning we were all up and ready for the second day's festivities. The prince had asked us to be at the windows by eight, to see a spectacle he had arranged for our entertainment. A quarter of an hour before that time, we heard something like a vast thunderstorm approaching from the east;

the earth trembled beneath our feet, and a great cloud of dust rose to the very heavens, obscuring the sun. In that cloud I began to make out a ripple of movement, and suddenly I realised that the steppe, as far as eye could see, was covered with a great herd of wild horses. I heard their neighs of terror or rage and watched them galloping in one huge mass towards the Volga. As the leaders reached the brink they hesitated for an instant, but the crowd behind forced them on and they launched themselves into the river, at this point almost two miles wide, until the Volga itself was cut in half by a broad belt composed of ten thousand horses, the leaders nearing the right bank while the stragglers were still on the left. The prince's riders who had rounded up this stampeding mass (fifty men at least), followed them into the water, slipping from their saddles and clutching their mounts by mane or tail as they swam across, until at last men and animals vanished into the distant forest. Never have I seen a sight so wild and magnificent, awe-inspiring in its splendid savagery.

At Prince Toumaine's suggestion we were rowed across the Volga, its waters still swirling from the passage of the wild horses, and as I sat facing the eight rowers I was struck, not for the first time, by the fact that all Kalmucks look exactly alike. When the great-uncle of the present prince came to Paris in 1814 he had his portrait painted by Isabey, but after the first few sittings he grew bored and sent a servant to take his place, yet the result was declared a perfect likeness of the royal visitor.

On the further shore we were entertained by displays of horsemanship, led by the prince himself, a sound though not spectacular rider. A few wild horses had been captured so that we could see them broken in by Kalmuck trainers, one of them a lad of ten who rode as though he and his mount were one. Kalmucks are trained to the saddle from their earliest days. The prince showed me the cradle used by his son, now six years old. It was a wooden contrivance hollowed out to support the child's back, with a padded projection on which he sits astride, held securely in place by a strap around his chest. At the back is a ring whereby the contraption can be hooked on the wall, baby and all. When he begins to walk he is placed on a sheep or a dog which he rides every day, till he is old enough to sit a horse.

While we enjoyed a picnic lunch—gigots of horsemeat, camel steaks, a sheep roasted whole and copious supplies of wine—the course was prepared for the camel race. On the Volga bank a great pole was erected with a long pennant streaming from the top—the winning post. Camels are half as fast again as the swiftest horse, and though the starting point was three miles upstream, only a few minutes after hearing the starter's shot we saw the leader outdistancing his 49 rivals to receive the prize of a splendid rifle. Then came a long programme of contests in which the riders, without dismounting, had to snatch scraps of paper from tent-pegs or pick up scattered coins from the bare ground.

The day was now far advanced, and the programme of festivities reached its climax—a wrestling match for which the prize was a magnificent leather cartridge belt, mounted in silver. "What a lovely trophy," said I, as the prince brought it over to show me. "Could I be allowed to compete for it?"

"Take it," the prince exclaimed. "I am delighted that it pleases you!"

"Your pardon, sire," I replied, "but taking it would not be the same. I should like to try to win it."

"Then," said he, "if you really mean to fight I will do myself the honour of being your opponent."

All one can do with a proposition like that is to accept it with good grace. The spectators took their seats and I entered the ring, followed by the prince, both of us stripped to our underpants. His skin was the colour of café-au-lait, and his limbs, though light and slender compared with his body, were far better proportioned than those of his subjects, probably because he had been well fed all his life. Before coming to grips we solemnly rubbed noses to show we were good friends, then amid the cheers of the onlookers the contest began. He was more accustomed to these exercises than I was, though perhaps not quite so strong. I rather think he gave me every possible advantage, and after five minutes he fell, his shoulders touched the ground and he acknowledged himself beaten. We both rose, rubbed noses again, and I went forward to receive the prize from the hands of the princess, who seemed astonished at the whiteness of my skin, compared to that of her husband.

The prince went to plunge in the river, but I had no wish to rival his hardihood in this respect, for only a mile or two away the Volga was frozen and I was glad to get back into my clothes. Once more we were rowed across to the castle where we sat down to another gargantuan meal, but when it was over the moment of parting could no longer be delayed. Sadly we left this hospitable home and made our way through the dusk to the landing stage, where our steamer, outlined with little lights and belching smoke from its funnel, waited impatiently. The prince and princess even came on board with us, to say goodbye. (It was the first time she had ever been on a steamer, and she had never seen a town, though Astrakhan itself was only a few hours journey from her home.) With tears in our eyes, Toumaine and I rubbed noses again and again—it was for the last time. The princess wept openly, and they both made me promise to come back one day. How I wish I could! (To satisfy them I had to swear by the Dalai-Lama, but perhaps such an oath is not binding for a Christian.) Salutes were fired as we drew away, and for two or three miles we could still see coloured flares shining beside the castle to bid us a last adieu. Then the river made an elbow bend and all was dark.

I was to see Prince Toumaine just once more. On our last day in Astrakhan, Tuesday, November 2nd, we called on M. Strouvé to say goodbye and found the prince with him, discussing some official matter. Over a glass of wine the conversation turned to the next stage of our journey, six days across the desert from Astrakhan to Kislar. There was danger, for certain tribes in the area were at war, and bands of robber Tatars are always lurking in ravines to prey on travellers, but I was far more concerned with the problem of food. We could carry with us enough bread and wine, but supplies of meat would not keep fresh for more than a day or two, and though we should hardly starve to death in the remaining four or five days, we should certainly develop a raging hunger. The prince smiled and said: "Do not give the matter another thought. I will see that you have fresh meat for dinner every evening until you reach Kislar."

He did not tell us how, and for a while I almost feared he might be joking, but he was as good as his word. When we stopped at the posthouse on our first evening in the desert, we were met by the prince's chief falconer, mounted on a racing camel and with hawk on wrist. He and his camel needed only four hours sleep a night, so long before dawn he was away scouring the desert in search of wild birds. He was also an excellent cook, and every day of our journey, when we reached the agreed posthouse at nightfall, there he would be, waiting for us with a goose or a couple of quail roasted to a turn. He stayed with us until we reached Kislar, where I handed him my rifle as a parting gift, and a note to thank Prince Toumaine.

So we said goodbye to Astrakhan, the last outpost of civilisation we should see for many a day. Our *tarantass* was loaded on to a barge (both provided by the civil authorities, to wit M. Strouvé), so were all the trunks and packing cases that could not go in the *tarantass* and would have to follow by *telega*. With sorrow in my heart I watched the first downward sweep of the oars—as symbolic of parting as the handful of earth sprinkled on a coffin—and saw the great port dwindle until it was lost in mist as we were rowed across the wide Volga for the last time. Then, in sand up to our knees, we turned our faces to the desert we had to cross, a land of nomads, camels and skin tents, where we and our tiny caravan were mere specks in the vast emptiness, but for news of our further travels you must read my next book of memoirs: *Adventures in the Caucasus*.

INDEX

Abbot of Valamo, 118–119

Abdication of Peter III, 104

Abo, Finland, 109; and Sweden, communications between, 109–110

Abuses, suppression of, 76, 84 (*See also* Local government)

Admiralty Building in St. Petersburg, 53

Adventures in the Caucasus, 194

Agriculture, 8; of Astrakhan, grapes, cultivation of, 175, 178, 179; of Finland, 125; of Gotland, 34; greenhouses in Ropcha, 107; labor shortage, effect of on, 148–149; neglect of, 8, 148–149

Aix-la-Chapelle, arrival in, 18

Alexander I, 11*n.;* emancipation of Estonians by, 36; Kazan University founded by, 163; statue of in St. Petersburg, 49

Alexander II, 49; bear hunting, skill of in, 63; emancipation decree of, 56; freeing of prisoners by, 80; lipsticks, use of by, 59; reforms of, 76; relaxing of bans by, 68

Alexandrovich, Dimitri, 79

Alexis, Michaelovitch, 69, 71

Alexis, Petrovitch, imprisonment of, 42; murder of, 42–43

America, bogus operations in, 81

Andrew of Radonega, Prince, 140

Angler, The, 100

Anne, Empress, enriching of shrine of St. Sergius by, 140; power given to Biren by, 31, 79

Annenkof, Alexis, 159

Annenkof, Pauline, 159

Aqueduct of Mytishchi, 138

Architecture, of churches, 34, 133, 162; of Valamo, 117–118

Armenians, culinary skills of, 179; lodgings for Cossack regiment provided by, 172; purity of race, preservation of, 178; visit to home of, 179

Army (*see* Russian Army)

Arnault, Naptal, M. and Mme., 105–106

Arsenal of St. Petersburg, 48, 50

Artists, early death of, 41–42

Ascher, 9, 16

Astrakhan, 8, 16; ancient prosperity of, 177; Armenians in, 178, 179; arrival in, 175; beds, lack of in, 176–177; Chief of Police of, 175–177; departure from, 194; festivities in, 175–194; fisheries in, 180–182; fishing seasons in, 181; grapes, cultivation of in, 175, 179; half-breeds in, 178; Indian tribes in, 178; irrigation system in, 175; Kalmucks in (*see* Kalmucks); metis in, 178; people of, blood mixture of, 177–178; pheasant shooting in, 180; post houses in, 169–170; roads of, 178; Russians in, physical appearance of, 180; seizure of by Ivan IV, 177; sheep breeding in, 178; Tatars in (*see* Tatars); trip to, 165–175; water shortage in, 178; watermelons, cultivation of in, 178; wines of, poor quality of, 175, 176

Astrakhan Region, area and population of, 177

Austria, saving of by Nicholas I, 60

Ava-Saxa, Mt., observation of astronomic phenomenon from, 32

Balder, firework display in memory of, 34–35

198

stadt, 82; in Moscow, 77, 129–131; setting of by serfs, 87, 95

Firework display in Visby, 34–35

Fisheries in Astrakhan, belonga, 181–182; sturgeon, 180–181

Fisherman, The, 96

Fishermen of Finland, 109–110

Fishing seasons in Astrakhan, 181

Fitz-James, Duke of, 106

Fleet, Russian, on maneuvers in Baltic, 38

Flight into Egypt, The, 38

Floods in St. Petersburg, 129

Florence, Daniel Home in, 13–14; memories of Dumas in, 25–26

Fontainebleau, parks of, 99

Fontanka Bridge, 59–60

Foreigners' Cemetery in Moscow, 132

Forest fires, 77, 79, 82, 87, 95, 111–113, 124, 125, 127, 129–131, 149

Fortress of St. Peter and St. Paul, 78–80

Fortress of Schlusselburg, 111, 112, 124

France, bogus operations in, 81; fire fighting in, 130–131; German invasion of, 20; Kirghis foray in, 169; veterans in, treatment of, 75

Free village, stay in, 149–150

French, M., 26

French huzzars, 23

Frigga, 34

Furs, sale of in Kazan, 162–163

Galitzine, Prince, 33–34

Gallinsky, de, Mlle., 158–159

Gambling by government officials, 83–84 (*See also* Local government)

Garrison in St. Petersburg, 54–55

Gautier, Théophile, 28

Generosity of Russians, 164, 172

German invasion of France, 20

Goatskins, use of for storing wines, 175, 176

Godounof, Boris, 134; tomb of, 140

Gods, false, casting of into Dnieper, 31

Golden Line in Moscow, 132–133

Gornestoef, designing of Valamo by, 117–118, 121

Gotland, agriculture of, 34; architecture of churches in, 34; firework display in, 34–35

Government, local (*see* Local government)

Granite cliffs in Finland, 123–124

Grapes, cultivation of in Astrakhan, 175, 179

Grass, M., 155–161, 164

Great Door of Ouspensky Cathedral, 139

Great Horde of Kirghiz, 169 (*See also* Kirghiz)

Greek sculpture in New Museum of Berlin, 28–29

Green paint, use of in St. Petersburg, 47, 54

Greenhouses in Ropcha, 107

Grégorovitch, 96–99, 101, 103, 105

Grousinsky, Knias, dethronement of, 160

Guise, de, Duke, 12

Gulf of Finland, effect of on Neva, 36

Gypsies, in Finland, 122; on Volga, 160

Half-breeds in Astrakhan, 178

Hamlet, 38, 55

Hares, in forest of Saint-Germain, 44; in Kazan, 164–165

Helen of Troy, elopement of, 42

Helena, Princess, 105

Heretics, 71 (*See also* Scopsi)

Hermitage in St. Petersburg, 52–53

Hippodrome in Nijni-Novgorod, 155

History of Russia, 42

Holy Inquisition, 14

Home, Daniel Dunglas, 13–17; favors bestowed on, 14; in Florence, 13–14; illness of, 13; meeting of, with Count and Countess Kouchelef, 14, 15, and with Dumas, 14–15; psychic powers of, 13–14, 108; seasickness suffered by, 33, 44, 48; wedding of, 11, 14, 17, 126n.

Honey, use of in trapping bears, 163

Horse races, Kalmuck, 186

Horsemanship of Kalmucks, 182, 184, 186, 188, 191–192 (*See also* Kalmucks)

Horsemeat, raw, use of as appetizer, 185

Horses, Kirghis, 169; permit for hiring of, 167–168; sacrificing of in Finland, 116; wild, roundup and training of, 190–191

Horses' Stone in Konnevitz, 116

Hospice of Konnevitz, 115–116

Hospice of Valamo, 119

Hospitality of Russians, 70, 96, 164, 171–173, 175

Hotel Pastoukov in Yaroslavl, 153

Humboldt, von, Friedrich, 27

Huns, inhabiting of Finland by, 109

Hunting expeditions, bear (*see* Bear hunting); falcon, 188–189, 194; in Jelpatievo, 137, 148; in Kazan, 164–165; pheasant, in Astrakhan, 180; wolf, 44–47

Imatra Falls, 126

Imperial Artillery, commander in chief of, 32

Imperial Winter Palace, 49, 59

Inauguration of breakwater in Astrakhan, 180

Independence, War of, 32

Indian tribes in Astrakhan, 178

Irrigation system in Astrakhan, 175

Isabey, portrait of Kalmuck painted by, 191

Ismailoff, General, 104

Issakov, M., 68

Ivan III (the Great), imperial emblem of, 41; marriage of to Princess Sophia, 41

Ivan IV (the Terrible), 10, 132; Astrakhan, seizure of by, 177; dedication of to St. Sergius, 140; father of, 132, 140; Kazan, capture of by, 133, 162; Kreml built by, 162; Polrovsky Cathedral built by, 133; son of, murder of, 151

Ivanovitch, Vasili, Prince, 132, 140

Jablonovsky, M., 162, 164

Jacquot Sans Oreilles, 160

Jagellon, 32

Jassy, death of Potemkin near, 53

Jelpatievo, arrival in, 147; departure from, 149; hunting in, 137, 148; trip to, 142–147

John III, statue of, 60

John the Baptist, scopsi belief in, 72, 73

Josse, M., 105

Joubert, Barthélemy, 62

Journalism, 101–102

Kaketia, wines of, 175

Kaliasin, stay in, 150–151

Kalino, 138, 141–143, 153, 166–168, 176, 190

Kalmucks, 171, 174–175, 177; attire of, 180, 182, 183; cradles used by, 191; cringing nature of, 180; diet of, 187; hands and feet of, effect of horseback riding on, 182; horsemanship of, 182, 184, 186, 188, 191–192; physical appearance of, 180, 182, 183, 191; prince of (*see* Toumaine, Prince); religion of, 169, 175, 180; religious ceremony of, 183–185; rubbing of noses by, 182, 183, 192; tea, making of by, 187; tents of, moving of, 186–187; women, horsemanship of, 184, 186, 188; women, intercourse of with Indian tribes, 178

Kama River, fish in, 165

Karabanovo, dissoluteness of, 155

Karamsino, M., 159

Katlof, M., 102

Kaulbach, von, Wilhelm, 28

Kazan, 17; arrival in, 161; capture of by Ivan IV, 133, 162; churches in, 161; departure from, 164–165; furs, sale of in, 162–163; hare hunting in, 164–165; Kreml in, 162; leatherwork of, 162; Medical Museum of, 163; monument to Russian soldiers in, 162; Moslem domination of, 161; Natural History Museum in, 163; population of, 161; religious amity in, 161; shops of, 162–163; stay in, 161–164, 171; Tatars in, 161–162 (*See also* Tatars); University of, 163; wine, drinking of in, 161–162

Keholm fortress in Finland, 124–125
Kent, Duke and Duchess of, 11*n*.
Kirghis, 167, 173; Chinese origin of, 169; foray of in France, 169; groups of, 169; horses of, 169; religion of, 169; thievery of, 169, 172
Kirghis Steppes, 167; billiard game in, 172–173; desolation of, 168–169; salt lakes in, 167, 170, 172–173
Kislar, 193, 194; wines of, 175
Kokchar, lighthouse at, 36
Konnevitz, 113–117; Horses' Stone in, 116; hospice of, 115–116; monks of, 114–115; pilgrimages to, 113, 117
Kostroma, stay in, 153–155
Kouchelef, Alexander (Sacha), 11, 12, 14, 18
Kouchelef, Alexandrina, 11; wedding of, 11, 14, 17, 126*n*.
Kouchelef, Count, 10–11, 38–39, 43, 54, 109, 110, 115–117; chamberlain to (*see* Dandré); country house of, 48, 50–51; meeting of, with Daniel Home, 14, 15, and with Dumas, 15–17; panama hat of, 58, 73; park around country house of, 54–56; servants in country house of, 50–51, 54, 96; valets to, 13, 18, 27; watchmen in country house of, 74–76
Kouchelef, Countess, 9–10, 12, 105; companion-housekeeper to, 12, 17–18; personal maids to, 13, 17–18, 20; pets of, 13, 14, 17–20, 26–27; ward of, 12; wardrobe of, 73
Kouchelef, M., 102
Koudriavtzef, Doctor, 12
Kraievsky, M., 101
Kreml in Kazan, 162
Kremlin, beauty of at night, 128–129; Napoleon in, 127, 132, 134
Kroll, de, Count, 11*n*.
Kronstadt, 36, 51; arrival in, 38; ceremonial honors accorded in, 39; corruption of government of, 81–82 (*See also* Local government); departure from, 38–39, 43; fires in, 82; naval base in, 38
Krylof, Ivan, 66; monument to, 61
Kuzaks, 167
Kyrile, Nathalia, 69–70, 140

Labanof, Prince, 167
Laborers (*See also* Serfs); shortage of, effect of on agriculture, 148–149; veterans hired as, 75, 76
Ladoga, Lake, 53, 109, 111–113; monasteries in (*see* Konnevitz; Valamo); seals in, 116, 120; storms on, 113–114, 117; transportation of marble on, 122
Lagoons of Finland, 125
Lahn, General, 164, 171
Lakes, salt, 167, 170, 172–173
Lama Buddhists, 169
Lapuchine, Abraham, 139–140
Lapuknin, Anna, 49
Lashing of criminals, 163
Lazaref, Michael, 82
Leather, Russian, odor of, 74
Leatherwork of Kazan, 162
Lefort, François, 104
Leopold I, campaign of against Turks, 37
Lermontov, translation of poems of, 151
Liberalism, preaching of, effects of, 83
Lindanisse, Castle of, seizure of by Waldemar I, 36
Lipsticks, use of by Alexander II, 59
Lissovsky, defense of Convent of St. Sergius led by, 31
Little Horde of Kirghis, 169 (*See also* Kirghis)
Little House of Peter I, 59–61, 77–78
Local government, 8; abuses in, suppression of, 76, 83; corruption in, forms of, 76, 81–95; economies in, urging of by Republicans, 83; extortion, from serfs, 86–88, and from women, 85–86; gambling, 83–84; investigation of by Nicholas I, 81–82; liberalism, effects of on, 83; reforms in, 76, 83; tax collections, forced, 84–85, 89–92
Longré, de, Mme., 21
Lost legion of Russian Army, 169
Lotsman, trip aboard, 159–160
Louis XV, 21, 101
Louis XVI, gift of to Archbishop Plato, 142

149; gypsies on, 160; overflowing of, 150, 161; shallowness of, 152, 154–155; source of, 165; thawing of, 150

Voltaire, de, François, treatise of on Peter I, 7, 42

Vuoksi, overflowing of, 126

Vyshniy-Volochok, thieves and receivers of stolen goods in, 127

Waldemar I, seizure of Castle of Lindanisse by, 36

War of Independence, 32

Watchmen, country, 74–76

Water closets in St. Petersburg, 61

Water shortage in Astrakhan, 178

Watermelons, cultivation of in Astrakhan, 178

White clergy, 115

White sturgeon, 165

Wild horses, roundup and training of, 190–191

Wild pigs, 126

Windsor Great Park, 99

Wines, of Astrakhan, poor quality of, 175, 176; Mohammedan ban on use of, 30, 161–162

Winter Palace, Imperial, 49, 59

Wolkonsky, Prince, 59

Wolf hunting, 44–47; by Prince Repnine, 45–47

Wolf tails, counterfeit, manufacture of, 148

Women, education of, 153; extortion paid by, 85–86; Finnish, national costume of, 125; Kalmuck, horsemanship of, 184, 186, 188; Kalmuck, intercourse of with Indian tribes, 178; prostitutes in Nijni-Novgorod, 156; sterilization of, 72, 112

Wrestling match, Dumas in, 192–193

Yaroslavl, stay in, 152–154

Young Patriot, The, 102

Yuri-Dolgoruki, 127

Zagrevsky, Count, 168

Zemledelcheskiai Gaseta, 102

Zenaida, Mme., 167